How to Talk So Teens Will Listen

& Listen So Teens Will Talk

**Adele Faber and
Elaine Mazlish**

Illustrations by Kimberly Ann Coe

Piccadilly Press • London

First published in Great Britain in 2006
by Piccadilly Press Ltd
5 Castle Road, London NW1 8PR
www.piccadillypress.co.uk

First published in 2005 by HarperCollins Publishers, 10 East 53rd Street,
New York, NY 10022

A catalogue record for this book is available from
the British Library

ISBN: 1 85340 857 3
ISBN-13: 978 1 85340 857 1

1 3 5 7 9 10 8 6 4 2

Printed and bound by in Great Britain by Bookmarque Ltd.

Cover design by Fielding Design

As parents, our need is to be needed; as teenagers their need is not to need us. This conflict is real; we experience it daily as we help those we love become independent of us.

—DR. HAIM G. GINOTT,
Between Parent and Teenager
(THE MACMILLAN COMPANY, 1969)

Contents

A Note to Readers of this Edition

Dear Friends,

We were delighted to learn that Piccadilly Press was planning to publish this book. We had received so many moving and thoughtful letters from parents in the UK in response to our earlier work that we were eager to share our latest book with you as well.

The subject of teenagers brings us all into new territory. We realize that there may be some differences in attitudes and practices between parents in the US and the UK. Yet despite any cultural differences which may divide us, there are more compelling basic realities which unite us.

The teen years can be difficult. Most parents feel the need to protect, safeguard and guide. Most teens feel the need to pull away, experiment and find their own direction.

Both parents and teenagers need caring, respectful communication skills to help them cope with the conflicts and frustrations that are a natural outcome of the teen growth and separation process. And this is what our book is all about. We hope it will be a source of support to all during these challenging years.

Warmest wishes,

Adele Faber and Elaine Mazlish

We'd Like to Thank . . .

Our families and friends, for their patience and understanding during the long writing process and for being nice enough not to ask, "So when exactly do you think you'll be finished?"

The parents in our workshops, for their willingness to try new ways of communicating with their families and for reporting their experiences back to the group. The stories they shared were an inspiration to us and to one another.

The teenagers we worked with, for everything they told us about themselves and their world. Their honest input gave us invaluable insights into their concerns.

Kimberly Ann Coe, our amazing artist, for taking all our stick figures and the words we put in their mouths and transforming them into a wonderfully varied cast of characters who bring the words to life.

Bob Markel, our literary agent and dear friend, for his enthusiasm for our project from the very beginning and for his unwavering support as we worked our way through the endless drafts that shaped this book.

Jennifer Brehl, our editor. Like the "perfect parent," she believed in us, affirmed our best, and respectfully pointed out where we might make "good" even better. She was right—every time.

Dr. Haim Ginott, our mentor. The world has changed dramatically since his passing, but his conviction that "to reach humane goals we need humane methods" remains forever true.

How This Book Came to Be

The need was there, but for a long time we didn't see it. Then letters like this began to arrive:

> *Dear Adele and Elaine,*
>
> *HELP! When my kids were little,* How to Talk . . . *was my Bible. But they're eleven and fourteen now, and I find myself facing a whole new set of problems. Have you thought about writing a book for parents of teenagers?*

Soon after there was a phone call:

> *"Our civic association is planning its annual Family Day Conference and we were hoping you'd be willing to give the keynote address on how to deal with teenagers."*

We hesitated. We had never presented a program that focused exclusively on teenagers before. Yet the idea intrigued us. Why not? We could give an overview of the basic principles of effective communication, only this time we'd use teenage examples and demonstrate the skills by role-playing with one another.

It's always a challenge to present new material. You can never be sure if the audience will connect with it. But they did. People listened intently and responded enthusiastically. During the question-and-answer period they asked our views on everything from curfews and cliques to answering back and grounding. Afterward we were surrounded by a small group of parents who wanted to talk to us privately.

"I'm a single mom, and my thirteen-year-old son has started hanging out with some of the worst kids in the school. They're into drugs and who knows what else. I keep telling him to stay away from them, but he won't listen. I feel as if I'm fighting a losing battle. How do I get through to him?"

"I am so upset. I saw an e-mail my eleven-year-old daughter received from a boy in her class: 'I want to sex you. I want to put my dinky in your cha-cha.' I don't know what to do. Should I call his parents? Should I report it to the school? What should I say to her?"

"I've just found out my twelve-year-old is smoking pot. How do I confront her?"

"I'm scared to death. I was cleaning up my son's room and found a poem he wrote about suicide. He's doing well in school. He has friends. He doesn't seem unhappy. But maybe there's something I'm not seeing. Should I let him know I found his poem?"

"My daughter has been spending a lot of time online lately with this sixteen-year-old boy. At least, he says he's sixteen, but who knows? Now he wants to meet her. I think I should go with her. What do you think?"

On the car ride home we talked nonstop: Look at what these parents are up against! . . . What a different world we live in today! . . . But have times really changed that much? Didn't we and our friends worry about sex and drugs and peer pressure and, yes, even suicide when our kids were going through their adolescence? But somehow what we had heard tonight seemed worse, scarier. There was even more to worry about. And the problems were starting earlier. Maybe because puberty was starting earlier.

———

A few days later there was another phone call, this time from a school principal:

"We're currently running an experimental program for a group of students in both our middle school and high school. We've given a copy of How to Talk So Kids Will Listen *to each of the parents in the program. Because your book has been so helpful, we were wondering if you'd be willing to meet with the parents and conduct a few workshops for them."*

We told the principal we'd give it some thought and get back to her.

———

Over the next few days we reminisced with each other about the teenagers we once knew best—our own. We turned back time and summoned up memories of our children's adolescent years that we had long since locked away—the dark moments, the bright spots, and the times we held our breath. Little by little, we reentered the emotional terrain of yesteryear and reexperienced the same anxieties. Once again we pondered what made this stage of life so difficult.

It wasn't as if we hadn't been warned. From the time our

kids were born we heard, "Enjoy them now while they're still small" . . . "Little children, little problems; big children, big problems." Over and over again we were told that one day this sweet child of ours would turn into a sullen stranger who would criticize our taste, challenge our rules, and reject our values.

So even though we were somewhat prepared for changes in our children's behavior, no one prepared us for our feelings of loss.

Loss of the old, close relationship. *(Who is this hostile person living in my home?)*

Loss of confidence. *(Why is he acting this way? Is it something I've done . . . or haven't done?)*

Loss of the satisfaction of being needed. *("No, you don't have to come. My friends will go with me.")*

Loss of the sense of ourselves as all-powerful protectors who could keep our children safe from harm. *(It's past midnight. Where is she? What is she doing? Why isn't she home yet?)*

And even greater than our sense of loss was our fear. *(How do we get our kids through these difficult years? How do we get ourselves through?)*

If that was the way it was for us a generation ago, what must it be like for mothers and fathers today? They're raising their kids in a culture that is meaner, ruder, cruder, more materialistic, more sexualized, more violent than ever before. Why wouldn't today's parents feel overwhelmed? Why wouldn't they be driven to extremes?

It's not hard to understand why some react by getting tough—why they lay down the law, punish any transgression, however minor, and keep their teens on a short leash. We can also understand why others would give up, why they'd throw up their hands, look the other way, and hope for the best. Yet both

of these approaches—"Do as I say" or "Do what you want"—
cut off the possibility of communication.

Why would any young person be open with a parent who is
punitive? Why would he seek guidance from a parent who is per-
missive? Yet our teenagers' well-being—sometimes their very
safety—lies in having access to the thoughts and values of their
parents. Teenagers need to be able to express their doubts, con-
fide their fears, and explore options with a grown-up who will
listen to them nonjudgmentally and help them make responsible
decisions.

Who, other than Mom and/or Dad, will be there for them
day in, day out, through those critical years to help them
counter the seductive messages of the media? Who will help
them resist the pressure of their peers? Who will help them cope
with the cliques and cruelties, the longing for acceptance, the
fear of rejection, the terrors, excitement, and confusion of adolescence? Who will help them struggle with the push to conform
and the pull to be true to themselves?

Living with teenagers can be overwhelming. We know. We
remember. But we also remember how we hung on during those
turbulent years to the skills we had learned and how they helped
us navigate the roughest waters without going under.

Now it was time to pass on to others what had been so meaningful to us. And to learn from this current generation what
would be meaningful to them.

We called the principal and scheduled our first workshop for
parents of teenagers.

Authors' Note

This book is based on the many workshops we've given around the country and those we've run for parents and teenagers, separately and together, in New York and Long Island. To tell our story as simply as possible, we condensed our many groups into one and combined the two of us into one leader. Though we have changed names and rearranged events, we have been faithful to the essential truth of our experience.

—Adele Faber and Elaine Mazlish

One

Dealing with Feelings

I didn't know what to expect.

As I ran from the parking lot to the school entrance, I held on tightly to my blowing umbrella and wondered why anyone would leave a warm home on such a cold, miserable night to come to a workshop on teenagers.

The head of the guidance department greeted me at the door and ushered me into a classroom where roughly twenty parents sat waiting.

I introduced myself, congratulated them all for braving the bad weather, and distributed name tags for everyone to fill out. As they wrote and chatted with one another, I had a chance to study the group. It was diverse—almost as many men as women, different ethnic backgrounds, some couples, some alone, some in professional attire, some in jeans.

When everyone seemed ready, I asked people to introduce themselves and tell us a little about their children.

There was no hesitation. One after the other, parents described kids who ranged in age from twelve to sixteen. Almost everyone commented on the difficulty of coping with teenagers in today's world. Still, it seemed to me people were being guarded, holding back, making sure they didn't disclose too much too soon to a room full of strangers.

"Before we go any further," I said, "I want to assure you that anything we discuss here will be confidential. Whatever is said within these four walls remains here. It's no one else's business whose kid is smoking, drinking, playing hooky, or having sex a lot earlier than we'd wish. Can we all agree to that?"

Heads nodded in assent.

"I see us as partners in an exciting venture," I went on. "My job will be to present methods of communication that can lead to more satisfying relationships between parents and teenagers. Your job will be to test these methods—to put them into action in your home and report back to the group. What was or wasn't helpful? What did or didn't work? By joining forces, we'll determine the most effective ways to help our kids make that tough transition from childhood to adulthood."

I paused here for the group's reaction. "Why does it have to be a 'tough transition'?" a father protested. "I don't remember having such a hard time when I was a teenager. And I don't remember giving my parents a hard time."

"That's because you were an easy kid," said his wife, grinning and patting his arm.

"Yeah, well maybe it was easier to be 'easy' when we were teenagers," another man commented. "There's stuff going on today that was unheard of back then."

"Suppose we all go back to 'back then'," I said. "I think there are things we can learn from our own adolescence that might give us some insight into what our kids are experiencing today. Let's start by trying to remember what was best about that time in our lives."

Michael, the man who had been the "easy kid," spoke first. "The best part for me was sports and hanging out with friends."

Someone else said, "For me it was the freedom to come and go. Getting on a subway by myself. Going to the city. Getting on a bus and going to the beach. Total fun!"

Others chimed in. "Being allowed to wear high heels and makeup and that whole excitement over boys. Me and my girlfriends would have a crush on the same guy, and it was, 'Do you think he likes me or do you think he likes you?' "

"Life was so easy then. I could sleep till noon on weekends. No worries about getting a job, paying the rent, supporting a family. And no worries about tomorrow. I knew I could always count on my parents."

"For me it was a time to explore who I was and experiment with different identities and dream about the future. I was free to fantasize, but I also had the safety of my family."

One woman shook her head. "For me," she said ruefully, "the best part of adolescence was growing out of it."

I looked at her name tag. "Karen," I said, "it sounds as if that wasn't the greatest time in your life."

"Actually," she said, "it was a relief to be done with it."

"Done with what?" someone asked.

Karen shrugged before answering. "Done with worrying about being accepted . . . and trying too hard . . . and smiling too hard so people would like me . . . and never really fitting in . . . always feeling like an outsider."

Others quickly built upon her theme, including some who only moments before had spoken glowingly of their teen years:

"I can relate to that. I remember feeling so awkward and insecure. I was overweight back then and hated the way I looked."

"I know I mentioned my excitement over boys, but the truth is, it was more like an obsession—liking them, breaking up with them, losing friends because of them. Boys were all I ever thought about, and my grades showed it. I almost didn't graduate."

"My problem in those days was the pressure I was under from the other guys to do stuff I knew was wrong or dangerous. I did a lot of stupid things."

"I remember always feeling confused. Who am I? What are my likes? My dislikes? Am I true or am I a copycat? Can I be my own person and still be accepted?"

I liked this group. I appreciated their honesty. "Tell me," I asked, "during those roller-coaster years, was there anything your parents said or did that was helpful to you?"

People searched their memories.

"My parents never yelled at me in front of my friends. If I did something wrong, like coming home really late, and my friends were with me, my parents waited until they were gone. Then they'd let me have it."

"My father used to say things to me like, 'Jim, you have to stand up for your beliefs . . . When in doubt, consult your conscience . . . Never be afraid to be wrong or you'll never be right.' I used to think, 'There he goes again,' but sometimes I really did hang on to his words."

"My mother was always pushing me to improve. 'You can do better . . . Check it again . . . Do it over.' She didn't let me get away with anything. My father, on the other hand, thought I was perfect. So I knew who to go to for what. I had a good mix."

"My parents insisted I learn all kinds of different skills—how to balance a checkbook, change a tire. They even made me read five pages of Spanish a day. I resented it then, but ended up getting a good job because I knew Spanish."

"I know I shouldn't be saying this, because there are probably a lot of working mothers here, including me, but I really liked having my mother there when I got home from school. If anything upsetting happened to me during the day, I could always tell her about it."

"So," I said, "many of you experienced your parents as being very supportive during your adolescent years."

"That's only half the picture," Jim said. "Along with my father's positive sayings, there was plenty of stuff that hurt. Nothing I did was ever good enough for him. And he let me know it."

Jim's words opened the floodgates. Out poured a torrent of unhappy memories:

"I got very little support from my mother. I had a lot of problems and needed guidance badly, but all I ever got from her were the same old stories: 'When I was your age . . . ' After a while I learned to keep everything inside."

"My parents used to lay these guilt trips on me: 'You're our only son . . . We expect more from you . . . You're not living up to your potential.' "

"My parents' needs always came before mine. They made their problems my problems. I was the oldest of six and was expected to cook and clean and take care of my brothers and sisters. I had no time to be a teenager."

"I had the opposite. I was so babied and overprotected, I didn't feel capable of making any decisions without my parents' approval. It took years of therapy for me to begin to have some confidence in myself."

"My parents were from another country—a whole other culture. In my house everything was strictly prohibited. I couldn't buy what I wanted, couldn't go where I wanted, couldn't wear what I wanted. Even when I was a senior in high school, I had to ask permission for everything."

A woman named Laura was the last to speak.

"My mother went to the other extreme. She was far too lenient. She didn't enforce any rules. I came and went as I pleased. I could stay out till two or three in the morning and nobody cared. There was never a curfew or any kind of intervention. She even let me get high in the house. At sixteen, I was doing coke and drinking. The scary part was how fast I went downhill. I still experience anger at my mother for not even trying to give me structure. She destroyed many years of my life."

The group was silent. People were feeling the impact of what they had just heard. Finally Jim commented, "Boy, parents may mean well, but they can really mess a kid up."

"But we all survived," Michael protested. "We grew up, got married, started families of our own. One way or another, we managed to become functioning adults."

"That may be true," said Joan, the woman who had referred to her therapy, "but too much time and energy went into getting past the bad stuff."

"And there are some things you never get past," Laura added. "That's why I'm here. My daughter is beginning to act out in ways that worry me, and I don't want to repeat with her what my mother did to me."

Laura's comment propelled the group into the present. Little by little, people began to voice their current anxieties about their children:

"What concerns me is my son's new attitude. He doesn't want to live by anyone's rules. He's a rebel. Same as I was at fifteen. But I hid it. He's out in the open. Insists on pushing the envelope."

"My daughter is only twelve, but her ego craves acceptance— especially from boys. I'm afraid that one day she'll put herself in a compromising position, just to be popular."

"I worry about my son's schoolwork. He's not applying himself anymore. I don't know if he's too into sports or just being lazy."

"All my son seems to care about now are his new friends and being cool. I don't like him hanging out with them. I think they're a bad influence."

"My daughter is like two different people. Outside the house she's a doll—sweet, pleasant, polite. But at home, forget it. The minute I tell her she can't do something or have something, she gets nasty."

"Sounds like my daughter. Only the one she gets nasty with is her new stepmother. It's a very tense situation—especially when we're all together for the weekend."

"I worry about the whole teen scene. Kids these days don't know what they're smoking or drinking. I've heard too many stories about parties where guys slip drugs into a girl's drink and about date rape."

The air was heavy with the group's collective anxiety.

Karen laughed nervously. "Well now that we know what the problems are—quick, we need some answers!"

"There are no quick answers," I said. "Not with teenagers. You can't protect them from all the dangers in today's world, or spare them the emotional turmoil of their adolescent years, or get rid of a pop culture that bombards them with unwholesome messages. But if you can create the kind of climate in your home where your kids feel free to express their feelings, there's a good chance they'll be more open to hearing your feelings. More willing to consider your adult perspective. More able to accept your restraints. More likely to be protected by your values."

"You mean there's still hope!" Laura exclaimed. "It's not too late? Last week I woke up with this terrible feeling of panic. All I could think was that my daughter wasn't a little girl anymore and there was no going back. I lay there paralyzed and thought about all the things I did wrong with her, and then I felt so depressed and so guilty.

"Then it hit me. Hey, I'm not dead yet. She's not out of the house yet. And I'm always going to be her mother. Maybe I can learn to be a better mother. Please, tell me it's not too late."

"It's been my experience," I assured her, "that it's never too late to improve a relationship with a child."

"Really?"

"Really."

It was time to start the first exercise.

———

"Pretend I'm your teenager," I said to the group. "I'm going to tell you a few things that are on my mind and ask you to respond in a way that's guaranteed to turn most kids off. Here we go:

"I don't know if I want to go to college."

My "parents" jumped right in:

"Don't be ridiculous. Of course you're going to college."

"That is the dumbest thing I've ever heard."

"I can't believe you would even say that. Do you want to break your grandparents' heart?"

Everyone laughed. I continued airing my worries and grievances:

"Why do I always have to be the one to take out the garbage?"

"Because you never do anything else around here except eat and sleep."

"Why do you always have to be the one to complain?"

"How come your brother doesn't give me a hard time when I ask him for help?"

"We had this long lecture on drugs today from a policeman. What a joke! All he did was try to scare us."

"Scare you? He's trying to knock some sense into your head."

"If I ever catch you using drugs, you'll really have something to be scared of."

"The trouble with you kids today is that you think you know everything. Well, let me tell you, you've got a lot to learn."

"I don't care if I've got a fever. No way am I missing that concert!"

"That's what you think. You're not going anywhere tonight— except bed."

"Why would you want to do anything that stupid? You're still sick."

"It's not the end of the world. There'll be plenty of other concerts. Why don't you play the band's latest album, close your eyes, and pretend you're at the concert."

Michael snorted, "Oh yeah, that oughta go down really well!"

"Actually," I said, "as your child, nothing I heard just now went down really well with me. You dismissed my feelings, ridiculed my thoughts, criticized my judgment, and gave me unsolicited advice. And you did it all so easily. How come?"

"Because it's what's in our heads," Laura said. "It's what we heard when we were kids. It's what comes naturally."

"I also think it's natural," I said, "for parents to push away painful or upsetting feelings. It's hard for us to listen to our teenagers express their confusion or resentment or disappointment or discouragement. We can't bear to see them unhappy. So it's with the best of intentions that we dismiss their feelings and impose our adult logic. We want to show them the 'right' way to feel.

"And yet, it's our listening that can give the greatest comfort. It's our acceptance of their unhappy feelings that can make it easier for our kids to cope with them."

"Oh boy!" Jim exclaimed. "If my wife were here tonight, she'd say, 'See, that's what I've been trying to tell you. Don't give me logic. Don't ask all those questions. Don't tell me what I did wrong or what I should do next time. Just *listen!*' "

"You know what I realize?" Karen said. "Most of the time I *do* listen—to everyone except my kids. If one of my friends were upset, I wouldn't dream of telling her what to do. But with my kids it's a whole other story. I move right in. Maybe it's because I'm listening to them as a parent. And as a parent, I feel I have to fix things.' "

"That's the big challenge," I said. "To shift our thinking from 'how do *I* fix things?' to 'how do I enable my kids to fix things for themselves?' "

I reached into my briefcase and handed out the illustrations I had prepared for this first meeting. "Here," I said, "in cartoon form are some basic principles and skills that can be helpful to our teenagers when they're troubled or upset. In each case you'll see the contrast between the kind of talk that can add to their distress and the kind that can help them to deal with it. There are no guarantees that our words will produce the positive outcomes you see here, but at the very least they do no damage."

Instead of Dismissing Feelings . . .

Mom doesn't want Abby to feel bad. But by dismissing her daughter's distress, she unwittingly adds to it.

Identify Thoughts and Feelings

Mom can't take away all of Abby's pain, but by putting her
thoughts and feelings into words, she helps her daughter
deal with reality and gather the courage to move on.

Instead of Ignoring Feelings . . .

Mom has good intentions. She wants her son to do well in school. But by criticizing his behavior, dismissing his worry, and telling him what to do, she makes it harder for him to tell himself what to do.

Acknowledge Feelings with a Word or Sound
(Oh . . . mmm . . . uh . . . I see.)

**Mom's minimal, empathic responses help her son feel
understood and free him to focus on what he needs to do.**

Instead of Logic and Explanations . . .

When Dad responds to his daughter's unreasonable request with a reasonable explanation, she becomes even more frustrated.

Give in Fantasy What You Can't Give in Reality

By giving his daughter what she wants in fantasy, Dad makes it a little easier for her to accept reality.

Instead of Going Against
Your Better Judgment . . .

**In order to make her son happy and avoid a battle,
Mom ignores her better judgment and takes the
path of least resistance.**

Accept Feelings as You Redirect Unacceptable Behavior

By showing empathy for her son's predicament, Mom makes it a little easier for him to accept her firm limits.

The comments began even before everyone had finished reading.

"You must've been in my house! Everything you shouldn't say sounds exactly like me."

"What bothers me is that all these scenarios have such happy endings. My kids would never give up or give in that easily."

"But this isn't about getting kids to give up or give in. It's about trying to really hear what they're feeling."

"Yeah, but to do that, you have to listen in a different way."

"And speak in a different way. It's like learning a whole new language."

"And to become comfortable with a new language," I said, "to make it your own, it helps to practice. Let's start now. Suppose I play your teenager again. I'll express my same concerns, only this time, Mom and Dad, you'll react by using any one of the skills you've just seen illustrated."

People immediately started thumbing through their pages of cartoons. I gave them a moment before launching into my list of worries. Some of the group's responses to me came quickly; others took time. People started, stopped, rephrased, and finally found the words that satisfied them.

"I don't know if I want to go to college."
"Sounds as if you're having some real doubts about it."
"You're wondering if college is right for you."
"Know what would be cool? If you could look into a crystal ball and see what your life would be like if you didn't go to college . . . or if you did."

"Why do I always have to be the one to take out the garbage?"
"Boy, I hear how much you resent it."

"It's not your favorite activity. Tomorrow let's talk about rotating chores. Right now I need your help."

"Wouldn't it be great if the garbage would take itself out?"

"We had this long lecture on drugs today from a policeman. What a joke! All he did was try to scare us."

"So you think he was exaggerating—trying to frighten kids into staying away from drugs."

"Scare tactics really turn you off."

"Sounds as if you wish adults would give kids straight information and trust them to make responsible decisions."

"I don't care if I've got a fever. No way am I missing that concert!"

"What rotten luck to be sick—on today of all days! You've been looking forward to that concert for weeks."

"I know. You had your heart set on going. The problem is, with a fever of 101, you belong in bed."

"Even though you know there will be plenty of other concerts, you sure wish you didn't have to miss this one."

When the exercise finally came to an end, people looked pleased with themselves. "I think I'm beginning to get it," Laura called out. "The idea is to try to put into words what you think the kid is feeling, but hold back on what *you're* feeling."

"Now that's the one part I object to," Jim said. "When do I get to talk about *my* feelings—to say what *I* want to say? For instance: 'Doing chores is a contribution to family life.' 'Going to college is a privilege; it can change your life.' 'Doing drugs is dumb; it can ruin your life.' "

"Yeah," Michael agreed, "after all, we're the parents. When do we get to talk about what *we* believe or what *we* value?"

"There will always be time for you to get your message across," I said, "but you have a better chance of being heard if you start by letting your kids know they've been heard. Even then there are no guarantees. They may accuse you of not understanding, of being unreasonable or old-fashioned. But make no mistake. Despite their put-downs and protests, your teenagers want to know exactly where you stand. Your values and beliefs play a vital role in determining their choices."

I took a deep breath. We had covered a lot of ground this evening. It was time for the parents to go home and test what they had learned. Up till now, they had been riding on the strength of my convictions. Only by putting the skills into action with their own teenagers and observing the results for themselves could they develop their own convictions.

"See you next week," I said. "I look forward to hearing about your experiences."

The Stories

I didn't know what would come of our first meeting. It's one thing to try to apply new principles to hypothetical problems when you're sitting around with other parents in a workshop. It's quite another when you're all alone at home, trying to cope with real kids and real problems. And yet, many of the parents did just that. Here, with slight editing, is a sampling of their experiences. (You'll notice that most of the stories come from the same people who participated actively in class. However, some come from parents who seldom joined the discussion but who wanted to share—in writing—how their new skills had affected their relationships with their teenagers.)

Joan

My daughter Rachel has seemed down in the dumps lately. But any time I'd ask her to tell me what was wrong, she'd say, "Nothing." I'd say, "How can I help you if you won't tell me?" She'd say, "I don't want to talk about it." I'd say, "Maybe if you talk about it, you'd feel better." Then she'd throw me a look and that ended that.

But after our discussion in class last week, I decided to try the "new approach." I said, "Rachel, you seem so unhappy lately. Whatever it is, something is making you feel really bad."

Well, the tears started rolling down her cheeks, and little by little the whole story came out. The two girls who had been her friends all through grade school and middle school were now part of the new popular crowd, and they were freezing her out. They didn't save a seat for her at lunch the way they used to, or invite her to any of their parties. They hardly even said hello to her anymore when they passed her in the hall. And she was positive it was one of them who sent an e-mail to some other kids about how the "dorky" clothes she wears make her look fat and don't even have brand names.

I was shocked. I had heard that this kind of thing went on in school, and I knew how cruel some girls could be, but I never imagined that anything like this would ever happen to my daughter.

All I wanted to do was take away her pain. Tell her to forget about those nasty, rotten girls. She'd make new friends. Better friends. Friends who would appreciate what a great kid she is. But I didn't say anything like that. Instead, I just talked about her feelings. I said, "Oh honey, that's rough. To find out that the people you trusted and thought were friends aren't really your friends has got to hurt."

"How could they be so mean!" she said and cried some more. Then she told me about another girl in her class they were "dissing" online—saying she had body odor and smelled of pee.

I could hardly believe what I was hearing. I told Rachel that this sort of behavior says everything about the kind of people they are and nothing about anybody else. Evidently the only way these girls can feel special, part of the "in-group," is to make sure everyone else is kept out.

She nodded her head, and we talked for a long time after that—about "true" friends and "false" friends and how to tell the difference. After a while I could see that she was starting to feel a little better.

But I couldn't say the same for myself. So the next day, after Rachel left for school, I contacted her guidance counselor. I told her that the call was confidential, but that I thought she might want to know what was going on.

I had no idea what kind of response I'd get, but she was great. She said she was very glad I had called because she had been hearing more and more stories lately about what she referred to as "cyber bullying" and that she had been planning to discuss the problem with the principal to see what could be done to help all the students understand how damaging this kind of online abuse and harassment can be.

By the end of our conversation I felt a whole lot better. I actually found myself thinking, *Who knows? Maybe something good will come of all this.*

Jim

My oldest son has a part-time job at a fast-food restaurant. Last Saturday, when he came home from work, he slammed his backpack on the table and began cursing out his boss. Every other word out of his mouth started with an *f* or an *s*.

It turns out that when his boss had asked him if he'd put in some extra hours on weekends, my son told him, "Maybe." But when he got to work on Saturday morning and was about to tell the boss he'd definitely do it, the "bastard" (to quote my son) had given away the overtime to someone else.

Well, the kid was lucky I didn't let loose with what I really wanted to say: "Why does that surprise you? What did you expect? Grow up! How's a man supposed to run a business with an employee who tells him 'maybe' he'll work. 'Maybe' doesn't cut it."

But I didn't chew him out. And I didn't even mention the cursing—this time. I just said, "So you didn't feel you had to give him a definite answer right away." He said, "No, I needed to think about it!"

I said, "Uh-huh."

He said, "I've got a life besides this job, you know!"

I thought, *This stuff isn't working.*

Then from out of the blue he says, "I guess I goofed. I should've called him when I got home and not left him hanging."

How about that? I showed him a little understanding, and he owned up to what he should've done in the first place!

Laura

A few days after our workshop I took my daughter shopping for jeans. Big mistake. Nothing she tried on was "right." It wasn't the right fit, or the right color, or the right designer label. Finally she found a pair she liked—a low-cut, skintight number that she could barely zip up and that outlined every part of her bottom.

I didn't say a word. I just left her in the dressing room and went out to look for a larger size. When I came back, she was still admiring herself in the mirror. She took one look at the pants I held up for her and started yelling, "I'm not trying those on! You want me to look like a nerd! Just because you're fat, you think everyone should wear big clothes. Well, I'm not gonna hide my body the way you do!"

I was so hurt, so angry, I came very close to calling her a little bitch. But I didn't. I said, "I'll wait for you outside." It was all I could manage.

She said, "What about my jeans?"

I repeated, "I'll wait for you outside," and left her in the dressing room.

When she finally came out, the last thing I wanted to do was "acknowledge her feelings," but I did anyway. I said, "I know you liked those jeans. And I know you're upset because I don't approve of them." Then I let her know how I felt. "When I'm spoken to that way, something in me shuts down. I don't feel like shopping anymore, or helping anymore, or even talking anymore."

Neither one of us said anything on the whole ride home. But just before we got to the house, she mumbled, "Sorry."

It wasn't much of an apology, but still, I was glad to hear it. I was also glad I hadn't said anything to her that I would've had to apologize for.

Linda

I don't know if my relationship with my son is any better, but I think I'm making some headway with his friends. They're thirteen-year-old twins, Nick and Justin, both very bright, but out of control. They smoke (I suspect more than cigarettes), they hitch rides, and once when their parents grounded them, they climbed out their bedroom window and went to the mall.

My son is flattered by their interest in him, but I'm worried. I'm sure he's been hitching rides with them, even though he denies it. If I had my way, I'd forbid him to see them outside of school. But my husband says that would only make things worse, that he'll find a way to see them anyway and lie about it.

So our strategy over the past month has been to invite the twins over for dinner every Saturday. We figure that if they're here, we can keep an eye on all of them and drive them to where they want to go. At least for one night we'd know they weren't standing on a dark corner somewhere with their thumbs out, waiting for some stranger in a car to pick them up.

Anyway, what all this is leading up to is that until now we could never get a conversation going with either of the twins. But after last week's workshop we actually made some progress.

The two of them were bad-mouthing their science teacher and calling him a stupid jerk. Normally we would've defended the teacher. But not this time. This time we tried to acknowledge how the twins felt about him. My husband said, "This is one teacher you really don't like." And they kept telling us more: "He's so boring. And he always yells at you for no reason. And if he calls on you and you don't know the answer, he puts you down in front of everybody."

I said, "Nick, I'll bet if you and Justin were teachers, you wouldn't yell at kids or put them down for not knowing an answer."

They both said, "Right!" at almost the same time.

My husband added, "And neither one of you would be boring. Kids would be lucky to have you two as their teachers."

They looked at each other and laughed. My son sat there with his mouth open. He couldn't believe his "cool" friends were actually having a conversation with his "uncool" parents.

Karen

Last night Stacey and I were looking through an old photograph album. I pointed to a picture of her on her bicycle when she was about six and said, "Look how cute you were!"

"Yeah," she said, *"then."* I said, "What do you mean *'then'*?" She said, "I don't look that good now." I said, "Don't be silly. You look fine." She said, "No, I don't. I look gross. My hair's too short, my boobs are too small, and my butt's too big."

It always gets to me when she talks that way about herself. It reminds me of my own insecurities when I was her age and how my mother was always at me with suggestions for how I could improve myself: "Don't slouch . . . Hold your shoulders up . . . Do something with your hair . . . Put a little makeup on. You look like the wrath of God!"

So yesterday when Stacey started picking herself apart, my first instinct was to reassure her: "There's absolutely nothing wrong with your butt, your hair will grow, and so will your breasts. And if they don't, you can always pad your bra."

Well, that's the kind of thing I *would've* said. But this time I thought, *Okay, I'll go with her feelings.* I put my arm around her and said, "You don't sound at all satisfied with the way you look. . . . You know what I wish? I wish that the next time you stand in front of a mirror that you'd be able to see what I see."

She suddenly looked interested. "What do you see?"

I told her the truth. "I see a girl who's beautiful—inside and out."

She said, "Oh, you're my mother," and left the room.

A minute later I saw her posing in front of the full-length mirror in the hall. She had her hand on her hip and she was actually smiling at herself.

Michael

Remember I mentioned my son's negative attitude toward school? Well, the morning after our workshop he came down to breakfast in his usual bad mood. He was stomping around the kitchen, complaining about all the pressure he was under. He had to take two big tests—Spanish and geometry—in one day.

I nearly told him what I always tell him when he carries on like that: "If you did your work and studied the way you should, you wouldn't have to worry about taking tests." But my wife poked me and gave me this look, and I remembered about the fantasy thing. So I said, "Wouldn't it be great if an announcement suddenly came over the radio—'Snow day today! Major storm expected. All schools closed!'"

That took him by surprise. He actually smiled. So I ramped it up. I said, "Know what would really be great? If *any* day you had a test turned into a snow day."

He gave a kind of half-laugh and said, "Yeah . . . I wish!" But by the time he left for school, he was in a better mood.

Steven

I've been remarried for over a year now, and Amy, my fourteen-year-old, has resented my new wife from day one. Every time I pick up Amy at her mother's house for her weekend with Carol and me, it's the same story. The minute she gets in the car she finds something to criticize about Carol.

And no matter what I say to Amy, I can't seem to get through. I point out how unfair she's being to Carol, how she doesn't give her a chance, how Carol has worked so hard to be her friend. But the more I talk, the more she tries to prove me wrong.

It's a good thing I came to the workshop last week, because the following Sunday, when I picked up Amy, she started right in: "I hate coming to your house. Carol is always hanging around. Why did you have to marry her?"

There was no way I could deal with this and drive, so I pulled over and turned off the ignition. All I could think was, *Take it easy. Don't argue with her. Don't even try to reason with her. Just listen this time. Let her get everything out.* So I said, "Okay, Amy, sounds like you've got a lot of strong feelings there. Is there anything else?"

She said, "You don't want to hear what I have to say. You never do."

"I do now. Because I can hear how angry and unhappy you are."

Well, that did it. Out came a long list of complaints: "She's not as sweet as you think . . . She's a big phony . . . All she cares about is you . . . She just pretends to like me."

I never once took Carol's side or tried to convince Amy she was wrong. I just *oh*-ed and *mmm*-ed and listened.

Finally, she sighed and said, "Oh, what's the use."

I said, "There *is* a use. Because knowing how you feel is important to me."

She looked at me, and I could see she had tears in her eyes. "Know something else?" I said. "We need to make sure we get to spend more time together on weekends—just the two of us."

"How about Carol?" she asked. "Won't she be mad?"

"Carol will understand," I said.

Anyway, later that day Amy and I took the dog for a long walk in the park. Now I can't prove there's any connection, but that weekend was the best Carol, Amy, and I ever had together.

Acknowledge Your Teenager's Feelings

Teen: Oh no! What'll I do? I told the Gordons I'd babysit for them Saturday, and now Lisa called and invited me to her sleepover!

Parent: What you should do is . . .

Instead of dismissing your teen's feelings and giving advice:

Identify thoughts and feelings:
"Sounds as if you're pulled in two directions. You want to go to Lisa's, but you don't want to disappoint the Gordons."

Acknowledge feelings with a word or sound:
"Uhh!"

Give in fantasy what you can't give in reality:
"Wouldn't it be great if you could clone yourself! One of you could babysit and the other could go to the sleepover."

Accept feelings as you redirect behavior:
"I hear how much you'd rather go to Lisa's. The problem is, you gave the Gordons your word. They're counting on you."

Two

We're Still "Making Sure"

I was eager to begin tonight's meeting. At the end of our last session, Jim had taken me aside to express his frustration at not being able to get his teenagers to do what he wanted them to do when he wanted them to do it. I acknowledged the difficulty and told him that if he could hang in there one more week, we'd go into the subject in depth.

As soon as everyone had assembled, I wrote the topic of the evening on the board:

Skills for Engaging Cooperation

"Let's start at the very beginning," I said. "When our kids were little, much of our time with them was spent 'making sure.' We made sure they washed their hands, brushed their teeth, ate their vegetables, went to bed on time, and remembered to say please and thank you.

"There were also things we made sure they didn't do. We made sure they didn't run into the street, climb on the table, throw sand, hit, spit, or bite.

"We expected that by the time they reached their adolescent years, most of the lessons would have been learned. But much to our frustration and exasperation, we find ourselves still on the job 'making sure.' True, our teenagers don't bite or climb on the table anymore, but most still need reminders to do their homework, do their chores, eat sensibly, bathe periodically, get enough sleep, and get up on time. We're also still making sure there are things they don't do. 'Don't wipe your mouth with your sleeve' . . . 'Don't throw your clothes on the floor' . . . 'Don't tie up the phone' . . . 'Don't use that tone of voice with me!'

"Each home is different. Each parent is different. Each teenager is different. What are the things you feel you need to 'make sure' your teenager does or doesn't do in the course of a day? Let's start with the morning."

Without a moment's hesitation, people began calling out:

"I make sure he doesn't fall back to sleep after the alarm goes off."
"Or skip breakfast."
"Or wear the same clothes three days in a row."
"Or hog the bathroom so no one else can get in."
"Or come late to his first class because he missed the bus again."
"Or pick a fight with her sister."
"Or forget to take her keys and lunch money."

"How about the afternoon?" I asked. "What's on your 'make sure' list?"

"Call me at work as soon as you get into the house."
"Walk the dog."
"Start your homework."
"Don't eat junk food."
"Don't have any friends over of the opposite sex when I'm not home."

"Don't forget to practice the piano (violin, saxophone)."
"Don't leave the house without telling me where you're going."
"Don't tease your sister."

"Now it's evening," I said. "Again, what are your do's and don'ts for your teens?" People thought for a moment and then . . .
"Don't hole up in your room. Spend time with the family."
"Don't drum on the table."
"Don't slump in your chair."
"Don't stay on the phone all night. Finish your homework."
"Don't stay online all night. Finish your homework."
"For once, say okay when I ask you to do something."
"For once, answer me when I ask you what's wrong."
"Don't use up all the hot water for your shower."
"Don't forget to put your brace on your teeth before you go to bed."
"Don't stay up late. You'll be exhausted in the morning."

"I'm exhausted just listening to this," Laura commented. "No wonder I'm so worn out by the end of the day."

"And it never lets up," a woman named Gail added. "I'm always after my boys—pushing, prodding, poking at them to get this done and that done. And it's been worse since my divorce. Sometimes I feel like a drill sergeant."

"I have another take on it," Michael said. "I think you're being a responsible parent. You're on the job, doing what a parent is supposed to be doing."

"So how come," Gail asked ruefully, "my kids don't do what *they're* supposed to be doing?"

"What my daughter thinks she's supposed to be doing," said Laura, "is give her mother a hard time. She'll argue with me over the least little thing. I'll say, 'Please take your dirty dishes out of your room,' and she'll say, 'Quit bugging me. You're always on my case.' "

There were murmurs of recognition from the group.

"So with teenagers," I said, "sometimes even the simplest, most reasonable request can trigger a short argument or a long battle. To get a better understanding of our kids' point of view, let's put ourselves in their shoes. Let's see how we'd react to some of the typical methods that are used to get teenagers to do what we want them to do. Suppose I play your parent. As you listen to me with your 'adolescent ears,' please call out your immediate, uncensored, visceral response."

Here are the different approaches I demonstrated, and here's how "my kids" reacted:

Blaming and accusing: "You did it again! You put oil in the pan, turned the burner on high, and left the room. What is wrong with you? You could've started a fire!"

"Stop yelling at me."
"I wasn't gone that long."
"I had to go to the bathroom."

Name-calling: "How could you forget to lock your brand-new bike? That was just plain stupid. No wonder it was stolen. I can't believe you could be so irresponsible!"

"I am stupid."
"I am irresponsible."
"I never do anything right."

Threats: "If you don't think it's important enough to do your chores, then I don't think it's important enough to give you your allowance."

"Bitch!"
"I hate you."
"I'll be glad when I'm out of this house."

Orders: "I want you to turn off the television and start your homework. Stop stalling. Do it *now!*"

"I don't want to do it now."
"Quit bugging me."
"I'll do my homework when I'm ready."

Lecturing and moralizing: "There's something we need to talk about. It's your burping at the table. It may be a joke to you, but the fact is, it's just bad manners. And whether we like it or not, people judge us by our manners. So if you must burp, at least cover your mouth with your napkin and say, 'Excuse me.' "

"What did you say? I stopped listening."
"I feel like burping."
"That's so shallow. Manners might be important to you, but they don't matter to me."

Warnings: "I'm warning you. If you start hanging out with that crowd, you're headed for big trouble."

"You don't know anything about my friends."
"What's so great about your friends?"
"I don't care what you say. I know what I'm doing."

Martyrdom: "I ask you to do one little thing for me and it's too much for you. I don't understand it. I work so hard to give you everything you need, and this is the thanks I get."

"Okay, so I'm a rotten kid."
"It's your fault I'm this way. You spoiled me."
"I feel so guilty."

Comparisons: "There's a reason your sister gets all the phone calls. Maybe if you made more of an effort to be friendly and outgoing the way she does, you'd be popular too."

"She's a big phony."
"I hate my sister."
"You always liked her more than me."

Sarcasm: "So you plan to go straight from basketball practice to the dance without showering. Well, you ought to smell wonderful! The girls will be lining up just to get near you."

"Ha, ha . . . you think you're soooooo funny."
"You don't smell so good yourself."
"Why don't you talk straight and say what you mean!"

Prophecy: "All you ever do is blame other people for your problems. You never take responsibility. I guarantee you, if you keep this up, your problems will only get worse and you'll have no one to blame but yourself."

"I guess I'm just a loser."
"I'm hopeless."
"I'm doomed."

"Enough! I'm having a guilt attack," Laura called out. "This is so much like the kind of stuff I say to my daughter. But just now, when I listened as a kid, I hated the way it sounded. Everything I heard made me feel so bad about myself."

Jim looked distressed.

"What are you thinking?" I asked him.

"I'm thinking that a lot of what you demonstrated sounds painfully familiar. As I mentioned last week, my father never hesitated to put me down. I try to be different with my own kids, but sometimes I hear his words come flying out of my mouth."

"I know! Sometimes I feel like I'm turning into my mother," Karen said. "And that's something I swore I'd never do."

"Okay, so now we know what *not* to say," Gail called out. "When do we get to what we *can* say?"

"Right now," I answered, holding up the illustrations I had prepared. "But before I distribute these, please keep in mind that none of the communication skills you're about to see work all the time. There are no magic words that apply to every teenager in every situation. That's why it's important to be familiar with a variety of skills. However, as you look through these pages, you'll see that the basic principle underlying all of these examples is respect. It is our respectful attitude and respectful language that makes it possible for our teenagers to hear us and to cooperate."

Instead of Giving Orders . . .

Orders often create resentment and resistance.

Describe the Problem

By describing the problem, we invite our teenagers
to become part of the solution.

Instead of Attacking the Teenager . . .

When we're angry, we sometimes lash out at our teenagers with words that attack or demean them. Result? They either withdraw or counterattack.

Describe What You Feel

When we describe what we feel, it's easier for the kids to hear us and to respond helpfully.

Instead of Blaming . . .

When teenagers are accused, they usually become defensive.

Give Information

When they're given information, simply and respectfully,
they're more likely to assume responsibility for
what needs to be done.

Instead of Threats or Orders . . .

**Many teenagers react to threats with
defiance or sullen compliance.**

Offer a Choice

We have a better chance of gaining their cooperation if we can substitute a choice that meets our needs and theirs.

Instead of a Long Lecture . . .

Teenagers tend to tune out long lectures.

Say It in a Word

**A short reminder focuses their attention and is more likely
to engage their cooperation.**

Instead of Pointing Out What's Wrong . . .

Teenagers tend to tune out critical comments.

State Your Values and/or Expectations

When parents state their expectations, clearly and respectfully, teenagers are more likely to listen and to try to live up to those expectations.

Instead of Angry Reprimands . . .

**Teenagers can be especially sensitive to
their parents' disapproval.**

Do the Unexpected

By substituting humor for criticism, we change the mood and encourage everyone's playful spirit.

Instead of Nagging . . .

**Some teenagers are slow to respond
to a reasonable reminder.**

Put It in Writing

Often the written word can accomplish what the spoken word cannot.

Comments flew as people leafed through the pages and studied the drawings:

"This isn't just for teenagers. I wouldn't mind if my husband used some of this stuff on me."

"*On* you?"

"Okay, *with* me. *For* me. The point is, it would probably improve a lot of marriages."

"I'll bet there are people who would look at these skills and say, 'There's nothing new here. It's just common sense.'"

"But it isn't common. If it were, we wouldn't all be here tonight."

"I'll never remember all this. I'm taping these cartoons to the inside of my closet door."

A father who was new to the group and who hadn't spoken before raised his hand. "Hi, I'm Tony, and I know I probably should keep my mouth shut because I wasn't here last week. But to me these examples only show how to handle the ordinary, everyday small stuff—a dirty backpack, a ripped shirt, bad table manners. I came here tonight because I thought I was going to find out how to deal with the kind of things teenagers do that worry the hell out of their parents—like smoking, drinking, having sex, taking drugs."

"Those are major worries today," I agreed. "But *it's how we handle the 'ordinary, everyday small stuff' that lays the groundwork for handling the 'big stuff.'* It's how we deal with the dirty backpack or ripped shirt or bad table manners that can either improve a relationship or worsen it. It's how we respond to our children's ups and downs that can cause them to pull away from us or to draw closer. It's how we react to what they've done or haven't done that can either stir up resentment or create trust and strengthen their connection to us. And sometimes it is only that connection that can keep our teenagers safe. When they're tempted, conflicted, or confused, they'll know where to turn for guidance. When the unwholesome voices in the pop culture call to them, they'll have another voice inside their heads—yours—with your values, your love, your faith in them."

After a long silence, Tony asked, "Is our meeting over?"

I checked my watch. "Just about," I told him.

"Good," he said, waving his set of cartoons, "Because I'm going to try some of this out tonight, and I want to get home while the kids are still up."

The Stories

In the following stories, you'll see how the parents used their new skills singly, in combination, and sometimes in situations that went beyond the "everyday, small stuff."

Gail

This last session was made-to-order for me. I'm recently divorced, just started working full-time, and if there's anything I desperately need now it's cooperation. Both my boys are in their teens, but they've never been big on helping out—which I know is my fault because I hate nagging, so I always end up doing things myself.

Anyway, Saturday morning I sat them both down and explained that there was no way I could manage my new job and keep on doing everything I did before. I told them I needed them to pitch in and that we all had to pull together now as a family. Then I listed all the chores that had to be done around the house and asked each of them to choose any three they'd be willing to be responsible for. Just three. They could even switch jobs at the end of each week.

Their first reaction was typical. Loud complaints about all

the pressure they were under at school and how they "never had time for anything." But finally each of them signed on for three chores. I posted the list on the refrigerator and told them that it was a huge relief just to think about coming home from work and finding the laundry done, the dishwasher unloaded, and the table cleared and set for dinner.

Well, that isn't exactly what happened. But they have been doing some of the chores, some of the time. And when they don't, I just point to the list and they get going.

Now if I had only known this years ago . . .

Laura

My daughter has a new way of letting me know that I've done something that "displeases" her. She gives me the silent treatment. If I dare to ask what's wrong, she shrugs and looks at the ceiling, which infuriates me.

But after last week's meeting, I was all fired up—determined to try something different. She was sitting at the kitchen table having a snack when I came in. I pulled up a chair and said, "Kelly, I don't like what's been going on between us."

She folded her arms and looked away. I didn't let that stop me. I said, "I do something that makes *you* mad; you stop talking to me, which makes *me* mad; then I end up yelling at you, which makes you even more mad. So, Kelly, what I realize now is that I need you to tell me directly if something is bothering you."

She shrugged and looked away again. This kid wasn't going to make it easy for me. "And if that's too hard," I said, "then at least give me a signal, some kind of sign. I don't care what. Knock on the table, wave a dish towel, put a piece of toilet paper on your head. Anything."

She said, "Oh, Mom, don't be crazy," and left the room.

I thought, *I do sound crazy*, but a few minutes later she came back into the kitchen with this funny look on her face and something white on her hair. I said, "What is that thing on your . . . oh, right . . . toilet paper." We both started to laugh. And for the first time in a long time we actually talked.

Joan

Last night my fifteen-year-old announced that she wanted to get her nose pierced.

I went berserk. I started screaming at her. "Are you out of your mind? God gave you a beautiful nose. Why would you want to put a hole in it? Why would you want to mutilate yourself? That is the stupidest idea I ever heard of!"

She screamed back at me. "All I want is one little ring for my nose! You should see what other kids have. Kim has a stud in her tongue, and Briana has a ring in her eyebrow, and Ashley has one in her belly button!"

"Well, they're stupid too," I said.

"I can't talk to you. You don't understand anything," she yelled and stomped out of the room.

I just stood there and thought, *And I'm the mother who's going to a class on communication. Wonderful!* But I wasn't about to give up. I just needed a better way to get through to her.

So I went on the Internet to see what I could find out about body piercing. Well, it turns out that it's illegal for anyone under eighteen in my county to have their bodies pierced, branded, or tattooed without a written, notarized letter from a parent or guardian. The only exception was for ear piercing. And there was this whole section on all the diseases you could get from un-clean instruments or unsanitary conditions—hepatitis, tetanus, infections, boils . . .

Well, when she finally came out of her room, I told her that I was really sorry for the things I had said about her and her friends, but there was information on the Internet I thought she should see. Then I pointed to the screen.

She looked at it and said, "Well, nobody I know ever got sick. Anyway, I'm willing to take a chance."

I said, "The problem is, *I'm* not willing to take a chance. Your health is too important to me."

She said, "Okay, so I'll go to a regular doctor and let him do it. All you'd have to do is give me written permission."

I said, "I can't go along with that. My original objection still stands. Besides, I know myself. Just seeing my daughter walking around with a ring sticking out of her nostril would be extremely upsetting to me. And I don't want to be upset every time I look at you. When you turn eighteen, if it's still important to you, you can decide then whether or not you want to do it."

Well, she wasn't exactly thrilled with my decision, but she seems to have accepted it. At least for now.

Tony

My fourteen-year-old, Paul, walks around the house as if he's off in another world. If I ask him to do something, he'll say, "Yeah sure, Dad," and that's the end of it. In one ear and out the other. So last weekend I "did the unexpected." Twice.

First time: in a loud, Count Dracula voice, I said, "I vont you to take out der garbage." He looked up at me and blinked. "And don't make me vait," I said. "Vaiting makes me *vild*!!!"

He laughed and said, "Vell, den I better do it."

Second time: I noticed a bowl with leftover cereal on the floor of his room. I pointed to it and in my regular voice I said, "Paul, do you know what this is?"

He said, "Yeah, a bowl."

I said, "Nope. It's a party invitation."

"A what?"

"An invitation to all the cockroaches in the neighborhood to come into Paul's room and party."

He grinned. "Okay, Dad, I get the message," and he actually picked up the bowl and brought it into the kitchen.

I know "funny" won't always work. But it's nice when it does.

Michael

My daughter hit me with a zinger this week. She said, "Now, Daddy, I'm going to ask you something and I don't want you to freak out and say no. Just listen."

"I'm listening," I said.

"For my sixteenth birthday party, I want to serve wine. Now, before you get all excited, you have to know that a lot of kids my age have wine at their birthday parties. It's a way of making the night special."

She must have read the disapproval on my face because she stepped up her campaign. "Okay, maybe not wine, but if I can't at least have beer, no one will even want to come. Actually, I wouldn't have to provide it, but if my friends could bring their own, that would be okay. Come on, Daddy. It's no big deal. No one will get drunk. I promise. We just want to have fun."

I almost gave her a flat-out no, but instead I said, "Jenny, I see that this is important to you. I need to think about it."

When I told my wife what Jenny wanted, she went right to her notes from last week and pointed to "put it in writing." She said, "If you write it, she'll read it. If you say it, she'll just argue with you."

Here's the letter I wrote:

Dear Jenny,

Your mother and I have given serious thought to your request that wine be served at your birthday party. For the following reasons, we can't say yes.

1. *In this state it is illegal to serve alcohol to anyone under twenty-one.*

2. *If we were to ignore the law and someone at your party had a car accident on the way home, we, as your parents, would be held legally responsible. Even more important, we'd feel morally responsible.*

3. *If we looked the other way and let your friends bring their own beer, in effect we'd be saying, "It's okay for you kids to break the law as long as we parents pretend we don't know what's going on." That would be dishonest and hypocritical.*

Your sixteenth birthday is a milestone. Let's talk about how we can celebrate the occasion in ways that are safe, legal, and fun for everyone.

Love,
Dad

I slipped the letter under her door. She never mentioned it, but later that day, after some phone calls with her friends, she came to us with a few proposals that "might make up for not having 'real' drinks"—an Elvis impersonator, a karaoke party, or someone who does horoscopes.

It's all still in the discussion stage. But one thing my wife and I know, whatever is decided, we plan to be around that night. We've heard that sometimes kids will leave a party, get a few drinks they've stashed in the car, and come back in—all smiling and innocent. We've also heard of kids bringing their own bottled water to a party, only the "water" is actually vodka or gin. So no, we won't be intrusive. We'll try to be discreet. But we'll be keeping our eyes open.

Linda

Remember I said I was going to tape the cartoons to the inside of my closet door? Well, that's what I did. And it was a big help. Whenever I was about to yell at the kids this week, I'd catch myself, go into my bedroom, open the closet, look over the cartoons, and even though my situation was different, I'd get a better idea of how to handle it.

But last Friday my son was late for school, which meant I was going to be late for work. And I lost it. "You're thirteen years old and still have no sense of time. Why do you always do this to me? I bought you a new watch. Do you ever wear it? No. And don't you dare walk away while I'm talking to you!"

He stopped, threw me a look, and said, "Ma, go read your door!"

To Engage a Teenager's Cooperation

Instead of ordering ("Turn that music down! And I mean *now*!!"), you can:

Describe the problem: "I can't think or have a conversation when the music is blasting."

Describe what you feel: "It hurts my ears."

Give information: "Frequent exposure to loud sound can damage a person's hearing."

Offer a choice: "What would you rather do—turn the volume way down or lower it a little and close your door?"

Say it in a word: "The volume!"

State your values and/or expectations: "We all need to tune in to each other's tolerance for loud music."

Do the unexpected: Put your hands over your ears, make a motion of turning the volume down, place palms together, and bow in a gesture of gratitude.

Put it in writing: Music this loud
May be cool for a crowd
But for just me and you
It is much too, too
LOUD!!!

Three

To Punish or Not to Punish

Our third session hadn't started yet. People were still clustered in small groups, deeply engrossed in conversation. Scraps of sentences reached my ears.

"After what she did, I'm grounding her for the month!"

"So I said to myself, No more Mr. Nice Guy. I've been too easy on this kid. This time he's going to be punished."

Well, I thought to myself, *we haven't talked about punishment yet, but it sounds as if some people are more than ready.*

"Laura, Michael," I said. "Would you be willing to let us all in on what your kids did that made you so angry at them?"

"I wasn't just angry," Laura sputtered. "I was worried sick! Kelly was supposed to be at her friend Jill's birthday party at six o'clock. At seven I got a call from Jill's mother. 'Where's Kelly? She knew we had to be at the bowling alley by seven-thirty. It was on the invitation. Now we're all standing around in our coats waiting for her.'

"My heart began to pound. I said, 'I don't understand. She left in plenty of time. She should have been there long ago.'

" 'Well, I'm sure there's nothing to worry about. I just hope she gets here soon,' Jill's mother said, and hung up.

"I made myself wait fifteen minutes before calling back. Jill answered the phone. 'No, Kelly still isn't here. And I even reminded her in school today not to be late.'

"Now I really started to panic. Horrible pictures flashed through my mind. Twenty agonizing minutes later the phone rang. It was Jill's mother. 'I thought you'd like to know that Kelly has finally arrived. Evidently she met some boy on the way here and was so busy talking to him she forgot we were waiting for her. I only hope we didn't lose our reservation at the bowling alley.'

"I apologized for my daughter and thanked her for calling. But when Kelly walked in after the party, I tore into her: 'Do you realize what you put me through? How could you be so inconsiderate? How could you be so irresponsible? You never give a thought to anyone but yourself. It was Jill's *birthday*. But did you feel an obligation to your friend? No! All you care about is boys and having fun. Well, the fun is over, young lady. You are grounded for the rest of the month! And don't think I am going to change my mind, because I won't.'

"Well, that's what I said to her then. But now I don't know. . . . Maybe I was too hard on her."

"Seems to me," Michael commented, "Kelly got exactly what she deserved. And so did my son."

All heads turned toward him. "What happened?" someone asked. "What did he do?"

"It's what he hasn't been doing," Michael answered. "Namely, his homework. Ever since Jeff made the team, soccer is all he cares about. Every day he comes home late from practice, disappears into his room after dinner, and when I ask him if he's keeping up with his homework, he says, 'Not to worry, Dad. I'm on top of it!'

"Well, Sunday, when Jeff was out, I walked by his room and noticed a letter lying on the floor near his door. I picked it up and saw it was addressed to me. It had been opened and was dated a week ago. Guess what? It was a warning notice from his math teacher. Jeff had handed in no homework—*none*—for the past two weeks. When I saw that, I hit the roof.

"As soon as he walked through the door, I was ready for him. I held up the letter and said, 'You lied to me about doing your homework. You opened mail that was addressed to me. And you never showed me this warning notice. Well, I have news for you, mister. No more soccer for you for the rest of the term. I'm call-ing the coach tomorrow.'

"He said, 'Dad, you can't do that to me!'

"I said, 'I'm not doing anything to you, Jeff. You've done it to yourself. Case closed.'"

"But is it really closed?" Laura asked.

"Jeff doesn't think so. He's been working on me all week to get me to change my mind. So has my wife." Michael glanced at her meaningfully. "She thinks I'm being too tough. Don't you, dear?"

"What do *you* think?" I asked Michael.

"I think Jeff knows now that I mean business."

"Yeah," Tony chimed in. "Sometimes punishment is the only way to get a kid to shape up—to be more responsible."

"I wonder," I asked the group, "does punishment make a child more responsible? Take a moment and think back to your own experiences when you were growing up."

Karen was the first to respond. "Punishment made me *less* responsible. When I was thirteen, my mother caught me with a cigarette and took away my phone privileges. So I smoked even more. Only I did it in the backyard where no one could see me. Then I'd come in and brush my teeth and say, 'Hi Mom,' with a big smile. I got away with it for years. Unfortunately, I'm still smoking."

"I don't know," Tony said. "To my way of thinking, there's a time and place for punishment. Take me, for instance. I was a bad kid. The gang I hung out with used to get into a lot of trouble. We were a wild bunch. One of the guys ended up in jail. I swear, if my father hadn't punished me for some of the things I did, I don't know where I'd be today."

"And I don't know where *I'd* be today," Joan said, "if I hadn't had therapy to help me undo the effects of all the times I was punished."

Tony looked startled by her comment. "I don't get it," he said to her.

"Both my mother and father," Joan explained, "believed that if a child did anything wrong and you didn't punish her, you weren't a responsible parent. And they always told me they were punishing me for my own good. But it wasn't good for me. I became an angry, depressed teenager who had no confidence in herself. And there was no one I could talk to at home. I felt very alone."

I found myself sighing. What people had just described was all the familiar fallout of punishment. Yes, some children become so discouraged by punishment and feel so powerless that they begin to lose faith in themselves.

And yes, some children, like Tony, conclude that they really are "bad" and need to be punished in order to become "good."

And yes, some, like Karen, become so angry and resentful that they continue their behavior but devise ways not to get caught. They become, not more honest, but more cautious, more secretive, more crafty.

Yet punishment is widely accepted as a preferred method of discipline. In fact, many parents see discipline and punishment as one and the same. How could I share my conviction that *in a caring relationship there is no room for punishment?*

Aloud I said, "If we were somehow forced to eliminate punishment as a disciplinary tool, would we then be completely helpless? Would our teenagers rule the roost? Would they become wild, undisciplined, self-absorbed, spoiled brats, devoid of any sense of right or wrong, who walk all over their parents? Or might there be methods other than punishment that could motivate our teenagers to behave responsibly?"

On the board I wrote:

Alternatives to Punishment

- State your feelings.
- State your expectations.
- Show how to make amends.
- Offer a choice.
- Take action.

I asked Laura and Michael if they'd be willing to try to apply these skills to their current situations with their children. They both agreed to take on the challenge. On the following pages you'll see, in cartoon form, the results of our struggle to work out scenarios that would meet the new guidelines. First we looked at how Laura might deal with her daughter Kelly, whose disregard for time had caused her mother such great concern.

Alternatives to Punishment

State Your Feelings

State Your Expectations

Show How to Make Amends

Offer a Choice

But suppose Kelly repeats her offense? Suppose Mom receives another "Where's Kelly" call? The next time Kelly wants to visit a friend, Mom can

Take Action

The group was impressed. Many comments ensued:

"I was afraid when you first talked about alternatives to punishment that you meant some kind of 'nicey-nice' approach where the parent gives the kid a little scolding and lets her off the hook. But this is strong. You say what you feel and what you expect and give her a way to take responsibility for her behavior."

"And you're not being mean or harsh or making the girl feel like a bad person. You're being tough, but respectful. Respectful to her and respectful to yourself."

"Yeah, it's not you, the parent, who's the enemy. You're on the kid's side, but you're holding her to a higher standard."

"And showing her how to meet it."

"And you're not sending the message 'I have all the power over you. I won't let you do this . . . I'm taking away that.' Instead, you're putting the power back in the teenager's hands. The ball is in Kelly's court. It's up to her to figure out exactly what she can do to give her mother peace of mind—like calling if she's delayed, and calling when she arrives, and making sure to call again before she leaves for home."

Laura groaned and held her hand to her head. "I don't know," she said. "Working it out here with all of you, I almost feel confident. But what happens when I'm faced with the real thing? This approach makes a lot of demands on a parent. It means you have to have a whole different attitude. The truth is, punishing a kid is a lot easier."

"Easier for the moment," I agreed. "But if your goals are to help your daughter to assume responsibility and at the same time to maintain a good relationship with her, then punishing her would be self-defeating.

"But you have a point, Laura. This approach does require a shift in our thinking. Suppose we get more practice. Let's see how the skills could be applied to the problem Michael is having with his son."

Alternatives to Punishment

State Your Feelings

State Your Expectations

Tony shook his head. "Maybe there's something I'm missing, but I don't see the difference between 'taking action' and punishing Jeff. Either way his father is keeping him off the team."

"Wait, I think I'm finally beginning to get it," Laura said, turning to Tony. "When you punish a kid, you close the door on him. He's got no place to go. It's a done deal. But when you take action, the kid might not like the action, but the door is still open. He still has a chance. He can face up to what he did and try to fix it. He can turn a 'wrong' into a 'right.'"

"I like the way you put that, Laura," I said. "Our goal in taking action is not only to put an end to unacceptable behavior but to give our kids a chance to learn from their mistakes. A chance to right their wrongs. Punishment may stop the behavior, but it may also stop children from becoming self-correcting."

I glanced at Tony. He still looked skeptical. I went on, determined to get through to him. "My guess is that the teenager who has just been grounded for a week does not lie up his room and think, *Oh, lucky me. I have such great parents. They've just taught me a valuable lesson. I'll never do that again!* It's far more likely that the young person will be thinking, *They're mean,* or, *They're unfair,* or, *I hate them,* or, *I'll get back at them,* or, *I'll do it again—only next time I'll make sure I don't get caught.*"

The group was listening intently now. I tried to sum up. "As I see it, the problem with punishment is that it makes it too easy for a teenager to ignore his misdeed and focus instead on how unreasonable his parents are. Worse yet, it deprives him of the work he needs to do to become more mature. More responsible.

"What is it that we hope will take place after a child transgresses? We hope he'll look at what he did that was wrong. That he'll understand why it was wrong. That he'll experience regret for what he did. That he'll figure out how to make sure it doesn't happen again. And that he'll think seriously about how

Alternatives to Punishment

State Your Feelings

State Your Expectations

Show How to Make Amends

Offer a Choice

What if Jeff does his homework, makes up his assignments, but little by little lets his schoolwork slide again? Dad can then

Take Action

Tony shook his head. "Maybe there's something I'm missing, but I don't see the difference between 'taking action' and punishing Jeff. Either way his father is keeping him off the team."

"Wait, I think I'm finally beginning to get it," Laura said, turning to Tony. "When you punish a kid, you close the door on him. He's got no place to go. It's a done deal. But when you take action, the kid might not like the action, but the door is still open. He still has a chance. He can face up to what he did and try to fix it. He can turn a 'wrong' into a 'right.'"

"I like the way you put that, Laura," I said. "Our goal in taking action is not only to put an end to unacceptable behavior but to give our kids a chance to learn from their mistakes. A chance to right their wrongs. Punishment may stop the behavior, but it may also stop children from becoming self-correcting."

I glanced at Tony. He still looked skeptical. I went on, determined to get through to him. "My guess is that the teenager who has just been grounded for a week does not lie up his room and think, *Oh, lucky me. I have such great parents. They've just taught me a valuable lesson. I'll never do that again!* It's far more likely that the young person will be thinking, *They're mean,* or, *They're unfair,* or, *I hate them,* or, *I'll get back at them,* or, *I'll do it again—only next time I'll make sure I don't get caught.*"

The group was listening intently now. I tried to sum up. "As I see it, the problem with punishment is that it makes it too easy for a teenager to ignore his misdeed and focus instead on how unreasonable his parents are. Worse yet, it deprives him of the work he needs to do to become more mature. More responsible.

"What is it that we hope will take place after a child transgresses? We hope he'll look at what he did that was wrong. That he'll understand why it was wrong. That he'll experience regret for what he did. That he'll figure out how to make sure it doesn't happen again. And that he'll think seriously about how he might make amends. In other words, *for real change to take place, our teenagers need to do their emotional homework. And punishment interferes with that important process."*

The room was silent. What were people thinking? Did they still have doubts? Had I been clear? Could they accept what they had heard? I looked at my watch. It was late. "We did a lot of hard work here tonight," I said. "I'll see you all next week."

Tony's hand went up. "One last question," he called out.

"Go ahead." I nodded.

"What if you use all the skills we worked on tonight, and the kid still doesn't shape up? Suppose he doesn't know how to be what you call 'self-correcting'? What then?"

"Then that's an indication that the problem needs more work. That it's more complex than it originally appeared and that you need to give it more time and gather more information."

Tony looked bewildered. "How?"

"By problem-solving."

"Problem-solving?"

"It's a process we'll be talking about next week. We'll be working on ways for parents and kids to join forces, explore possibilities, and solve the problem together."

For the first time that evening Tony smiled. "Sounds good to me," he said. "This is one meeting I'm not gonna miss."

The Stories

In the week that followed our session on alternatives to punishment, several people reported how they put their new skills into action.

This first story was told by Tony about his fourteen-year-old son, Paul.

Tony

Paul and his friend Matt came running down the driveway, out of breath, grinning from ear to ear. I said, "What's up, guys?" They said, "Nothing," and looked at each other and laughed. Then Matt whispered something to Paul and took off.

"What did he tell you not to tell me?" I asked Paul. He didn't answer. So I said, "Just tell me the truth. I won't punish you."

Finally, I got it out of him. The story was that he and Matt biked over to the community pool for a swim, but it was closed for the night. So they tried all the doors, found one that wasn't locked, and let themselves in. Then they turned on all the lights and ran around, whooping it up, knocking over all the lounge chairs, throwing cushions everywhere—including into the pool. And to them it was one big joke.

The kid was lucky I promised not to punish him, because believe me, when I heard what he did, I wanted to throw the book at him—cut off his allowance, take away his computer, ground him indefinitely—anything to wipe that stupid smile off his face.

I said, "Listen to me, Paul. This is serious. What you did has a name. It's called vandalism."

His face turned red. He yelled, "See I *knew* I shouldn't have told you. I *knew* you'd make a big deal out of it. It's not like we stole anything or peed in the pool!"

"Well, congratulations for that," I said, "but, Paul, it *is* a big deal. A lot of people in this community worked their tails off to raise enough money to build a pool for their families. They're proud of it, and they work hard to maintain it. And it also happens to be the pool where you learned how to swim."

Paul said, "What are you trying to do? Guilt me?"

"You bet I am," I said, "because what you did was wrong and now you need to make it right."

"What do you want me to do?"

"I want you to go back to the pool—*now*—and put everything back the way you found it."

"Now?! . . . Jeez, I just got home!"

"Yes, now. I'm driving you."

"What about Matt? It was his idea. He should come too! I'm calling him."

Well, he did call, and at first Matt said, "No way," that his mother would kill him if she found out. So I got on the phone. I said, "Matt, the two of you did it, and the two of you need to fix it. I'll pick you up in ten minutes."

Anyway, I drove the kids back to the pool. Luckily, the door was still open. The place was a wreck. I told the boys, "You know what you have to do. I'll wait in the car."

About twenty minutes later, they came out and said, "It's all done. Wanna see?" I said, "Yeah, I do," and went inside to check.

Well, the whole place was straightened up. The lounge chairs were all lined up, and the cushions were back where they belonged. I said, "Good. Everything looks normal. Turn off the lights and let's go."

On the way home the boys were quiet. I don't know about Matt, but I think Paul finally understood why he shouldn't have done what he did. And I think he was glad he had a chance to, as you say, "make amends."

Joan

I was making dinner when Rachel walked through the door. I took one look at her bloodshot eyes and dopey smile, and I knew she was "high." I wasn't sure it was pot, but I was hoping it was nothing worse.

I said, "Rachel, you're stoned."

She said, "You're always imagining things about me," and disappeared into her room.

I just stood there. I couldn't believe it. This was the same child who just last month had confided to me, "Swear you won't tell anybody, Mom, but Louise started smoking pot. Can you believe it? Isn't that terrible?"

I remember thinking *Thank God, it's not my daughter*. And now this! I didn't know what to do. Should I ground her? Forbid her to go anywhere after school? (Certainly not to Louise's!) Insist that she come straight home from now on? No, that would only lead to arguments and tears. Besides, it wasn't realistic.

But I couldn't pretend it didn't happen. And I knew there was no point in trying to talk to her until the effects of whatever she had taken or smoked had worn off. Also, I needed time to think. Should I tell her about my own "experimenting" as a teenager? And if I do, how much should I tell her? Would it help her to know? Or would she use it as an excuse to justify what she was doing ("You did it and you're okay")? Anyway, over the next few hours, I had a dozen imaginary conversations with her. Finally, after dinner, when she seemed more herself, we talked. Here's how the real thing went:

"Rachel, I'm not looking for a confession, but I saw what I saw and I know what I know."

"Oh, Mom, you're so dramatic! It was just a little pot. Don't tell me you never tried it when you were my age."

"Actually, I was a lot older. Sixteen, not thirteen."

"*See* . . . and you're okay."

"I wasn't so okay then. My old friends, what you'd call the 'good kids,' stopped being friends with me, and my grades went way down. The truth is, when I started I had no idea what I was getting myself into. I thought it was harmless. Not as bad for you as cigarettes."

"So what made you stop?"

"Barry Gifford, a boy in my class. He crashed his car into a tree after leaving a party where everyone was getting high. Anyway, Barry ended up in the hospital with a ruptured spleen. Then a few days later we all had to go to this drug awareness program, and they handed out these pamphlets. After that I decided it wasn't worth it."

"Oh, they were probably just trying to scare you."

"That's what I thought. But then I read the whole pamphlet. Some of it I already knew, but there was a whole lot of stuff I didn't know."

"Like what?"

"Like how pot can stay in your system for days after you take it. How it messes up your memory and your coordination, and even your menstrual cycle. And how it's even worse for you than cigarettes. I had no idea that marijuana had more cancer-causing chemicals than tobacco. That was a big surprise to me."

Rachel suddenly looked worried. I put my arm around her and said, "Listen, daughter of mine, if I could, I'd follow you around day and night to make sure that nobody ever gives you or sells you anything that could do you harm. But that would be pretty crazy. So I have to count on you to be smart enough to protect yourself from all the garbage that's out there. And I believe you will. I believe you'll do what's right for your life—no matter how much people pressure you."

She still looked worried. I gave her a big hug and that was that. We didn't talk about it anymore. I think what I said had an impact, but I'm not taking any chances. Kids lie to their parents about drugs (I know—I did), so even though I have mixed feelings about snooping, I think I'll be checking her room every so often.

Gail

Neil, my fifteen-year-old, asked me if Julie, his friend since childhood, could sleep over on Saturday. Her parents were going to an out-of-town wedding, and her grandmother, who had planned to stay with her, got sick and couldn't come.

I thought, *Why not?* My younger son would be spending the weekend at his father's house, so Julie could have his room. Of course I checked with Julie's mother to see how she felt about it. She jumped at the offer—relieved that a responsible adult would be looking after her daughter for the night.

When Julie came, I showed her where she'd be sleeping. Then the three of us had a nice dinner and watched a video.

The next morning Julie's mother called to say she was back home and could she speak to Julie. I went upstairs to get her. The door of her room was half-open, and the bed had not been slept in! The pillows that I had arranged so carefully the day before were exactly as I had left them. As I stood there with my mouth open, I heard laughter coming from Neil's bedroom.

I rapped hard on his door and yelled out that Julie's mother was on the phone and wanted to speak to her.

When the door finally opened, Julie came out looking rumpled and embarrassed. She avoided my eyes, ran downstairs to talk to her mother, ran back upstairs to get her backpack, thanked me "for everything," and went home.

As soon as she left the house, I exploded. "Neil, how could you do this to me!? I gave Julie's mother my word that I would be responsible for her. That she'd be safe and protected!"

Neil said, "But Mom, she . . ."

I cut him off. "Don't 'but Mom' me. What you did was inexcusable."

"But, Mom, nothing happened."

"Oh, *right*. Two teenagers spend the night together in the same bed and nothing happened. You must think I'm pretty stupid. Well, I'll tell you something that won't be happening next weekend. You're not going on the ski trip with your class."

I said it, and I meant it, and I felt it was exactly what he deserved. Then I left the room so I wouldn't have to listen to him carry on about how unreasonable I was being.

A few minutes later I changed my mind. How could keeping Neil from his ski trip help him realize why he shouldn't have done what he did? So I walked back into his room and said, "Listen, Neil, forget what I said about the ski trip. Here's what I really want to say: I know sex is a normal, healthy part of life, but the fact is, parents worry when it comes to their kids. They worry about their daughters becoming pregnant, about their sons becoming fathers. They worry about AIDS and all the other . . ."

He didn't let me finish. He said, "Ma, enough! I don't need a sex education lecture. I know all that stuff. Besides, I'm trying to tell you, *nothing happened*! We were just lying on the bed, watching TV."

Well, maybe they were and maybe they weren't. I decided to give him the benefit of the doubt. I said, "I'm glad to hear it, Neil. Because when you invited Julie to spend the night in our home, you took on a responsibility—to both Julie and her mother . . . and *me*. A responsibility that needed to be honored."

Neil didn't say anything, but from the expression on his face, I could see that my words hit home. And that was enough for me. I was able to drop it.

Jim

My wife and I thought we had covered all bases when we bought our new computer. We put it in the family room (over the objections of twelve-year-old Nicole, who lobbied hard to have it in her bedroom); we installed the latest filtering software (we heard there were at least three million porn sites a kid could accidentally tap into); and we worked out a loose schedule to try to meet the needs of everyone in the family. We also made it clear to Nicole that the computer was strictly off-limits after nine P.M. and was only to be used for schoolwork or to go online with friends.

Sounds good, doesn't it? Well, a few nights ago I woke up a little after midnight, saw a light in the family room, got up to turn it off, and found Nicole glued to the computer. She was so absorbed, she didn't even hear me. I stood behind her and read the screen: "Courtney, you sound so cute and funny and sexy. When can I meet you?" The second she realized I was there, she typed in "pos" (I later learned that means "parent over shoulder") and blanked out the screen.

I broke out in a cold sweat. I've heard too many news reports about what happens to young girls who meet teenage boys in chat rooms. The boy flatters her, tells her how much they have in common, makes her feel special, and little by little gets her to the point where she agrees to meet him. Only it turns out he's not a cute teenage boy but some old guy, a sexual predator who's out to do who-knows-what to her.

I said, "Nicole, what the hell do you think you're doing? Do you have any idea what kind of danger you're exposing yourself to? I ought to take away your computer privileges indefinitely!"

She immediately went on the defensive. She said there was

nothing to get so excited about, that she was only having a little fun, that she hadn't even used her real name, and that she was smart enough to know the difference between a "sicko creep" and a normal person.

I said, "Nicole, listen to me. There is *no way* you can tell the difference! The worst 'sickos' are capable of sounding completely normal and charming. They know exactly how to go about fooling a young girl. They've had lots of practice." Then I told her that I wanted her password because from now on her mother and I would be checking regularly to see where she'd been online.

Her reaction? I didn't trust her . . . I had no right . . . I was taking away her privacy, etc., etc. But by the time I finished telling her some of the horror stories I had heard about how these "normal" guys turn out to be stalkers, kidnappers, rapists, or worse, all she could manage to say, in a weak little voice, was, "Well, you can't believe everything you hear."

I guess she was trying to save face. But I think a part of her was actually relieved that her father was looking out for her and that he wasn't a pushover.

Alternatives to Punishment

Teen: You swore you'd quit smoking, and you're still do-
          ing it! You are such a phony. You are so full of it!

Parent: And *you*, big mouth, are grounded this weekend!

Instead:

State your feelings:
"That kind of talk makes me angry."

State your expectations:
"When I'm trying to stop smoking, what I expect from my son is
support—not an attack."

Offer a choice:
"Name-calling hurts. You can either talk to me about what you
think might help me quit or you can put it in writing."

Show how to make amends:
"When you realize you've offended someone, it's a good idea to
apologize."

But what if the teenager continues to speak disrespectfully?

Take Action (as you leave the room):
"This conversation is over. I'm not available for insults."

Four

Working It Out Together

Karen began the session even before everyone had settled down. "I couldn't wait to get here tonight. Remember last week when Tony asked what if none of the alternatives to punishment work? You said something about problem-solving. Anyway, I've got a big problem going on now with Stacey, and I have no idea how to solve it."

"The good news," I said, "is that you don't have to solve it by yourself. The five-step method you'll be learning today shows how parents and teens can sit down and tackle the problem together."

"Sit down?" Laura exclaimed. "Who has time to sit down? In my house everyone is always rushing off somewhere. We talk to each other on the run."

"People do have hectic schedules these days," I said. "It isn't easy to find the time. Yet time is what this process requires. You can't think together creatively if either one of you is rushed or agitated. For this approach to yield results, it's best to wait until both parties are relatively calm."

"Yeah," Tony said, "but the minute you let a kid know you

want to talk to him about something he's doing that you don't like, no matter how calm *you* are about it, *he's* not going to be so calm anymore."

"And that," I said, "is why your very first step, after bringing up the problem, is to invite your teenager to tell his or her side of the story. That means putting your feelings on hold, temporarily, and listening to her. Once she knows her point of view has been heard and understood, she'll be much more likely to be able to hear what you have to say."

"And then?" Karen asked impatiently.

"And then," I said, "it's a matter of the two of you putting your heads together and trying to figure out something that might work for both of you. Suppose I illustrate by using an example from my own home.

"When my son was about fourteen, he discovered heavy metal. He'd play that music—if you can call it that—so loud the windows rattled. I asked him to please turn it down. Nothing. I yelled at him to turn it down. Still nothing. I tried all of the skills we talked about in our session on engaging cooperation: I described, I gave information, I offered choices, I wrote a note . . . I even used humor. I thought I was very funny. He didn't.

"One night I lost it. I stormed into his room, unplugged his tape player, and threatened to take it away permanently. You can imagine the screaming match that followed.

"I had a hard time falling asleep that night. The next day I decided to try the one approach I hadn't used—problem-solving. I waited until after breakfast before even venturing to bring up the subject. But the minute I mentioned the word 'music,' his back went up. He said, 'Oh no, not that again!' I said, 'Yes, *that* again. Only this time I want to try to see things from your point of view. . . . I'd like to really understand where you're coming from.'

"That took him by surprise. He said, 'It's about time!' Then he let me know exactly how he felt: 'I think you're much too sensitive. The music isn't *that* loud—it has to be loud enough to feel the beat and hear the lyrics. Because the lyrics are great, even though you hate them. But if you ever really listened to them, maybe you'd like them too.'

"I didn't argue with him. I acknowledged everything he said, and then I asked if he could listen to how I felt.

"He said, 'I know how you feel. You think it's too loud.'

" 'You're right. I try not to let it bother me, but it does.'

" 'So wear earplugs.'

"Again I didn't argue. I wrote it down and said, 'That's our first idea! Let's see what else we can think of that might work for both of us.'

"Well, we came up with all kinds of possibilities—everything from his wearing headphones to soundproofing his room to putting a rug on his floor to turning down the volume *a little,* to closing bedroom and kitchen doors.

"When we finally reviewed our list, we quickly eliminated earplugs for me (I didn't want to walk around with my ears plugged up), headphones for him (loud volume could damage his hearing), and soundproofing (too expensive). However we did agree that a rug on his floor, closing doors, and lowering the volume—even a little—would help. But it turned out that what he really wanted was for me to listen to his music with him—to 'at least give it a chance.'

"Well, I did listen, and after a while I could sort of see why the music might appeal to him. I even began to understand why the words that were so distasteful to me might be satisfying to kids. I guess teenagers relate to lyrics that express their anger and frustration.

"Did I grow to love his music? No. But I did become more accepting of it. And I think that because I was willing to spend time with him in his world, he became more willing to accommodate me. Sometimes he'd even ask, 'Mom, is this too loud for you?'

"Well, that was my experience. Now let's see how the same approach might apply to a situation that most of you are probably familiar with—the mess, disorder, chaos, or whatever you call it in a teenager's room."

People laughed knowingly. Michael said, "I call it the 'garbage dump.'"

"In our house," Laura added, "we call it the 'black hole.' Whatever goes in, never comes out."

"And what do you call the kids?"

From around the room I heard, "Slob" . . . "Pig" . . . "You live like an animal" . . . "The way you keep your room, who'd ever want to marry you?"

I reached into my briefcase. "Here's an alternative to that kind of talk," I said and handed out the illustrations that would show the problem-solving process in action—step by step.

On the next few pages you'll see what I distributed to the group.

Working It Out Together

Step I

Invite Your Teen to Give His Point of View

Step II

State Your Point of View

Step III

Invite Your Teenager to Brainstorm with You

Step IV

Write Down All Ideas—Silly or Sensible— Without Evaluating

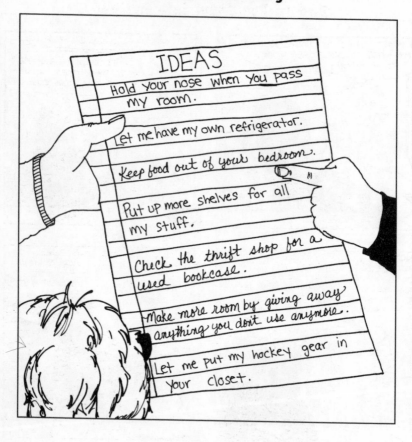

IDEAS

Hold your nose when you pass my room.

Let me have my own refrigerator.

Keep food out of your bedroom.

Put up more shelves for all my stuff.

Check the thrift shop for a used bookcase.

Make more room by giving away anything you don't use anymore.

Let me put my hockey gear in your closet.

Step V

Review Your List. Decide Which Ideas You Can Both Agree to and How to Put Them into Action.

"I don't mean to be negative," Karen said, "because I can see how this approach could work with a kid whose room is a mess. But that's not a serious problem. Stacey did something this week that really worried me. And I know I got excited and made things worse. But I still don't see how I could have used any of this with her."

"So what did she do?" Laura asked. "Don't keep us in the dark."

Karen took a deep breath. "Okay, here goes. Last Friday my husband and I went out to dinner and a movie. Before we left, Stacey, who's thirteen, asked if two of her girlfriends could come over, and of course we said yes. The movie ended early, and when we got back to the house, we saw two boys running out the side door. My husband ran after them. I went inside.

The minute I opened the door I knew something wasn't right. The windows were wide open, the house was freezing cold, the whole place smelled of cigarette smoke, and Stacey and her girlfriends were in the kitchen stuffing beer cans into the bottom of a garbage bag and covering them with newspapers.

"As soon as she saw me, she said, 'It wasn't my fault.' "

"I said, 'We'll talk later,' and sent the girls home. The minute they were out the door Stacey started telling me this whole long story and giving me all kinds of excuses.

"I told her I wasn't buying any of it and that she knew the rules and deliberately broke them. And then I let her know that her father and I weren't finished with her yet. So that's why I'm here tonight. But problem-solving? I don't know. I really don't see how that could help."

"We won't know unless we try," I said. "Would you be willing to role-play with me?" I asked.

Karen looked uncertain. "What part would I play?"

"Whatever part you want."

She thought a moment. "I guess I should be Stacey. Because I know the kind of thing she'd say. So how do I begin?"

"Since I'm your mom," I said, "and I'm the one who's worried about the problem, it's up to me to start the conversation."

I pulled my chair up to Karen. "I hope this is a good time for you, 'Stacey,' because we need to talk about last night."

Karen (now Stacey) slumped in her chair and rolled her eyes. "I tried to talk to you, but you wouldn't listen!"

"I know," I said, "and that can be frustrating. But I'm ready to listen now." Here's how our dialogue continued:

Stacey:	Like I said, I didn't expect those boys to come. I don't even know them. They're not in any of my classes. They're older.
Mother:	So the boys were a complete surprise to you.
Stacey:	That's right! When I opened the door for Jessie and Sue, these two guys were standing behind them. I never invited them in. I told Jessie my parents would be pissed if I let boys in the house.
Mother:	So you made it very clear that you wanted them to leave.
Stacey:	Yeah, but they said they were just going to stay for a few minutes.
Mother:	And you thought they meant it.
Stacey:	I did. Like, you know, I didn't think they were going to smoke or drink. When I told them not to, they laughed. I didn't even know that Jessie smoked.
Mother:	So you made a real effort to stop them, but no matter what you said, no one would listen. You were in a tough position, Stacey.

Stacey: I really was!

Mother: Stacey, here's how it was for me. It was a shock
             to come home and see boys running out the
             door and to smell smoke in the house and find
             beer cans in the garbage and . . .

Stacey: But, Mom, I just told you, it wasn't my fault!!

Mother: I understand that now. But I want to make sure
             it doesn't happen again. So to me the big ques-
             tion is, how can you feel comfortable about hav-
             ing your friends over, and how can Dad and I
             feel confident that our rules are being
             respected—whether we're home or not?

Stacey: Mom, it's no biggie. All I have to do is tell Sue
             and Jessie they can't ever bring boys over when
             you're not home.

Mother: Okay, I'll write that down. It's the first sugges-
             tion for our list. Now *I* have a thought: install a
             peephole in the door. That way you can see
             who's out there before you open it.

Stacey: And if anyone wants to smoke, I'll tell them
             they have to go outside.

Mother: We could make some NO SMOKING signs and put
             them around the house. You could tell everyone
             your mean mother made you do it. . . . What
             else?

Suddenly Karen broke out of character. "I know . . . I know
we're not finished, and I know we're supposed to go over all the
suggestions and decide which ones are best and all that, but I
have to tell you what was happening to me when I was playing
Stacey. It was so amazing. I felt so respected . . . that my mother
really listened to me . . . that it was safe to tell her how I really

felt and that she wasn't going to jump down my throat . . . and that I was smart for coming up with some ideas, and that my mother and I were a real team."

I beamed at Karen. In her own inimitable way, she had expressed the core of what I had been hoping to communicate.

I thanked her for throwing herself so fully into her part and for sharing her inner process with us. Several people applauded.

Karen grinned at them. "Don't applaud yet," she said. "The big performance is still ahead. Now the real mother has to go home and pull it off with the real Stacey. Wish me luck, everybody."

From around the room came shouts of, "Good luck, Karen!"

On that high note, the meeting ended.

The Stories

When parents took the time to sit down with their teenagers and try out their new problem-solving skills, they experienced a number of new insights. Here are the highlights of what they reported:

Karen: Problem-solving can help you learn what's really going on.

When I left the session last week, I didn't know whether Stacey would even be willing to talk to me. There was so much bad feeling between us. But as soon as I did the very first step of "the method"—you know, really listening to her point of view and accepting all her feelings—she turned into another person. Suddenly she was telling me things she never would have told me before.

I found out that one of the boys was Jessie's new boyfriend, and that she was laughing and being silly and hanging all over him, and that when he offered her a cigarette she took it and smoked it.

I didn't say a word. I just listened and nodded my head. Then she told me that the boys had a six-pack with them, and when they finished that, they started looking around for something else to drink. One of them found the liquor cabinet, and they both helped themselves to some Scotch. They tried to talk the girls into having "a shot," but only Jessie did.

Boy, did I have to exercise self-control! But I'm glad I did, because the more we talked, the more I understood where Stacey was coming from. I could see that part of her was excited by the whole experience, but mostly I think she was scared and overwhelmed.

Just knowing that made the rest of our discussion a lot easier. I didn't have to spend time explaining how I felt (Stacey already knew my views about smoking and drinking), and it didn't take long for us to come up with a list of solutions. Here's what we both agreed to:

- No boys allowed in the house unless parents are home.
- No alcoholic beverages allowed.
- Anyone who *must* have a cigarette has to go outside.
- Mom will tell Sue and Jessie about the new house rules (in a friendly way).
- Dad will install a lock on the liquor cabinet.
- If adult help is needed and parents can't be reached, call any of the numbers listed on the refrigerator door.

By the time we finished our list, we both felt pretty good. We had worked things out together. Instead of me laying down the law, Stacey had a say in what the law should be.

Laura: It isn't always necessary to go through every step of problem-solving in order to arrive at a solution.

When Kelly came waltzing into my room to model her new outfit for me, she was bubbling over with excitement. "Mom, look what I bought with my birthday money! Isn't it cool? It is so totally in fashion! Don't you love it?"

I took one look at her and thought, *Thank goodness her school has a dress code.* My next thought was, *Okay, maybe this is the time for mother and daughter to do some problem-solving.* I started with the first step—her feelings. "I hear you, Kelly. You love the way that little T-shirt goes with those hip-hugger jeans."

Then I expressed my feelings. "I think that look is too suggestive. I don't want my daughter walking around in public with all that bare skin and her belly button showing. I think it sends the wrong message."

She didn't like hearing that. She plopped down in a chair and said, "Oh, Mom, you are so out of it."

"That may be true," I said, "but can we possibly come up with any kind of solution that would . . ." Before I could even finish my sentence, she said, "So I won't wear it 'in public.' Only in the house, when I'm hanging out with my girlfriends. Okay?"

"Okay," I said. And that ended it. At least temporarily. Because I know the scene today. The girls walk out the door looking like what my mother would call "perfect little ladies." But as soon as they turn the corner, the T-shirts get rolled up, the jeans get yanked down, and once again, the belly button is on display.

Jim: Don't reject any of your teenager's suggestions. Sometimes the worst ideas can lead to the best.

Jared, my fourteen-year-old, has suddenly started complaining that his sister, who's twelve, is driving him crazy. Whenever his friends are in the house, she manages to find reasons to walk into his room and get herself noticed. I understand what's going on, but it makes Jared furious. He yells at her to get out and yells at my wife to keep her out.

One night after dinner I decided to try problem-solving with him. The first step took some self-control. I had to make myself sit there and listen to all his complaints about his sister. And once he got started, he couldn't stop. "She's such a pest . . . She's always hanging around when my friends are over . . . She makes up any excuse to come into my room . . . She needs paper or she wants to show me something . . . And she never knocks . . . And when I tell her to leave, she just stands there like an idiot."

I acknowledged how frustrating that must be for him, but decided to say nothing about how frustrating it was for me to hear him talk that way about his sister. I knew he was in no mood to hear my feelings.

The first thing he said when I told him that we needed some creative ideas to solve this was "send her to Mars."

I wrote it down, and he broke into a big smile. The rest of the list came fast.

- Hang a KEEP OUT sign on my door. (Jared)
- Dad should tell her she *can never* come into my room unless I say so. (Jared)
- Jared should tell his sister himself, calmly and *diplomatically*, that he wants his privacy respected when his friends visit. (Dad)

- Make a deal with her. If she leaves me alone with *my* friends, I won't tease *her* friends when they come over. (Jared)

We left it there. That was a few days ago. Since then, Jared did have a talk with Nicole, and so did I. But the big test is still ahead. His friends will be over for band practice on Saturday.

Michael: When you use the problem-solving approach with your teenagers, they're more likely to try the same approach with you.

I overheard Jeff on the phone telling his friend about this "awesome" rock concert they *had* to go to. When he hung up, he said, "Dad, I really need to talk to you."

I thought, *Uh-oh, here we go again. We're going to have the same old argument: You never let me go anywhere. Nothing terrible is going to happen. Nobody else's father . . . etc., etc.*

But to my amazement, he said, "Dad, Keith wants me to go to a concert this Saturday night. It's in the city. But before you say anything, I want to hear all your objections. All the reasons you wouldn't want me to go. I'll write them down. You know, the way you did with me last week."

Well, I had a long list for him. I told him that I worry about two fifteen-year-old boys standing alone, late at night, at a bus stop. I worry about all the drugs that are passed around at concerts. I worry about muggers and pickpockets looking for easy targets. I worry about injuries from that thing called mosh pits where kids throw themselves off the stage and other kids catch them. Maybe. And I object to the hate lyrics that put down women, police, gays, and minorities.

When I was finished, he looked at his scribbled notes and he actually addressed each of my concerns.

He said he'd make sure that he and Keith stood with other people at the bus stop; that he'd keep his wallet in the inside pocket of his jacket and keep his jacket zipped up; that he and his friends aren't into drugs; that he didn't know if there was going to be a mosh pit, but if there was he'd just watch; and that he's not so weak-minded that some dumb words in a song are going to turn him into a bigot.

I was so impressed by how mature he sounded that I agreed to let him go—under certain conditions: instead of the boys taking the bus, his mother and I would drive them to the city, go to a movie while they were at the concert, and pick them up afterward. "If that plan is okay with you," I said, "then all you'll need to do is call the box office and find out what time the concert lets out."

He thanked me. And I thanked him for taking my concerns seriously. I told him that the way he had approached me helped me to think things through.

Joan: There are some problems that go beyond problem-solving. Sometimes professional help is needed.

At first I thought Rachel had lost weight because of all the exercise she was doing lately. But I couldn't understand why she was tired all the time or why she had no appetite. No matter what I made—even her favorite foods—she'd take one or two bites, push the rest around on her plate, and when I'd urge her to eat more, she'd say, "I'm really not hungry" or "Anyway, I'm too fat."

Then one morning I accidentally walked in on her as she was getting out of the shower and I couldn't believe what I saw. Her body was emaciated. She was skin and bones.

I was completely unnerved. I didn't know if this was the kind of problem we could sit down and solve together, but I had to try. The very first step—acknowledging her feelings—backfired. I said, "Honey, I know I've been on your case lately about how you haven't been eating, and I know that can be irritating, and I can understand why you'd . . ."

Before I could get one more word out of my mouth, she flared up at me: "I don't want to talk about this. It's not your concern. It's *my* body and what I eat is *my* business!" Then she went into her room and slammed the door.

That was when I called our family doctor. I told him what was going on and he urged me to bring Rachel in for a checkup. When she finally came out of her room, I said, "Rachel, I know you don't think your eating should be my concern. But the fact is, I *am* concerned. You're my daughter and I love you and I want to help you, but I don't know how and that's why I made an appointment with the doctor."

Well, she gave me a hard time. ("I don't need help! *You're* the one who has a problem, not me.") But I didn't back down. And when we finally saw the doctor, he confirmed my worst fears. Rachel had an eating disorder. She had lost twelve pounds, missed her last few periods, and her blood pressure was low.

The doctor was very direct with her. He told her she had a potentially serious health problem that required immediate attention, that it was good it was caught early, and that he was referring her to a special program. When she asked, "What kind of program?," he explained that it was a "team" approach—a combination of individual, group, and nutritional counseling.

As we were leaving, Rachel looked overwhelmed. The doctor smiled at her and took her hand. He said, "Rachel, I've known you since you were a little girl. You're a spunky kid. I've got a lot of confidence in you. When you go into this program, you're going to make it work for you."

I don't know if Rachel was able to take in what he said, but I was grateful for his words and very relieved. I wouldn't have to face this alone. There was help out there.

Working It Out Together

Parent: This is the second time you missed your curfew! Well, you can forget about going anywhere next Saturday night. You're in for the weekend.

Instead:

Step 1: Invite your teenager to give her point of view.

Parent: Something is making it difficult for you to meet your curfew.

Teen: I'm the only one who has to be home by ten. I always have to leave when everyone is having fun.

Step 2: State your point of view.

Parent: When I expect you home at a certain time and you're still not here, I worry. My imagination goes into over-drive.

Step 3: Invite your teenager to brainstorm with you.

Parent: Let's see if there are any ideas we can come up with that would give you a little more time with your friends and give me peace of mind.

Step 4: Write down all ideas—without evaluating.

1. Let me stay out as long as I want and don't wait up for me. (teen)
2. Never let you out again until you're married. (parent)
3. Move my curfew up to eleven. (teen)
4. Extend your curfew to ten-thirty—temporarily. (parent)

Step 5: Review your list and decide which ideas you want to put into action.

Teen: Ten-thirty is better. But why temporarily?

Parent: We can make it permanent. All you'd have to do is prove you can be on time from now on.

Teen: It's a deal.

Five

Meeting the Kids

I wanted to meet the kids.

I'd been hearing about them, talking about them, thinking about them, and now I wanted to experience them for myself. I asked the parents how they'd feel about my scheduling a few sessions with their children—one to get acquainted, one to teach them some basic communication skills, and then one where we would all meet together.

The response was immediate: "That would be wonderful!" . . . "Great idea!" . . . "I don't know if I can get her to go, but I'll give it my best shot" . . . "Just tell me when. He'll be there."

We set three dates.

As I watched the kids pile into the room, I immediately started matching children to parents, trying to figure out who belonged to whom. Was the tall, skinny boy Tony's son Paul? He sort of looked like Tony. Was the girl with the friendly smile Laura's daughter Kelly? But then I thought, *No, don't go there. Get to know these young people as individuals, not as extensions of their mothers or fathers.*

When everyone had settled down, I said, "As your parents have probably told you, I teach methods of communication that can help people of all ages to get along better. But as you well know, 'getting along better' isn't always easy. It means we need to be able to hear each other and, at the very least, make an effort to understand the other person's point of view.

"Now, parents certainly understand their own point of view. But I think what many of them are missing—and that includes me—is a deeper understanding of the younger generation's point of view. That's where all of you come in. I'm hoping today to get a better sense of whatever it is that you believe to be true—either for yourself or for your friends."

The boy who looked like Tony grinned. "So what do you want to know? Just ask me. I'm an expert."

"Yeah, sure," another boy snickered. "On what?"

"We'll soon find out," I said as I handed out the page of questions I had prepared. "Please look these over, see what you're comfortable answering, and then we'll talk."

A hand shot up.

"Yes?"

"Who gets to see what we write?"

"Only me. You don't have to put your name on the paper. No one will know who wrote what. All I care about is your honest feedback."

I wasn't sure they'd want to write after a long school day, but they did. They studied each question, stared out the window, bent over their papers, and wrote quickly and earnestly. When everyone was finished, we went down the list of questions together and discussed each one. Most of the kids read their answers aloud; others added their thoughts spontaneously; and a few listened quietly, preferring to hand in their responses in writing. Here are the highlights of what they had to say:

What do you think people mean when they make a comment like, "Oh well, he's a teenager"?

"That we're immature, that we're all brats and a pain in the neck. But I don't agree. Anyone can act like that, no matter what age they are."

"That all teens are trouble. But that's wrong. It's a put-down. There isn't just one kind of teenager. We're all different."

"They always say, 'You should know better,' or, 'Act your age.' But this is our age."

"It's demeaning and insulting when adults think so little of our capabilities."

"They think they know us. They say, 'We had the same problems when we were young.' But they don't realize that times have changed and problems have changed."

What do you think is the best part of being your age— for either you or your friends?

"Having more privileges. Fewer limits and boundaries."

"Having fun and doing what I like to do."

"Having boyfriends."

"Staying out later on weekends and going to the mall with my friends."

"Enjoying life without the responsibilities I know I'll have later on."

"Getting closer to being able to drive."

"There's the freedom to experiment, but also the security and love of your family to come back to when something goes wrong."

What are some of the things kids your age worry about?

"Not fitting in."

"Not being accepted socially."

"Losing friends."

"Kids worry about what others think about them."

"We worry about the way we look—clothes, hair, shoes, brand names."

"Girls have to be skinny and pretty, and guys have to be cool and athletic."

"We worry about academic competition and having to do a ton of homework every night and passing all our subjects."

"Our future and getting good grades."

"I worry about drugs and violence and terrorists attacking us and stuff like that."

"I worry that there's going to be a school shooting and a lot of people are going to be killed. It's so easy to get a gun."

"Teenagers have a lot of stress. Maybe more stress than their parents. They can say whatever they want to say to us, but no way can we say what we want to say to them."

Is there anything your parents say or do that is helpful to you?

"My parents discuss things with me, and we try to come up with solutions."

"My mom knows when I'm in a bad mood and leaves me alone."

"My mom always tells me I look good—even if I don't."

"My dad helps me if I don't understand my homework."

"Once my dad told me about trouble he got into when he was a kid. That made me feel better when I got into trouble."

"My mother talks to me about things to say if people want me to try drugs."

"My parents always tell me, 'Have an aim or goal in life. As long as you have one, it will keep you on track.' "

Is there anything your parents do or say that's unhelpful?

"They blame things on me that aren't true. Also, when I tell them about something that makes me mad, they say, 'Take a rest,' or, 'Forget about it.' That really pisses me off."

"I hate when they tell me I have a bad attitude. Because no child comes into the world with a bad attitude. That's not how you are inside. Sometimes it's the parents' fault. They can be a bad example."

"My parents criticize my study habits, which is unfair because I do okay in school."

"I hate it when my parents yell at me."

"My parents work too hard. There is never enough time to talk to them. I mean, about everyday stuff."

"Parents shouldn't always criticize and correct their kids. My brother was raised up that way. And now he has trouble with authority. He quit all his jobs because he can't handle authority. I'm like that too. I can't hear correction. I hate correction."

If you could give advice to parents, what would it be?

"Don't say, 'You can tell me anything,' and then freak out and lecture us when we do."

"Don't say things like, 'Are you still on the phone?' or 'Are you eating again?' when you can see that we are."

"Don't tell us not to do something and then do it yourself, like drink or smoke cigarettes."

"If you come home in a bad mood, don't bring your troubles down on us or blame us for your bad day."

"Parents shouldn't act nice on the outside and then at home call you names and hit you and take your respect away. If kids are

mean, it could be because that's what they see at home. So even if parents get frustrated and want to say something mean, they should really try to hold that back."

"Parents should believe in us. Even if we do something wrong, it doesn't mean we're bad people."

"Don't criticize our friends. You don't really know them."

"Don't make us feel guilty if we'd rather hang out with our friends than be with the family."

"If you want your kids to tell you the truth, then don't ground them for every little thing."

"Even though your kids aren't little anymore, tell them that you love them."

"If there is some way to let your children experience life without being in danger, find that plan and follow it, because that's what we need."

If you could give advice to other teenagers, what would it be?

"Don't do dumb things, like drugs, just to get other kids to like you."

"Be friendly to everyone, even the kids who aren't popular."

"Don't join in when kids pick on someone."

"Don't get other kids in trouble by e-mailing bad stuff about them."

"Develop true, good friendships. Then when life is hard and you have no one else, they'll be there."

"If you want your parents to give you a later curfew, start coming home on time."

"If your boyfriend says he'll dump you if you don't have sex with him, then you should dump him."

"Don't think you can just smoke a few cigarettes once in a while and that's it. Because my friend started out that way, and now she's up to a pack a day."

"If you drink or take drugs, just know that you could be messing up your health and your future. Some kids say, 'I don't care. It's my body and I'll do what I want with it.' But they're wrong. It's not just them who will be hurt. All the people who care about them will be let down and disappointed."

What do you wish could be different about your life—at home, in school, or with friends?

"I wish my parents would realize I'm not a baby anymore and let me do more things, like go to the city with my friends."

"I wish my teachers would ease up on the homework. They all act like theirs is the only subject we take. We have to stay up so late at night to finish everything. No wonder we're tired in class."

"I wish my schedule wasn't so packed with studying and music lessons and that I had more free time to hang out with my friends."

"I wish kids wouldn't act nice to your face and then talk about you behind your back."

"I wish my friends would all get along and not try to make me take sides."

"I wish people didn't judge you by how you look or what you wear. That's why I like to go online. Because then, even if you look weird or ugly, it doesn't matter."

"I wish kids didn't fight over stupid things like, 'I saw you with my guy.' Fights don't solve anything. All that happens is you end up getting suspended, and then your parents punish you too."

"I wish parents wouldn't pressure their kids to be perfect. I mean, we only live this life once, so why can't we just sit back a little and enjoy being a teenager? Why do we have to excel all the time? Yes, we have goals and dreams, but can't we reach them without all this stress?"

When the last question had been answered, everyone looked at me expectantly. I said, "Know what I wish? I wish parents and teenagers everywhere could have heard what you had to say this afternoon. I think they would have gained some important insights that could be very helpful to them."

The kids seemed pleased by my comment. "Before we leave," I asked, "is there anything we haven't talked about that you think parents should be aware of?"

A hand went halfway up, then down, then up again. It was the boy who looked like Tony. "Yeah, you tell them that sometimes we yell and say things that get them all upset. But they shouldn't take it personally. A lot of times we don't even mean it."

"That's right," said the girl whose smile was so much like Laura's. "And tell them not to get crazy when we don't clean our room or do stuff to help out. It's not because we're brats. Sometimes we're too tired or we have things on our mind or we need to talk to our friends."

Another girl chimed in. "And ask the parents how they'd like it if the second they got home from work we'd say to them, 'You left your dirty dishes in the sink again!' or, 'I want you to start making dinner *right now!*' or, 'No TV until you've finished paying all your bills!' "

Everyone laughed.

"Actually," she added, "my mother isn't yelling as much since she's been going to your class. I don't know what she's learning there, but she doesn't go ballistic so much anymore."

"What your mother and all the other parents are learning," I said, "are the same communication skills I look forward to sharing with you next week. We'll be exploring ideas that can help people get along better in all of their relationships."

"All?" one of the girls asked. "Does that mean with our friends too?"

"With your friends too," I assured her. Yet there was something about the way she asked the question that gave me pause.

I hadn't planned to focus on friends in our next session, but suddenly it occurred to me that maybe I ought to. Maybe I should take my cue from the kids. Hearing their many comments today about the importance of their friendships jolted me into a fresh awareness of how much emotion teenagers invest in their interactions with their peers.

"How would you all feel," I asked the group, "about using our next session to see how these communication skills might apply to your relationships with your friends?"

No one answered immediately. The kids looked at one another and then back at me. Finally, someone said, "That's cool." Heads nodded in agreement.

"Then that's what we'll do," I said. "See you next week."

Six

About
Feelings,
Friends,
and Family

"Move your ass, retard!"

"Shut your face, trailer trash!"

The words hit me as I made my way past groups of teenagers milling around their lockers at the end of the school day. The guidance counselor ran down the hall toward me. "I'm so glad I caught you!" she exclaimed. "You're meeting in 307 today. Don't worry, I contacted all the kids and told them about the change."

I thanked her and hurried up the stairs, trying to avoid the stampede of pushing, shoving kids who were racing down.

"Ouch, watch where you're going, dirtbag."

"Watch yourself, loser."

"Hey, butthead, wait for me!"

What was going on? Was this the way teenagers talked to one another today?

By the time I got to room 307, most of the kids were already there waiting outside the door. I waved them in and, as they were settling down, described what I had just heard. "Tell me," I inquired, "is this kind of talk typical?"

They laughed at my naïveté.

"Doesn't it bother you?" I asked.

"Nah, it's just joking around. Everybody does it."

"Not everybody."

"But a lot of kids do."

That stymied me. "As you know," I said, "my work is about relationships. About how the words we use to communicate affect the way we feel about each other. So I need to ask you, seriously, are you telling me you really don't mind getting up and going to school each day knowing that there's a good chance that before the day is over, someone will call you a 'loser' or a 'dirtbag' or something worse?"

One of the boys shrugged. "It doesn't bother me."

"Me either," someone added.

I couldn't let it go. "So no one here objects to this kind of talk?"

There was a short pause.

"I do sometimes," a girl admitted. "And I know I shouldn't because my friends and I, we always call each other names, and it's like we're just kidding around. You know, having fun. But if you fail a test and someone calls you a 'retard'—that happened to me once—or like the time I got a bad haircut and my friend said I looked like a weirdo, then it wasn't so funny. I made believe it didn't bother me. But that was on the outside."

"What do you think would happen," I asked her, "if you didn't make believe, if instead you told your friends how you felt on the inside?"

She shook her head. "That wouldn't be good."

"Because? . . ."

"Because they'd put you down or make fun of you."

"Yeah," another girl agreed. "They'd think that you were too sensitive and that you were trying to be different or better, and then they wouldn't want to be your friends anymore."

Many hands flew up. People had a lot to say:

"But those aren't real friends. I mean, if you have to be phony and pretend you don't care, just to fit in, that sucks."

"Yeah, but a lot of kids will do anything to be accepted."

"That's right. I know someone who started drinking and doing other stuff only because his friends did."

"But that's so dumb, because you should be able to do what you think is right and let your friends do whatever they want to do. I say, 'Live and let live!' "

"Yeah, but that's not the way it works in real life. Your friends have a lot of influence over you. And if you don't go along, you could be cut out."

"So what? Who wants friends like that? I think a real friend is someone you can be yourself with, someone who doesn't try to change you."

"Someone who listens to you and cares about how you feel."

"Yeah, someone you can talk to if you have a problem."

I was touched by what the kids were saying. Their friends were so important to them that some of them were willing to give up a part of themselves in order to be part of the group. And yet they all knew, on some level, what gave meaning to a mutually satisfying friendship.

"We must be on the same wavelength," I said. "Ever since our last meeting, I've been doing a lot of thinking about how the skills I teach to adults might work in teenage relationships. You made it very clear just now that the quality you most value in a friend is the ability to hear, accept, and respect what you have to say. Now, how can that idea be put into practice?"

I reached into my briefcase and pulled out the material I had prepared. "You'll see several examples here of one friend trying to get through to another. You'll also see the contrast between the kind of response that can undermine a relationship and the kind that gives comfort and support.

"Let's go over these pages together," I said as I distributed them to the group. "Would any of you be willing to act out the different parts?"

There wasn't a moment of hesitation. They all wanted to "act it out." Amid bursts of laughter, they read their parts with energy and dramatic flare. As I sat there, looking at the illustrations and listening to the voices of real kids, I felt as if I were watching an animated cartoon.

Instead of Put-downs . . .

When people are upset, questions and criticism
can make them feel worse.

Listen with a Nod, a Sound, or a Word

Sometimes a sympathetic sound, grunt, or word can help a
friend feel better and think better.

Instead of Dismissing Thoughts and Feelings . . .

When a friend brushes your feelings aside, you're not likely to want to continue the conversation.

Put Thoughts and Feelings into Words

It's much easier to talk to someone who accepts your feelings and gives you a chance to come to your own conclusions.

Instead of Dismissing Wishes . . .

When a friend dismisses your wishes and puts you down
for even having them, you can feel demeaned and
frustrated.

Give in Fantasy What You Can't Give in Reality

It's easier to deal with reality if a friend can give us what we want in fantasy.

"So what do you think of these examples?" I asked. The kids' responses came slowly.

"It's not the way we talk, but maybe it would be good if we did."

"Yeah, because the example showing the 'wrong' way really makes you feel like junk."

"But you can't just say the 'right' words. You have to mean them or people will think you're being phony."

"In a way a lot of it doesn't sound natural. It's a different way of talking. But maybe if you get used to it . . ."

"I could get used to hearing it. I don't know if I could get used to saying it, and I don't know what my friends would think if I did."

"I think the whole thing is awesome. I wish everybody would talk to everybody this way."

"Would that include kids talking 'this way' to their parents?" I asked.

That stopped them. "Like when?" someone questioned.

"Like when your mother or father is upset about anything."

I could see by their puzzled expressions that this was a new direction for them.

"Just imagine," I went on, "that one night your mother or father comes home from work tired and full of complaints about the day: the traffic was heavy, the computer was down, the boss didn't stop yelling, and everybody had to stay late to make up for lost time.

"Well, you could react by saying, 'You think *you* had a bad day? Mine was a lot worse.' Or you could show you understand with a sympathetic 'Oh,' or by putting your parent's thoughts and feelings into words, or by giving them in fantasy what you can't give in reality."

The group was intrigued by my challenge. There was a short

pause, and then, one by one, they reached out to their imaginary parents:

"Boy, Mom, sounds like you had a hard day."

"It's a real pain when the computer goes down."

"You must hate it when the boss yells."

"It's no fun being stuck in traffic."

"I bet you wish you had a job where you could walk to work."

"And that you never had to stay late again!"

"And that your old boss would retire and you'd get a new one who doesn't yell."

They were all grinning at me now, obviously pleased with themselves.

"Know what?" a girl said. "I'm going to try this tonight with my mother. She's always complaining about her job."

"I want to try it with my dad," a boy said. "A lot of times he comes home late and talks about how tired he is."

"I suspect," I said, "that there are going to be some very appreciative parents out there tonight. And don't forget to bring them to our final meeting next week. It will be interesting to see what happens when we all put our heads together."

Feelings Need to Be Acknowledged

Girl: Briana is such a snob! She walked right by me when she saw me in the hall. She only says hello to the cool kids.

Friend: Don't let it get to you. Why should you care about her?

Instead of denying feelings:

Acknowledge feelings with a sound or word:
"Ucch!"

Identify feelings:
"Even though you know what a snob she is, it can still make you mad. Nobody likes being ignored."

Give in fantasy what you can't give in reality:
"Don't you wish one of the popular kids would give Briana a taste of her own medicine? Walk past her as if she doesn't exist. Then smile and give a big hello to somebody else."

Seven

Parents and Teens Together

Tonight was a first for all of us. As each family entered the room and took their seats, there was an undercurrent of tension. No one knew what to expect. Least of all me. Would the parents be inhibited by the presence of their teenagers? Would the kids hold back knowing their parents were watching them? Could I help both generations feel comfortable with each other?

After welcoming everyone, I said, "We're here tonight to explore ways of talking and listening that can be helpful to all members of the family. Now, that doesn't sound as if it should be hard, but sometimes it is. Mostly because of the simple fact that no two people in any family are the same. We're unique individuals. We have different interests, different temperaments, different tastes, and different needs that often collide and conflict with one another. Spend enough time in any home and you'll hear exchanges like:

'It's so hot in here. I'm opening the window.'
'No! Don't! I'm freezing!'

'Turn that music down. It's too loud!'
'Loud? I can hardly hear it.'

'Hurry up! We're late!'
'Relax. We've got plenty of time.'

"And during the teen years, new differences can develop. Parents want to keep their children safe, protected from all the dangers in the outside world. But teens are curious. They want a chance to explore the outside world.

"Most parents want their teenagers to go along with *their* ideas about what's right or wrong. Some teenagers question those ideas and want to go along with what their friends think is right or wrong.

"And if that isn't enough to fuel family tensions, we also have to deal with the fact that parents these days are busier than ever and under more pressure than ever."

"You can say that again!" Tony called out.

The teenager sitting next to Tony muttered, "And kids these days are busier than ever and under more pressure than ever."

There was a chorus of "yeahs" from the other teenagers.

I laughed. "So it's no mystery," I continued, "why people in the same family, who love one another, could also irritate, annoy, and occasionally infuriate one another. Now then, what can we do with these negative feelings? Sometimes they come bursting out of us. I've heard myself say to my own kids, 'Why do you always do that?' . . . 'You'll never learn!' . . . 'What is wrong with you?' And I've heard my kids say to me, 'That's stupid!' . . . 'You're so unfair!' . . . 'Everyone else's mother lets them' . . ."

There were smiles of recognition from both generations.

"Somehow," I went on, "even as these words are coming out of our mouths, we all know, on some level, that this kind of talk only makes people more angry, more defensive, less able to even consider one another's point of view."

"Which is why," Joan sighed, "we sometimes sit on our feelings and say nothing—just to keep the peace."

"And sometimes," I acknowledged, "deciding to 'say nothing' is not a bad idea. At the very least, we don't make matters worse. But fortunately, silence is not our only option. If ever we find ourselves becoming annoyed or angry with anyone in the family, we need to stop, take a breath, and ask ourselves one crucial question: *How can I express my honest feelings in a way that will make it possible for the other person to hear me and even consider what I have to say?*

"I know what I'm proposing isn't easy. It means we need to make a conscious decision not to tell anyone what's wrong with him or her, but to talk only about yourself—what you feel, what you want, what you don't like, or what you would like."

I paused here for a moment. The parents had heard me expound on this topic many times before. The kids were hearing it for the first time. A few of them looked at me quizzically.

"I'm going to hand out some simple illustrations," I said, "which will show you what I mean. To me, they demonstrate the power that both parents and teenagers have to either escalate or deescalate angry feelings. Take a few minutes to look at these examples and tell me what you think."

Here are the drawings I distributed to the group.

Sometimes Kids Make Parents Angry

When parents are frustrated, they sometimes
lash out with angry accusations.

Instead of Accusing . . . Say What You Feel and/or Say What You'd Like

Teenagers are more likely to hear you when you tell them how you feel, rather than how rude or wrong they are.

Sometimes Parents Make Kids Angry

When teenagers are insulted, they're sometimes tempted to
return the insult.

Instead of Counterattacking . . . Say What You Feel and/or Say What You'd Like

Parents are more likely to listen when you tell them what you feel, rather than what's wrong with them.

I watched as people studied the pages. After a few minutes I asked, "What do you think?"

Tony's son Paul was the first to respond. (Yes, the tall, skinny boy was Tony's son.) "I guess it's okay," he said, "but when I get mad, I don't think about what I should or shouldn't say. I just shoot my mouth off."

"Yeah," Tony agreed. "He's like me. Quick on the trigger."

"I understand," I said. "It's very hard to think or speak rationally when you're feeling angry. There have been times my own teenagers have done things that have made me so furious, I've yelled, 'Right now, I'm so mad, I'm not responsible for what I might say or do! You'd better stay far away from me!' I figured that gave them some protection and gave me a little time to simmer down."

"Then what?" Tony asked.

"Then I'd go for a run around the block or take out the vacuum and do all the floors—anything physical, anything that would keep me moving. What helps you cool off when you're really, really angry?"

There were a few sheepish grins. The kids were the first to respond:

"I shut my door and blast my music."
"I say curses under my breath."
"I go for a long bike ride."
"I bang on my drums."
"I do push-ups till I drop."
"I pick a fight with my brother."

I gestured toward the parents. "And you?"
"I go right to the freezer and finish off a pint of ice cream."
"I cry."
"I yell at everyone."

"I call my husband at work and tell him what happened."
"I take a couple of aspirin."
"I write a long, mean letter, and then I tear it up."

"Now imagine," I said, "that you've already done whatever it is you do to take the edge off your anger and that you're a little more able to express yourself helpfully. Can you do it? Can you tell the other person what you want, or feel, or need, instead of blaming or accusing them? Of course you can. But it does take some thought, and it does help to get some practice."

"In the cartoons I just handed you, I used examples from my own home. Now I'd like to ask all of you to try to recall something that goes on in your home that bothers, irritates, or upsets you. As soon as you think of it, please jot it down."

The group seemed startled by my request. "It can be a big thing or a little thing," I added. "Either something that has happened or even something that you imagine could happen."

Parents and kids glanced at each other self-consciously. Someone giggled, and after a few moments everyone started writing.

"Now that you've zeroed in on the problem," I said, "let's try two different ways of dealing with it. First write down what you could say that you suspect would only make matters worse." I paused here to give everyone time to write. "And now what you could say that might make it possible for the other person to hear you and consider your point of view."

The room fell silent as people grappled with the challenge I had set for them. When everyone seemed ready, I said, "Now, will each of you please take your papers and find a parent or a child who is *not* your own and sit next to him or her."

After a few minutes of general confusion—amid sounds of shifting chairs and shouts of, "I still need a kid!" and, "Who

wants to be my parent?"—people finally settled down with their new partners.

"Now," I said, "we're ready for the next step. Please take turns reading your contrasting statements to each other and notice your reactions. Then we'll talk about it."

People were tentative about getting started. There was much discussion about who would begin the scene. But once the decision had been made, both parents and teenagers assumed their new roles with conviction. They spoke softly to each other at first and little by little became more animated and louder. A mock fight between Michael and Paul (Tony's son) drew all eyes in their direction.

"But you always put it off till the last minute!"

"I do not! I told you I'll do it later."

"When?"

"After dinner."

"That's too late."

"No, it isn't."

"Yes, it is!"

"Just quit hassling me and leave me alone!!"

Suddenly they both stopped, aware that the room was silent and everyone was looking at them.

"I'm trying to get my kid to start his homework earlier," Michael explained, "but he's giving me a hard time."

"That's because he won't get off my back," Paul said. "He doesn't realize that the more he bugs me to do it, the more I put it off."

"Okay, I give up," Michael said, "now let me try the other way." He took a deep breath and said, "Son, I've been thinking . . . I've been pushing you to start your homework early because that's what feels right to me. But from now on, I'm going to trust you to get started when the time seems right to you. All

I ask is that it get done sometime before nine-thirty or ten at the latest, so that you can get a decent night's sleep."

Paul flashed a big grin. "Hey, 'Pop,' that was much better! I like that."

"So I did okay," Michael said proudly.

"Yeah," Paul replied. "And you'll see, I'll do okay too. I'll do my homework. You won't have to remind me."

The group seemed galvanized by the demonstration they had just witnessed. Several teams of parents and kids volunteered to read their contrasting statements aloud. We all leaned forward and listened intently.

Parent *(accusing):*

"Why do you always have to give me an argument when I ask you to do anything? You never offer to help. All I ever hear from you is, 'Why me? Why not him? I'm busy.'"

Parent *(describing feelings):*

"I hate getting into an argument when I ask for help. It would make me so happy to hear, 'Say no more, Mom. I'm on the job!'"

Teen *(accusing):*

"Why didn't you give me my messages? Jessica and Amy both said they called, and you never told me. Now I missed the game and it's all your fault!"

Teen *(describing feelings):*

"Mom, it's really important to me to get all my messages. I missed out on the game because they changed the day and I didn't find out until it was too late."

Parent *(accusing):*
"All I ever hear from you is 'Give me . . . ,' 'Get me . . . ,'
'Take me here,' 'Take me there.' No matter what I do for you,
it's never enough. And do I ever get a thank-you? No!"

Parent *(describing feelings):*
"I'm happy to help whenever I can. But when I do, I'd like to
hear a word of appreciation."

Teen *(accusing):*
"Why can't you be like the other mothers? All my friends can
go to the mall by themselves. You treat me like a baby."

Teen *(describing feelings):*
"I hate being home on Saturday night when my friends are all
having fun at the mall. I feel I'm old enough now to take care
of myself."

Laura, who had been listening with special interest as her own daughter read the last statement, suddenly let out a shriek. "Oh no, Kelly Ann! I don't care what you say or how you say it, I am not letting a thirteen-year-old go to the mall at night. I'd have to be crazy—with what's going on in the world today."

Kelly turned red. "Mom, *please*," she entreated.

It took us all a moment to figure out that what had been a practice exercise for the group was a very real and current conflict between Laura and her daughter.

"Am I wrong?" Laura asked me. "Even if she's with friends, they're still kids. It's just plain irresponsible to let young girls go wandering around the mall at night."

"Ma, nobody wanders," Kelly retorted heatedly. "We go into

stores. Besides, it's perfectly safe. There are tons of people around all the time."

"Well," I said, "we have two very different viewpoints here. Laura, you're convinced that the mall is no place for an unsupervised thirteen-year-old at night. You foresee too many potential dangers.

"Kelly, to you the mall seems 'perfectly safe,' and you feel that you should be allowed to go there with your friends." I turned to the group. "Are we deadlocked here, or can we think of anything that would satisfy the needs of both Kelly and her mother?"

The group didn't waste a minute. Both parents and teenagers waded in to solve the problem.

Parent (to Laura): I'll tell you what I do with my daughter. I drive her and her friends there and tell them they can stay two hours. But she has to call me after one hour and call again when she's ready to be picked up. I know it's a pain in the neck for her, but it gives me peace of mind.

Teenage girl (to Laura): You can get Kelly a cell phone. That way, she could call you if she has a problem or you could reach her anytime.

Another parent (to Laura): How about you taking the girls and dropping them off? Hang out with them a little while. Then you do a little shopping for yourself and set a time and place to meet them and bring them home.

Teenage boy (sixteen, tall, and handsome, speaking to Kelly): If you want to go to the mall with your friends, why don't you let your mom come with you?

Kelly: Are you kidding?! My friends would freak out.

Laura: Why? All your friends like me.

Kelly: No way. That would be too embarrassing.

Same handsome teen (smiling at Kelly): Suppose you tell
            your friends to put up with it, just once or twice,
            so your mom can see the scene—where you go,
            what you do. That way, maybe she'll relax.

Kelly (charmed by him): I guess. (*looks questioningly at
            her mother*)

Laura: I would do that.

I was impressed by what I had just witnessed. Even more
striking to me than the swift resolution of the conflict was the
way the group had responded to the standoff between Laura
and Kelly. No one took sides. Everyone showed great respect for
the strong feelings of both mother and daughter.

"You've all just given a clear demonstration," I said, "of a
very civilized way of dealing with our differences. It seems we
have to override our natural tendency to prove ourselves right
and the other person wrong: 'You're wrong about this! And
you're wrong about that!' Why do you suppose it isn't just as
natural for us to point out what's right? Why aren't we just as
quick to praise as we are to criticize?"

There was a short pause and then a flurry of responses. First
from the parents:

"It's a lot easier to find fault. That doesn't take any effort.
But to say something nice takes a little thought."

"That's true. Like last night my son turned his music way
down when he noticed I was on the phone. I appreciated his doing that, but I never bothered to thank him for being so consid-
erate."

"I don't know why kids have to be praised for doing what
they're supposed to do. Nobody praises me for getting dinner on
the table every night."

"My father thought praise was bad for kids. He never complimented me because he didn't want me to get a 'swelled head.'"

"My mother went to the other extreme. She never stopped telling me how great I was: 'You're so pretty, so smart, so talented.' I didn't get a swelled head, because I didn't believe her."

Teenagers joined the discussion:

"Yeah, but even if a kid did believe her parents and thought she was so special, when she goes to school and sees what other kids are like, she could be in for a big letdown."

"I think parents and teachers, they say stuff like, 'Terrific,' or 'Great job,' because they think they're supposed to. You know, to encourage you. But me and my friends, we think it sounds phony."

"And sometimes grown-ups praise you to get you to do what they want you to do. You should've heard my grandmother the time I got this really short haircut. 'Jeremy, I hardly recognized you. You look so handsome! You should keep your hair that way all the time. You look like a movie star!' Yeah, right."

"I don't think there's anything wrong with a compliment if it's sincere. I know I feel great when I get one."

"Me too! I like it when my parents say something nice about me to my face. Actually, I think most kids can use a little praise—now and then."

"I have news for you kids," Tony said. "Most *parents* can use a little praise—now and then."

There was a burst of applause from the parents.

"Well," I said, "you've certainly expressed a wide range of feelings about praise. Some of you like it and wouldn't mind hearing a lot more of it. And yet for some of you it's uncomfortable. You experience praise as either insincere or manipulative.

"Could the difference in your responses have something to do with *how* you're being praised? I believe it does. Words like,

'You're the greatest . . . the best . . . so honest . . . smart . . . generous . . . ' can make us uneasy. Suddenly we remember the times we weren't so great or honest or smart or generous.

"What can we do instead? We can describe. We can describe what we see or what we feel. We can describe a person's effort, or we can describe his achievement. The more specific we can be, the better.

"Can you hear the difference between 'You're so smart!' and 'You've been working on that algebra problem for a long time, but you didn't stop or give up until you got the answer'?"

"Yeah, sure," Paul called out. "The second thing you said is definitely better."

"What makes it better?" I asked.

"Because if you tell me I'm so smart, I think, *I wish*, or, *She's trying to butter me up*. But the second way, I think, *Hey, I guess I am smart! I know how to hang in there until I get the answer.*"

"That does seem to be the way it works," I said. "When someone describes what we've done or are trying to do, we usually gain a deeper appreciation of ourselves.

"In the cartoons I'm handing out now, you'll see examples of parents and teenagers being praised—first with evaluation, then with description. Please notice the difference in what people say to themselves in response to each approach."

When Praising Kids

Instead of Evaluating . . .

Describe What You Feel

Different kinds of praise can lead kids to very different
conclusions about themselves.

When Praising Kids

Instead of Evaluating . . .

Describe What You See

Evaluations can make kids uneasy. But an appreciative
description of their efforts or accomplishments is
always welcome.

When Praising Parents

Instead of Evaluating . . .

Describe What You Feel

People tend to push away praise that evaluates them. An honest, enthusiastic description is easier to accept.

When Praising Parents

Instead of Evaluating . . .

Describe What You See

Words that describe often lead people to a greater
appreciation of their strengths.

I noticed Michael nodding his head as he looked over the illustrations.

"What are you thinking, Michael?" I asked.

"I'm thinking that before tonight I would've said that any kind of praise was better than none. I'm a big believer in people giving each other a pat on the back. But I'm beginning to see there are different ways to go about it."

"And better ways!" Karen announced, holding up her cartoons. "Now I understand why my kids get so irritated when I tell them they're 'terrific' or 'fantastic.' It drives them crazy. Okay, so now I've got to remember—*describe, describe*!!"

"Yeah," Paul called out from the back of the room. "Cut out the gushy stuff and say what you like about the person."

I seized upon Paul's comment. "Suppose we all do exactly that—right now," I said. "Please return to your real family. Then take a moment to think about one specific thing that you like about your parent or teenager. As soon as it comes to mind, put it in writing. What could you actually say to let the other person know what it is that you admire or appreciate?"

There was a wave of nervous laughter. Parents and kids looked at each other, looked away, and then down at their papers. When everyone had finished writing, I asked them to exchange papers.

I watched quietly as smiles grew, eyes filled, and people hugged. It was sweet to see. I overheard, "I didn't think you noticed" . . . "Thank you. That makes me really happy" . . . "I'm glad that helped" . . . "I love you too."

The custodian poked his head in the door. "Soon," I mouthed to him. To the group I said, "Dear people, we have come to the end of our final session. Tonight we looked at how we can express our irritation to each other in ways that are helpful rather than hurtful. And we also looked at ways to express our appreciation so that each person in the family can feel visible and valued.

"Speaking of appreciation, I want you to know what an enormous pleasure it's been for me to work with all of you over these many weeks. Your comments, your insights, your suggestions, your willingness to explore new ideas and take a chance with them have made this a very gratifying experience for me."

Everyone applauded. I thought people would leave after that. They didn't. They hung around, talked to one another, and then each family lined up to say good-bye to me personally. They wanted me to know that the evening had been important to them. Meaningful. The kids as well as the parents shook my hand and thanked me.

When everyone had gone, I stood lost in thought. Almost everything in the media these days gives a picture of parents and teenagers as adversaries. Yet here tonight I had witnessed a very different dynamic. Parents and teens in partnership. Both generations learning and using skills. Both generations welcoming the opportunity to talk together. Happy to connect with each other.

The door opened. "Oh, we're so glad you didn't leave yet!" It was Laura and Karen. "Do you think we could have one more meeting next Wednesday—just for parents?"

I hesitated. I hadn't planned to go on.

"Because we were all talking in the parking lot about the stuff going on with our kids that we didn't think we should bring up tonight with them sitting there."

"And you wouldn't have to worry about contacting people. We'd take care of that."

"We know it's last-minute, and some people said they couldn't make it, but it's *really* important."

"So would that be okay with you? We know how busy you are, but if you have the time . . ."

I looked into their anxious faces and mentally rearranged my schedule.

"I'll make the time," I said.

Expressing Your Irritation

To Your Teenager

Instead of accusing or name-calling:
"Who's the birdbrain who left the house and forgot to lock the door?!!"

Say what you feel: "It upsets me to think that anyone could have walked into our home while we were away."

Say what you'd like and/or expect: "I expect the last person who leaves the house to make sure the door is locked."

To Your Parent

Instead of blaming or accusing:
"Why do you always yell at me in front of my friends? No one else has parents who do that!"

Say what you feel: "I don't like being yelled at in front of my friends. It's embarrassing."

Say what you'd like and/or expect: "If I'm doing something that bothers you, just say, 'I need to talk to you for a second,' and tell me privately."

Expressing Appreciation

TO YOUR TEENAGER

Instead of evaluating her:
  "You're always so responsible!"

Describe what she did: "Even though you were under a lot of pressure at your rehearsal, you made it your business to call when you knew you were going to be late."

Describe what you feel: "That phone call saved me a lot of worry. Thank you!"

TO YOUR PARENT

Instead of evaluating him:
  "Good job, Dad."

Describe what he did: "Boy, you spent half your Saturday setting up that basketball hoop for me."

Describe what you feel: "I really appreciate that."

Eight

Dealing with Sex and Drugs

The group was smaller tonight. Small enough for us to move to the library and sit comfortably around a conference table. Several people started talking about last week's meeting. How much they had enjoyed it. How much better things were going at home. How, since then, both they and the kids would catch themselves repeating some of the same old negative stuff, smile self-consciously, say, "Do-over!" and start again. And even though the new words sounded a little awkward or unfamiliar, they still felt good.

Karen tried to listen patiently, but I could see that she could barely contain herself. At the first break in the conversation, she blurted out, "I'm sorry to be negative, and I'm even sorrier to bring the subject up, but I'm still upset over something that went on at a party that Stacey was at last week." She paused here and took a deep breath. "I heard that one of the girls in her class was giving oral sex to a few of the boys. Now, I'm not a prude, and I don't think I'm naïve. I know all kinds of things go on with teenagers today that were unheard of when I was a kid. But twelve and thirteen years old! In our community! At a birthday party!"

Everyone at the table wanted to weigh in on the topic:

"It's hard to believe, isn't it? But according to what I've been reading, it's happening everywhere. And with kids who are even younger. And not only at parties. They're doing it in the school bathroom, on the bus, and in the house before their parents come home from work."

"What I find so disturbing is that the kids don't even see it as that big a deal. Oral sex to them is like what a good-night kiss was to us. They don't even think of it as sex. After all, it isn't intercourse, so you're still a virgin. And you can't get pregnant, so they figure it's safe."

"It's *not* safe. That's what's so scary to me. My brother is a doctor, and he told me the kids can get some of the same diseases from oral sex as they can from regular sex—like oral herpes or gonorrhea of the throat. He said that the only protection is a condom. And even that's not 100 percent safe. A boy could have genital warts or lesions on his scrotum, and no condom will help since it doesn't cover that area."

"I feel sick just listening to this. The whole situation is a nightmare. As far as I'm concerned, the only real protection is not doing it at all."

"Yeah, but face it. It's a different world today. And according to what I've been hearing, it's something the girls do for the boys—not the other way around. Some of the girls even do it publicly."

"I've heard that too. Evidently the girl feels pressured to 'perform' in order to be popular. What she doesn't realize is that word gets around, and she gets a reputation for being 'trashy' or a 'slut.'"

"But the boy's reputation gets a boost. He gets bragging rights."

"I worry about both the boys and the girls. How do they feel about themselves afterward—like when they see each other in the hall the next day? And how does having this kind of sex now—and it *is* sex, because if it involves sex organs it's sex—affect their future relationships?"

With each person's comment, Karen grew more visibly agitated. "Okay, okay," she said. "So it's widespread and a lot of kids are into it, but what am I supposed to do about it? I can't ignore it. I know I have to talk to Stacey about what went on at that party. But I don't even know where to begin. The truth is, I'm embarrassed about even bringing up the subject with her."

There was a long pause. People looked at one another blankly and then at me. This wasn't easy. "The one thing I'm sure of," I began, "is what *not* to say: 'Stacey, I know all about what went on at that party you were at last week, and I am shocked and revolted. That is the most disgusting thing I have ever heard! Was there only one girl doing "you know what" to the boys? Are you sure? Did anyone ask you to do it? And did you? Don't lie to me!'

"Instead of giving her your revulsion or the third degree, you'd have a far better chance of having a productive conversation if you tell yourself to keep your tone neutral and your questions general rather than personal. For example, 'Stacey, I just heard something that took me by surprise, and I want to check it out with you. Someone told me that oral sex is going on at kids' parties—even the one you were at last week.'

"Whether she confirms or denies it, you can continue the conversation—again, keeping your tone nonjudgmental: 'Ever since I heard I've been wondering if this is something the girls do because they feel pressured by the boys? Or is it because they think it will make them popular? I've also been wondering what happens if a girl refuses.'

"After Stacey tells you as much as she's comfortable telling, you can express your point of view. But since the subject can be difficult for parents, you might want to take some time beforehand to decide exactly what it is you want to communicate."

"I know what I want to communicate," Karen said ruefully. "I just don't think she could hear it."

Laura looked puzzled. "What couldn't she hear?"

"That I feel it's wrong for one person to use another to satisfy a sexual urge. Or for anyone to 'service' anyone else just to be popular. To me that's demeaning. It's not being respectful to yourself. And that goes for a boy as well as a girl."

"Sounds good to me," Laura said. "Why couldn't you say that to Stacey?"

"I suppose I could." Karen sighed. "But I know my daughter. She'd probably tell me I was being uptight and old-fashioned, that I just didn't 'get it,' and the kids today don't think it's such a big deal. It's just what they do at some parties. So what do I say to that?"

"You can start," I said, "by acknowledging her perspective: 'So to you and a lot of the kids you know it's no big deal.' Then you can go on to share your adult perspective. 'As I see it, oral sex is a very personal, intimate act. Not a party game. Not something you do for fun. And I can't help but wonder if some of the kids who participate don't feel bad about it afterward and wish they hadn't.' No matter what Stacey says after that, you've given her something to think about. At the very least, she knows where her mother stands."

"Right on!" Michael said. "And while you're at it, Stacey should also be told about the health risks. About the STDs kids can get from oral sex. Or any kind of sex, for that matter. She needs to understand that some of the diseases are curable, but some aren't. Some are life-threatening. That's nothing to fool around with."

Laura shook her head. "If it were my kid, she'd have her hands over her ears by now. She could never stand to hear me go on and on about all the horrible diseases she could get."

"But we're the parents!" Michael exclaimed. "Whether the kids like it or not, there's a lot we need to tell them about sex for their own protection."

Laura looked pained. "I know you're right," she acknowledged, "but the truth is, I dread having the 'big talk' with my daughter."

"You're not alone," I said. "The 'big talk' can be embarrassing for both parents and kids. Besides, the subject of sex is too important and too complex to try to tackle in one sitting. Instead, be on the lookout for opportunities that can lead to some 'little' talks. For instance, when you're watching a movie or a TV program together, or listening to the news on the radio, or reading an article in a magazine, you can use what you're seeing or hearing to get a conversation going."

My suggestion sparked an immediate response. Evidently several people were already using this approach with their children. Here, in cartoon form, are some of the examples they shared with the group.

Instead of the One "Big Talk" . . .

The onetime talk about sex can be hard for a parent to
deliver and hard for a teenager to listen to.

Look for Opportunities to Have "Small Talks"

While Listening to the Radio

While Reading a Newspaper

While Watching a Sitcom Together

While Driving a Car

Joan raised her hand. "My mother could never, *ever,* have brought up any of these topics with me. She would have died of embarrassment. She did do one thing, though. When I was about twelve, she gave me a book about the 'facts of life.' I pretended I wasn't interested, but I read it from cover to cover. And whenever my girlfriends came over, we'd close the bedroom door, take out 'The Book,' read it again, and giggle over all the pictures."

"What I like about a book," Jim said, "is that it gives the kid a little privacy—a chance to look over the material without someone looking over his shoulder. But no book is going to be a substitute for a parent. Kids want to know what their parents think. What their parents expect of them."

"That's the part that worries me," Laura said. "The 'expect' part. I mean, if you're talking to your kids about sex and giving them books about it with pictures, won't they get the idea that you *expect* them to be having sex and that they've got your permission?"

"Not at all," Michael said. "Not if you make it clear that what you're giving them is information, *not* permission. Besides, it seems to me that if we don't give our kids some basic facts, we could be putting them at risk. If there's anything we believe they should know for their own protection, the only way we can ever be sure they'll know it is to give them the information ourselves."

Michael paused here, searching his mind for an example. "For instance, how many boys know how to use a condom safely— how to actually put it on and take it off? And how many are aware that they need to check the expiration date on the package? Because a dried-out condom is as good as no condom at all."

"Wow," Laura said, "*I* didn't even know that. . . . And I wonder how many girls realize that, no matter what their friends tell them, they *can* get pregnant the first time they have sex— even if they've got their period."

Michael nodded vigorously. "That's just the kind of thing I

mean," he said. "And here's something else. I'll bet it doesn't occur to most kids that even if they're having sex with a person who may have had sex with only one other person, that one other person could have had sex with lots of other people. And who knows what diseases got passed down along the way!"

Tony frowned. "Everything you all said just now is very important. I mean, you're right. You gotta tell your kids about the dangers. But shouldn't you also tell them that there's a good part about sex? That it's normal, natural . . . one of life's pleasures. Hey, it's how we all got here!"

After the laughter subsided, I said, "Nevertheless, Tony, those 'normal, natural' feelings can sometimes overwhelm our kids and play havoc with their judgment. Today's teenagers are under enormous pressure. Not only from their hormones and their peers but from a sexualized pop culture that bombards them with explicit, erotic images on television, in movies, in music videos, and on the Internet.

"So, yes, it's normal for kids to want to experiment, to act out what they've seen or heard. And yes, we do want to convey that sex is 'one of life's pleasures.' But we also need to help our teenagers set boundaries. We need to share our adult values and give them some guidelines to hang on to."

"For instance?" Tony said.

I thought a moment. "Well . . . for instance, I think young people should be told that it's never okay to let anyone pressure them into doing anything sexual that they're not comfortable with. They don't have to be unpleasant about it. But they can let the other person know how they feel. They can simply say, 'I don't want to do this.'"

"I totally agree," Laura exclaimed. "And anyone who doesn't respect that isn't a person they should ever go out with again. . . . And I also think kids should be made to understand that sex isn't something you do just because you think everybody else is doing it. You need to do what's right for you. Besides, who knows what's really going on? Maybe some kids *are* having sex, but I'll bet a lot of them aren't and are lying about it."

"And speaking of 'doing what's right for you,'" Joan added, "before kids even think of turning their bodies and souls over to someone else, they ought to ask themselves some serious questions, like, 'Is this a person who really cares about me?' . . . 'Is this someone I can trust?' . . . 'Is this someone I can be myself with?'"

"To me," Karen said, "the main message kids ought to hear from their parents is *'Slow down. There's no need to rush.'* I think it's a big mistake for them to be having sex or hooking up or whatever they call it today, when they're still so young."

"I couldn't agree more!" Joan exclaimed. "These are the years they should be concentrating on their studies and getting involved in different kinds of activities—sports, hobbies, clubs—and doing volunteer work in the community. It's not a time for them to be complicating their lives with sexual relationships. I know they don't want to hear it from us, but still, we should tell them that some things are worth waiting for."

"But there are always going to be some kids who won't wait," Michael pointed out. "And if that's the case, if they're determined to 'go all the way,' they should hear some straight talk from their parents. I'd spell it out for them. I'd tell them they need to have a serious discussion with their prospective partner so that they can decide together just what kind of contraception *each of them* plans to use. Then *both of them* need to check it out with a doctor. My point is, if teenagers think they're grown-up enough to have sex, then they have to be prepared to act like grown-ups. And that means thinking about consequences and taking responsibility."

Jim nodded appreciatively. "Boy, Michael, that really lays it on the line. And of course, everything you said just now goes for all kids—whether they're straight or gay."

There was a sudden silence. Several people looked uneasy.

"I'm glad you added that, Jim," I said. "We do have to recognize the possibility that a young person might be homosexual and that all the precautions Michael recommended just now would apply equally to him or her."

Jim looked hesitant. "I guess the reason I even brought it up," he said, "is because I was thinking of my nephew. He just turned sixteen, and a few weeks ago he confided in me that he's gay. He said the reason he was telling me was because, knowing me, he was pretty sure I'd be okay with it, but he was worried about how his parents would take it. It seems he had been wanting to tell them for a long time but was afraid. Not of his mother's reaction so much. But he didn't know what his father would do if he found out.

"We talked for a long time about the possible fallout, and at one point he said, 'I'm gonna do it, Uncle Jim. I'm gonna tell them.'

"Well, he did. He told them. He said they were both very upset at first. His father wanted him to see a therapist. His mother tried to reassure him. She explained that it wasn't at all unusual for a teenager to feel an occasional attraction to a person of the same sex, but it was probably just a passing thing.

"Then he told her that it wasn't a passing thing, that he'd been having these feelings for a long time now, and he hoped they'd both understand. It must've been very hard for them to hear that, but little by little they seemed to come around. In the end his father was the one who really surprised him. He said that, no matter what, he'd always be their son and that he'd always have their love and support.

"I can tell you that was one relieved young man. And I was

one very relieved uncle. Because if his mother or father had ever turned their back on him over this, I don't know what would have happened. I've read too many stories about kids going into a major depression or even becoming suicidal when their parents reject them because they're gay."

"Your nephew was fortunate," I said. "Coming to terms with a teenager's homosexuality is never easy for any parent. But if we can accept our children for who they truly are, then we've given them a great gift—the strength to be themselves and the courage to begin to deal with the prejudice of the outside world."

Another long silence. "There's something else," Joan said slowly. "Whether our kids are straight or gay, they all need to be made aware that once they decide to add sex to a relationship it's never the same. Everything gets more complicated. All the feelings become more intense. If anything goes wrong, if there's a breakup—which happens all the time with teenagers—it can be devastating for them.

"I remember what went on with my best friend in high school. She was crazy about this boy, let herself get talked into sleeping with him, and after he dumped her for someone else, she went to pieces. Her grades went down, she couldn't eat, sleep, study, or concentrate on anything for the longest time."

Jim threw up his hands. "Well," he announced, "after listening to all this, I'm beginning to think there's a good case to be made for abstinence. Face it, it's the only method that's 100 percent safe. I know someone here is going to tell me that kids are reaching puberty earlier and marrying later and that it's unrealistic to expect them to abstain for so many years, but abstinence doesn't mean they can't go near each other. They can still hold hands, or hug, or kiss, or maybe even go to what we used to call first base. That would be okay . . . I mean, okay for everyone except *my* daughter."

People smiled. Laura looked troubled. "It's easy for us to sit around a table and decide what we should tell our kids they can or can't do. But there's no way we can follow them around twenty-four hours a day. And no matter what we tell them, who says they'll listen?"

"You're right, Laura," I said. "There are no guarantees. No matter what a parent says, some kids will test the limits and some will go beyond the limits. Nevertheless, all the skills you've been putting into practice these past few months make it far more likely that your kids *will* be able to listen to you. But even more important, they'll have the confidence to listen to themselves and set their own limits."

Tony nodded. "I sure as hell hope that what you said just now applies to drugs too, because I'm getting a bad feeling about some of the kids my son is starting to hang out with. They don't have the greatest reputation—one of them was suspended for getting high in school—and I don't want my boy influenced by him. I mean, if they're trying to get him to use drugs, I want to know what I can do to head them off. Like what should I say to him?"

"What would you like to say?" I asked.

"What my father said to me."

"What was that?"

"That he'd break every bone in my body if he ever caught me using drugs."

"Did that stop you?"

"No. I just made sure he never caught me."

I laughed. "So at least now you know what not to do."

Laura jumped in. "How about if you tell him, 'Listen, if anyone tries to talk you into doing drugs, just say *no*.'"

Tony gave me a what-do-you-think look.

"The problem with that approach," I said, "is that by itself it's not enough. Kids need to hear more than a simple 'just say no.' They're under enormous pressure today to just say yes. The combination of all the messages in the pop culture and the easy availability of drugs and the urging of their peers can be hard to resist: 'You gotta try this' . . . 'Trust me, you'll like it' . . . 'This stuff is really great' . . . 'It feels sooo good!' . . . 'Helps you relax' . . . 'Come on, don't be a wimp.'

"And as if that weren't enough, scientists are now telling us that although a teenager may appear physically mature, his brain is still in the process of being formed. The part that controls impulses and exercises judgment is one of the very last areas of the brain to develop."

"That's so scary," Laura said.

"Yes, it is," I agreed, "but the good news is that you all have more power than you realize. Your kids care deeply about what you think. They may not always show it, but your values and convictions are very important to them and can be the determining factor in their decision to either use or avoid drugs and alcohol. For example, Tony, you can tell your son, 'I sure hope your friend isn't into drugs anymore. He's a nice kid, and I hate to think of him messing up his future because of what he's putting into his body today.'

"And it's not only our words that can keep our children from risky behavior, it's also what we model. It's what our kids see us do or not do that speaks volumes to them."

"Now that hits home," Joan commented. "My father once grounded me because he found out I had one little drink at a party. But I used to see him every night with his cocktail before dinner and beer with dinner, so I figured if it was okay for him, it was okay for me."

"At least your father had an idea about what was going on with you," Laura said, "and was trying to be responsible. A lot of parents today are clueless. They figure that if their kid *seems* to be doing everything right, then everything is right. But you can't ever really be sure. I read an article recently about these teenagers from a wealthy community. They were on the honor roll, on all the teams, and every weekend they were binge drinking. And the parents had no idea until a few of them ended up in the hospital and one of them nearly died.

"That story is a wakeup call," I said. "Binge drinking goes on in many communities today. It's a major concern for parents, especially since we now know that teen drinking is more dangerous than we previously thought. All the recent studies show that the adolescent brain is in a critical stage of development. Alcohol destroys brain cells, causes neurological damage, memory loss, learning problems, and puts a youngster's overall health at risk. There's also new evidence that the earlier kids start drinking, the greater the chance of their becoming alcoholics as adults."

"Oh great!" Tony said. "Now that we know all that, how do we get it into the heads of our dopey kids? They don't think anything could ever happen to them. They'll go to a party and dare one another to see who can drink the most before throwing up or passing out."

"Which is why," I said, "we need to be very clear and very specific when we tell our children, *'Binge drinking can kill you. Putting a large amount of alcohol into your body at any one time can lead to alcohol poisoning. And alcohol poisoning can lead to coma or death. That's a medical fact.'*"

Joan put her hands to her head. "This is too much for me," she groaned. "Alcohol by itself is bad enough, but everything I've been reading says that teenagers who do a lot of drinking are also into doing drugs. And there's so much new stuff out there that I never even heard of before. It's not just pot or crack or LSD anymore. Now there's ecstasy, and . . ."

People were quick to add to Joan's list: ". . . and roofies, the date rape drug."

"And something called Ketamine, or 'Special K.'"

"And how about methamphetamines? That's supposed to be even more addictive than cocaine."

"I heard about something new the kids inhale to get high. It's called poppers or liquid gold."

"Boy," Tony said, shaking his head, "there's a helluva lot to know, isn't there."

"It can seem overwhelming," I said, "but the information is all out there—in books, in magazines, and on the Internet. You can call a substance abuse hotline and ask for their current pamphlets. You can talk to other parents in your community and find out what they know. And while you're at it, you can ask your son what he knows about what the kids in his school are using today."

"Well," Tony said, "looks like I've got my work cut out for me."

"All parents of teenagers," I said, "have their work cut out for them. We all need to make it clear to our kids that their mothers and fathers are informed, involved, ready to do whatever it takes to protect them.

"And once again, a onetime lecture won't do the job. Kids need to hear your thoughts about drugs in different ways and at different times. They need to feel comfortable enough to ask you questions, to answer your questions, and to explore their own thoughts and feelings.

"So . . . on to our final challenge! How can we take advantage of a small opportunity that might present itself in the course of a day to engage our children in a dialogue about drugs? What kinds of conversations can we imagine having with our teenagers?"

After much back and forth, the group envisioned the following scenarios.

Take Advantage of Small Opportunities to Talk About Drugs

Reading a Newspaper

Watching a Commercial

Commenting on Something You Notice

Looking at a Magazine

Setting an Example

Commenting on a Radio Program

As we were discussing our last example, Laura's hand shot up. "So far all we've been talking about is how to steer our kids away from using drugs. But what if a kid is already using stuff? I mean, what if it's too late?"

"It's never too late to exercise your power as a parent," I said. "Even if it's a onetime only 'experiment,' it can't be ignored. You need to confront your teenager, review the risks, and reaffirm your values and expectations.

"If, however, you suspect that your teenager is already using drugs with some frequency, if you notice changes in behavior, grades, appearance, attitude, friends, sleeping patterns, or eating habits, then it's time to take action: Let your child know what you've observed. Listen to his or her side of the story. Learn whatever you can about what's really going on. Call a local or national drug abuse program for additional information. Consult with your doctor. Investigate whatever services are available in your community that can offer professional counseling and treatment. In other words, get help. You can't do it alone."

"I hope I never have to do it at all." Laura sighed. "Maybe I'll get lucky and my kids will turn out just great."

"You have more than luck to depend upon, Laura," I said. "You've got skills. And even more important, you understand the attitude that gives heart to the skills. All of you do. Over these past few months you've made many changes in the way you communicate with your children. And all of these changes—both large and small—can make a profound difference in your relationship with them.

"By being responsive to your teenagers' feelings, by working out problems together, by encouraging them to reach for their goals and realize their dreams, you let your kids know every day how much you respect and love and value them. And young people who feel valued by their parents are more likely to value themselves, more likely to make responsible choices, less likely to get involved in behavior that would work against their own best interests or jeopardize their future."

Silence. It had been a long session, yet everyone seemed reluctant to leave.

"I'm going to miss these classes." Laura sighed. "Not just for the skills but for all the support I've gotten from everyone here." Her eyes welled up. "And I'm going to miss hearing about everybody's kids."

Karen hugged her. Michael did too.

"What I'll miss most," Joan said, "is knowing I have people I can talk to if a problem comes up."

"And as we all well know," Jim commented ruefully, "with teenagers there are always going to be new problems. That's why it's been great to have a place to go where you can get some feedback from people who are in the same boat."

"Hey," Tony said, "who says we have to quit? How about we keep on meeting—not every week maybe, but like every month or two?"

Tony's suggestion was met with an immediate, enthusiastic response.

Everyone looked at me expectantly.

I thought for a moment. What these parents wished for themselves was what I wished for all parents of teenagers—an ongoing support system. The relief of no longer feeling isolated. The comfort of being able to unburden yourself to people you know will understand. The hope that springs from exchanging ideas and seeing new possibilities. The pleasure of sharing small triumphs with one another.

"If that's what you all want," I said to the group, "keep me posted. I'll be there."

Sex and Drugs

Instead of One Big Lecture ("I know you think you know all about sex and drugs, but I think it's time we had a talk")

LOOK FOR SMALL OPPORTUNITIES TO GET A CONVERSATION GOING

Listening to the radio: "Do you think what that psychologist said just now is right? Do kids have a hard time refusing drugs because they don't want to look geeky or lose friends?"

Watching television: "So, according to this commercial, all a girl has to do to get a guy interested in her is wear the right color lip gloss."

Reading a magazine: "What do you think of this? It says here, 'Sometimes kids take drugs just to feel good. But then they have to use drugs—just to feel normal.'"

Watching a movie: "Did that last scene seem realistic? Would two teenagers who just met jump into bed together?"

Reading a newspaper: "When you have time, take a look at this article about teens and binge-drinking. I'd be interested in your reaction."

Listening to music: "How do you feel about these lyrics? Do you think they could affect the way guys treat girls?"

Next Time We Meet . . .

In the days that followed I found my thoughts returning to the group again and again.

We had been on a long journey together. Different people had started out with different hopes, different fears, and different destinations in mind. Yet no matter what their original reasons for coming to the workshop meetings, they all had the satisfaction of seeing not only that their new skills improved their relationships with their teenagers, but that their teenagers were behaving more responsibly. Accomplishments we could all feel good about!

Still, I was glad we'd be meeting again. It would give me a chance to share with the parents what had been welling up within me with increasing clarity—the larger view of what our work together had been about.

Next time I'll tell them that if it is indeed true that "children learn what they live," then what their children had been living and learning over these past few months were the most basic principles of caring communication. Every day, in the push and pull of family life, their teenagers were learning that:

- **Feelings matter.** Not just your own, but those of people with whom you disagree.
- **Civility matters.** Anger can be expressed without insult.
- **Words matter.** What you choose to say can cause resentment or generate goodwill.
- **Punishment has no place in a caring relationship.** We're all people in process—capable of making mistakes and capable of facing our mistakes and making amends.
- **Our differences needn't defeat us.** Problems that seem insoluble can yield to respectful listening, creativity, and persistence.
- **We all need to feel valued.** Not only for who we are now, but for who we can become.

Next time we meet, I'll tell the parents that each day offers new opportunities. Each day gives them a chance to demonstrate the attitude and language that can serve their teenagers in the present moment and in all the years ahead.

Our children are our gift to tomorrow. What they experience in our homes today will empower them to bring to the world they inherit the ways that affirm the dignity and humanity of all people.

That's what I'll tell the parents—next time.

Additional Reading
That May Be Helpful

Elkind, David, PhD. *Parenting Your Teenager in the 1990s: Practical Information and Advice About Adolescent Development and Contemporary Issues.* Cambridge, MA: Modern Learning Press, 1993. Dr. Elkind addresses many of the issues that continue to confront parents of teenagers a decade later. He offers insights and advice in a supportive, readable manner.

Faber, Adele, and Elaine Mazlish. *How to Talk So Kids Will Listen and Listen So Kids Will Talk.* London: Piccadilly Press, 2001. Recommended for two reasons:

1. The chapter on autonomy—how to help a child become a separate, independent individual who can one day function on his own—is especially relevant during the teen years.

2. The chapter on how to free a child from being trapped in a role (for example, lazy, complainer, princess, disorganized) applies to teenagers as well. It's never too late to help a young person see himself differently and realize his potential.

———. *How to Talk So Kids Can Learn: At Home and in School.* London: Piccadilly Press, 2003. Describes the kind of communication that motivates students to think, learn, persist, and believe in themselves.

Giannetti, Charlene, and Margaret Sagarese. *The Roller-Coaster Years: Raising Your Child Through the Maddening Yet Magical Middle School Years.* New York: Broadway Books, 1997. A lively, practical book that deals with the wide range of issues affecting most middle-schoolers and their parents.

Hersch, Patricia. *A Tribe Apart: A Journey into the Heart of American Adolescence.* New York: Ballantine Books, 1998. A gifted journalist takes you deep inside the world of eight very different teenagers and reveals the passions and pressures that shape their personality and character during their adolescent years.

Lopez, Ralph, MD. *The Teen Health Book: A Parents' Guide to Adolescent Health and Well-being.* New York: W. W. Norton & Co., 2002. An excellent resource. Written in a clear and friendly style, it addresses both the physical and emotional concerns of teenagers.

McGraw, Jay. *Closing the Gap: A Strategy for Bringing Parents and Teens Together.* New York: Fireside/Simon & Schuster, 2001. Advice to both parents and teens from the personal perspective of a young college student.

Pipher, Mary, PhD. *Reviving Ophelia: Saving the Lives of Adolescent Girls.* New York: Ballantine Books, 1995. A look at the harm done to our daughters by the current culture, along with sensible strategies for how to help them.

Pollack, William, PhD. *Real Boys: Rescuing Our Sons from the Myths of Boyhood.* New York: Owl Books, Henry Holt and Company, 1999. A logical companion to *Reviving Ophelia, Real Boys* makes clear how our gender stereotypes harm our sons and offers a wealth of caring alternatives.

Richardson, Justin, MD, and Schuster, Mark A., MD, PhD. *Everything You Never Wanted Your Kids to Know About Sex (But Were Afraid They'd Ask): The Secrets to Surviving Your Child's Sexual Development from Birth to the Teens.* New York: Three

Rivers Press, 2003. The title says it all. Sound, sensible advice on dealing with a tough topic.

Sheras, Peter, PhD, with Sherill Tippins. *Your Child: Bully or Victim? Understanding and Ending Schoolyard Tyranny.* New York: Fireside/Simon & Schuster, 2002. A thoughtful exploration of the causes and effects of bullying and suggestions for how to deal with it.

Taffel, Dr. Ron, with Melinda Blau. *The Second Family: Reckoning with Adolescent Power.* New York: St. Martin's Press, 2001. Dr. Taffel takes an unflinching look at how peers and the current pop culture can push parents to the sidelines of their teenagers' lives. He recommends a variety of ways to renew and strengthen the connection between the generations.

Walsh, David, PhD. *Why Do They Act That Way?: A Survival Guide to the Adolescent Brain for You and Your Teen.* New York: Free Press, 2004. Dr. Walsh draws upon the latest research about the adolescent brain as well as his own extensive experience with troubled teens to give parents valuable insights, information, and guidelines.

To Learn More . . .

If you are interested in having a chance to discuss and practice the communication skills in this book with others, please visit www.fabermazlish.com. There you'll find information about:

- Group workshops for parents and professionals
- Individual workshops
- Books for parents and professionals
- Books for kids
- Audio- and videotapes
- Creative solutions to parenting problems
- Adele and Elaine's newsletter, the *Faber/Mazlish Forum*
- And much more!

Index

OTHER BOOKS BY ADELE FABER AND ELAINE MAZLISH

HOW TO TALK SO KIDS WILL LISTEN AND LISTEN SO KIDS WILL TALK

ISBN: 1 85340 705 4
ISBN-13: 978 1 85340 705 5

The bestselling book that gives you the knowhow you need to be effective with your children. Enthusiastically praised by parents and professionals around the world, the down-to-earth, respectful approach of Faber and Mazlish makes relationships with children of all ages less stressful and more rewarding.

"No peace-loving parent should be without a copy." Good Housekeeping

SIBLINGS WITHOUT RIVALRY
How to Help Your Children Live Together So You Can Live Too

ISBN: 1 85340 630 9
ISBN-13: 958 1 85340 630 0

Guides the way to family peace and tranquility with humour and compassion for both parents and children. Illustrated, action-oriented and easy to understand, it's packed with sensitive yet sensible ways to turn quarrelling siblings and frustrated parents into an open, communicative family.

"A very human book about one of the toughest problems parents have to handle."
Dr Benjamin M Spock

LIBERATED PARENTS, LIBERATED CHILDREN
Your Guide to a Happier Family

ISBN: 1 85340 707 0
ISBN-13: 958 1 85340 707 9

Wisdom, humour and practical advice abound in this indispensible book that demonstrates the kind of communication that guides self-esteem, inspires confidence, encourages responsibility and makes a major contribution to the stability of today's family.

"A real find . . . What Faber and Mazlish have to offer is a wealth of specific solutions to difficult situations and challenging behaviour, which they encourage readers to tailor to their own personality." Time Out

HOW TO TALK SO KIDS CAN LEARN
At Home and in School

ISBN: 1 85340 704 6
ISBN-13: 958 1 85340 704 8

Using the unique communication strategies, down-to-earth dialogues and delightful cartoons that are their hallmark, the leading experts on parent-child communication show parents and teachers how to help children handle the everyday problems that interfere with learning and how to inspire kids to be self-directed, self-disciplined and responsive to the wonders of learning.

CHRISTOPHER GROENHOUT

Sculptures at Tongdosa temple (p242), Gajisan
Provincial Park

Hikers on Namsan (p205), Seoul

PHILIP GAME

Passenger ferry arrives in Busan (p227), Gyeongsangnam-do

TONY WHEELER

330

MARTIN MOOS

The ruggged peaks of Wolchulsan National Park
(p266), Jeollanam-do

Ancient Korean sculpture
(p55)

MARTIN MOOS

The bright lights of Gwangju (p251), Jeollanam-do

BILL WASS

Statue of a *haenyeo* (traditional female diver; p284), Jejudo

Harubang (lava-rock statue; p272), Jejudo

Yongduam Rock (p278), Jejudo

Seonunsa temple (p303), Seonunsan Provincial Park

JEFF YATES

Gochang fortress wall (p304), Jeollabuk-do

MARTIN MOOS

Reclining gold Buddhas, Seonunsa temple (p303), Seonunsan Provincial Park

BILL WASSMAN

Yongmun Pokpo (p312), Gyeryongsan
National Park

Traditional building, Bomunsan (p309), Daejeon

Beopjusa temple (p328), Songnisan National Park

JOHN BORTHV

Bulguksa temple (p202), Gyeongju

Monk playing drum, Girimsa temple (p203), Gyeongju

MARTIN MOOS

RICHARD I'ANSON

Buddha rock carving, Beopjusa temple (p328), Songnisan National Park

Mansudae Grand Monument (p362),
Pyongyang, North Korea

Waterfall (p373), Paekdusan, North Korea

Yanggakdo Football Stadium (p367), Pyongyang, North Korea

Arirang Mass Games (p355), Pyongyang, North Korea

TONY WHE

Myohyangsan (p370), north of Pyongyang,
North Korea

JANE SWEENEY

Sonjuk Bridge (p369), Kaesong, North Korea

TONY WHE

(Continued from page 328)

From Danyang it's a 30-minute boat ride to Janghoe ferry terminal, where the rocky cliffs are the most scenic. If you exit the terminal at Janghoe then turn right and continue 100m, opposite the bus stop is the ticket office for the western part of **Woraksan National Park** (adult/youth/child W1600/600/300; ☺ sunrise-sunset). A 2.5km hike up Jebibong (721m) takes three hours return.

From Janghoe to the next ferry pier, Cheongpung, takes another a half hour. Nearby is a folk village and across the bridge is a resort with a bungy jump. After another hour the boat arrives at Chungju ferry terminal. Only seven buses a day (W950, 30 minutes) run from here to Chungju bus terminal, so you may have to wait some time. A taxi costs W13,000.

Going the other way, from Chungju ferry terminal ferry boats go to the Woraksan terminal (W8000 return), Cheongpung (W9000), Janghoe (W13,000) and Danyang (W18,000). The ferry boats run at least twice a day, but the schedule depends on the number of passengers. If the ferry isn't running to Danyang, take a ferry to Janghoe and a bus to Danyang.

MARTIAL ARTS FIESTA

Every October since 1997, Chungju has hosted a week-long **World Martial Arts Festival** (☎ 850 6740; www.martialarts.or.kr) together with a cultural festival that features food stalls, music and dances. Martial arts exponents from Korea and around the world flock to the city, where they demonstrate their amazing and varied skills. See displays of Chinese *wushu*, Malaysian *silat*, Brazilian *capoeira*, Indian *kalan*, Uzbekistan *kurash* and other martial arts from as far apart as Venezuela, the Ukraine and the Philippines. See also p384.

Sleeping & Eating

Titanic Motel (타이타닉모텔; ☎ 842 5858; r W25,000; ✗ 🖵) Chungju's flashiest motel is adorned with white castle battlements and blue turrets outside. Inside is a disco-décor lift and a flame-effect corridor leading to luxury rooms with ornate furniture and snazzy black-and-white tiles in the bathrooms that feature all-body showers. More spacious rooms with

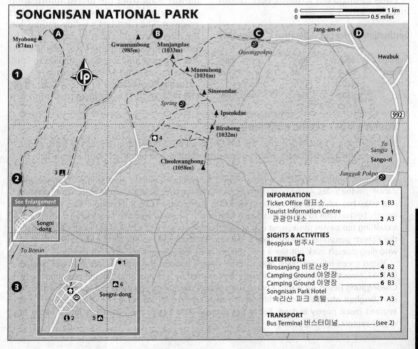

SONGNISAN NATIONAL PARK

INFORMATION	
Ticket Office 매표소	**1** B3
Tourist Information Centre	
관광안내소	**2** A3
SIGHTS & ACTIVITIES	
Beopjusa 법주사	**3** A2
SLEEPING 🏠	
Birosanjang 비로산장	**4** B2
Camping Ground 야영장	**5** A3
Camping Ground 야영장	**6** B3
Songnisan Park Hotel	
속리산 파크 호텔	**7** A3
TRANSPORT	
Bus Terminal 버스터미널	(see 2)

a computer or Jacuzzi are W5000 extra. Opposite the train station, Titanic (named after the love-story movie rather than the sinking ship) is a 15-minute walk or W2000 taxi ride from the bus terminal.

Pongaksan (폰각산; Aehyangdaero; meals W4000-10,000; ⏲ 24hr; ♿) A large family restaurant that serves just about everything; it's along the road facing the train station. Always busy despite the dull decor, it has a children's play area plus every child's dream: free self-serve ice cream!

Getting There & Away
BUS
Chungju's new bus terminal is a 15-minute walk or a W2000 taxi ride from the motels in front of the train station. Local buses from outside the bus terminal run to Suanbo Hot Springs (W1000, 35 minutes, every 40 minutes) and to Songgye-ri in Woraksan National Park (W1000, 45 minutes, five daily). From across the road outside the bus terminal, bus 301 (W950, 25 minutes, seven daily) leaves for Chungju Dam and the Chungju Lake ferries.

From Chungju bus terminal, destinations include:

Destination	Price (W)	Duration	Frequency
Cheongju	6400	1½hr	every 20min
Daejeon	8000	2¼hr	hourly
Danyang	6200	1½hr	hourly
Seoul	6200	2hr	every 20min

TRAIN
Mugunghwa (semi-express) trains (W11,700, five daily) run to Seoul.

SUANBO HOT SPRINGS 수안보
This relaxing spa resort, 21km southeast of Chungju, is small enough to walk round, and its restaurants specialise in rabbit, duck and pheasant meals. Nearby is Woraksan National Park and a small ski resort. The **tourist information centre** (☎ 845 7829) is on the main street near the bus terminal.

Less than 2km from Suanbo Hot Springs is **Sajo Ski Resort** (사조스키리조트; ☎ 846 0750; www.sajoresort.co.kr), which is very modest in scale, a big handicap in a country that believes bigger is better. There are seven slopes and three lifts, and ski equipment can be hired. Night skiing is also possible. Near the slopes is a hotel and a youth hostel, but the best plan is to stay in Suanbo and use the free shuttle buses that run during the ski season.

Sleeping & Eating
Sinheung Hotel (신흥호텔; ☎ 846 3711; fax 846 1760; r W25,000; ♿) On the main road, a one-minute walk from the tourist information centre, is the best (and about the only) budget *yeogwan*. The corridors need upgrading, but the rooms are light and straightforward. The small *oncheon* (hot spring bath) downstairs is free to guests and is open from 6am to 7pm. Prices increase W10,000 on Saturdays.

Suanbo Royal Hotel (수안보로얄호텔; ☎ 846 0190; r W50,000; ♿) On the main road is this new

---

KOREA'S MOST SCENIC BOAT RIDE

Stalls and shops clustered around the ferry terminal at Chungju Dam (p328) sell Darth Vader sun visors, fried grasshoppers, Frisbee-sized slabs of toffee and bottles of North Korean 'Bilberry Bog Wine'.

Stepping onto a ferry boat, a gang of jolly Korean pensioners is already in party mode and dancing in the aisles. As the boat skims along the lake at over 20 knots, an old man, nattily dressed in a trilby hat, white baggy trousers and a lilac waistcoat, and with more gold than ivory in his mouth, beckons me to get up and dance with him. A wrinkled grandma in colourful trousers and a clashing top passes me a paper cup of *soju* (Korean vodka) and a couple of biscuits. Fortunately the Korean pensioner dancing style is nothing like ballroom, so I hope that my uncoordinated wriggling doesn't stick out like a sore thumb, even if my height and Western face does.

Virgin green hillsides reach down to the water's edge of the artificial lake that was created in 1985. Here the pristine forest scenery isn't marred by gas stations or plastic greenhouses. At Cheongpung Resort we watch a brave soul leap off the 60m bungy jump. But the trip's highlight is at Janghoe where the rocky cliffs were greatly admired by Joseon-era poets and painters and inspired much poetry and art. Today the magical cliffs inspire the pensioners into a frenzy of digital-camera button-pushing.

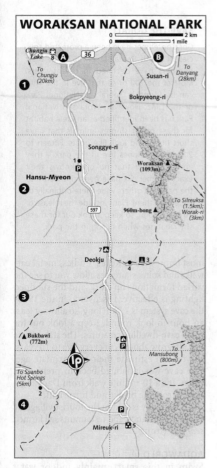

WORAKSAN NATIONAL PARK

meal consisting of pheasant served up in seven different ways: kebabs, dumplings, meatballs, barbecued, *shabu shabu*-style, raw and in soup. It costs W50,000 and is meant for sharing. Walk down the Suanbo Sangnok Hotel road to the three green signs, look left and it's the restaurant with black tiles on the roof.

Getting There & Away
Local buses (W1000, 35 minutes, every 40 minutes) leave from outside Chungju bus terminal to Suanbo Hot Springs. Intercity buses depart from Suanbo bus terminal to destinations such as Daegu (W11,800, three hours, six daily) and Dong-Seoul (W9900, 2½ hours, hourly).

WORAKSAN NATIONAL PARK
월악산국립공원
Woraksan, which means 'Moon Crags Mountains', offers fine hiking through picturesque forests, with lake views and the slim chance of seeing an endangered goral antelope (p340). Tickets can be purchased at the **ticket office** (☎ 653 3250; adult/youth/child W1600/600/300; ☑ sunrise-sunset).

A road runs right through the park, so access is no problem. **Mireuk-ri**, the tourist village at the southern entrance, is 11km southeast of Suanbo Hot Springs. Scattered near the tourist village is **Mireuksaji**, the remains of a temple that was originally built in the late-Shilla or early-Goryeo period. A couple of stone pagodas and a stone Buddha are the main relics, though a replacement shrine hall is being built.

The most popular hiking route starts deeper in the park at another small tourist village, **Deokju**, which has a camping ground. Follow the trail up to **Dongmun**, the east gate of an ancient

and bright hotel containing smallish rooms that have large bathrooms equipped with electronic bidets. The *oncheon* and sauna is W3000 for guests, W5000 for nonguests.

Suanbo Sangnok Hotel (수안보상록호텔; ☎ 845 3500; fax 845 7878; r from W130,000; ✖ ▢) Appealing, comfortable rooms can be found here, but the main attraction is the *oncheon* spa and sauna (W6000 and only available to guests). The restaurant serves local specialities such as pheasant or duck *shabu shabu* (beef and noodle casserole; W60,000), which are meant for sharing.

Satgatchon (삿갓촌; meals W5000-50,000; ☑ 7.30am-10pm) This small, rustic restaurant is the best place for *kkwong* (꿩; pheasant) *shabu shabu* (샤브샤브), a seven-course mountain fortress, whose walls stretched for 10km, that dates back to the Goryeo dynasty. Further on is a temple, **Deokjusa**, after which you bear left to the uninspiringly named peak '960m-*bong*' – Korea has so many mountain peaks that it's run out of names. Carry on to **Woraksan** (1093m) and then descend the steep slope back down to the access road and **Song-gye-ri**, another tourist village at the northern entrance to the park. The total distance is around 10km and takes about six hours.

There are shops, restaurants and *minbak* (private homes with rooms for rent) in Song-gye-ri, Deokju and Mireuk-ri, plus two camping grounds (W3000 to W6000 per night).

Local buses (W1000, 45 minutes, five daily) leave from outside Chungju bus terminal to Mireungni and through the park to Songgye-ri. They can also be picked up in Suanbo's main street (W1000, 10 minutes, five daily).

DANYANG 단양
pop 41,000

Danyang is a resort town nestled in the mountains on the edge of Chungju Lake (p328). Lakeside motels are as retro as the town itself, but you can spend a couple of pleasant days exploring the sights. Visit at least one of the limestone caves and don't miss the awesome temple complex, Gu·insa (p327).

Information

Nonghyup Bank Changes major currencies.
Post office Uphill from the bus terminal.
Tourist information centre (☎ 422 1146) Located just over the bridge.

Sights & Activities
GOSU DONGGUL 고수동굴
This spectacular limestone **cave** (☎ 422 3072; adult/youth/child W4000/2500/1500; ⏱ 9am-5pm) is the

---

---

most impressive in Korea. Endless metal catwalks and spiral staircases allow you to see the varied formations up close, and the subdued lighting is effective. Discovered in the 1970s the cave system is 1.7km long, so allow at least an hour to look round. Keep a look out for small cave-dwelling creatures. The stalagmites usually grow about 1cm every five to 10 years, so you can estimate their approximate age. The cave was inhabited back in prehistoric times. It's a 10-minute walk from Danyang – walk across the bridge and turn right.

Local honey is sold in the tourist village by the cave's entrance, and restaurants sell farmed *seong·eo* (trout).

AQUAWORLD 아쿠아월드
Swim in this smart, mainly indoor **water park** (☎ 420 8311; adult/child W15,000/10,000 Mon-Fri, W20,000/15,000 Sat & Sun; ⏱ 10am-8.30pm or longer), which has linked pool areas. Immerse yourself in pine-needle, sulphur and Jacuzzi baths, and then steam away any remaining stress in jade, charcoal and amethyst saunas (W3000 extra). Play pool and four-ball or release vocal energy in the *noraebang* (karaoke) next to the restaurants and shops. Up above are resort condos (p342).

LAKESIDE WALK 호수주변산책로
Take an evening stroll along the promenade – lined with trees, flowerbeds and lighting – that runs along the lake from outside the bus terminal, past an artificial waterfall and outdoor concert area to the tourist hotel.

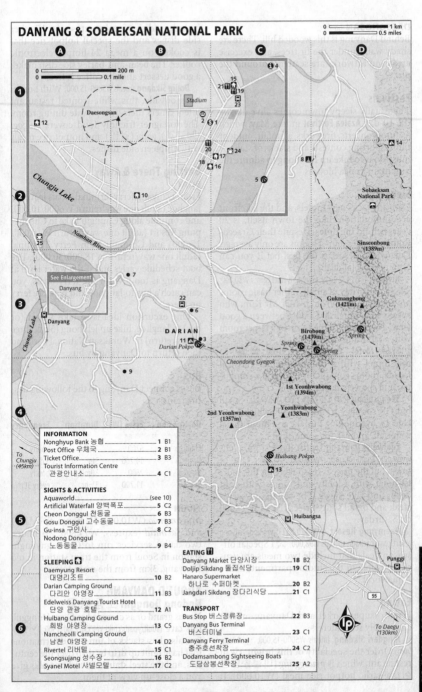

DANYANG & SOBAEKSAN NATIONAL PARK

INFORMATION
Nonghyup Bank 농협 **1** B1
Post Office 우체국 **2** B1
Ticket Office **3** B3
Tourist Information Centre
관광안내소 **4** C1

SIGHTS & ACTIVITIES
Aquaworld ....(see 10)
Artificial Waterfall 양백폭포 **5** C2
Cheon Donggul 천동굴 **6** B3
Gosu Donggul 고수동굴 **7** B3
Gu·insa 구인사 **8** C2
Nodong Donggul
노동동굴 **9** B4

SLEEPING
Daemyung Resort
대명리조트 **10** B2
Darian Camping Ground
다리안 야영장 **11** B3
Edelweiss Danyang Tourist Hotel
단양 관광 호텔 **12** A1
Huibang Camping Ground
회방 야영장 **13** C5
Namcheolli Camping Ground
남천 야영장 **14** D2
Rivertel 리버텔 **15** C1
Seongsujang 성수장 **16** B2
Syanel Motel 샤넬모텔 **17** C2

EATING
Danyang Market 단양시장 **18** B2
Doljip Sikdang 돌집식당 **19** C1
Hanaro Supermarket
하나로 수퍼마켓 **20** B2
Jangdari Sikdang 장다리식당 **21** C1

TRANSPORT
Bus Stop 버스정류장 **22** B3
Danyang Bus Terminal
버스터미널 **23** C1
Danyang Ferry Terminal
충주호선착장 **24** C2
Dodamsambong Sightseeing Boats
도담삼봉선착장 **25** A2

CHUNGCHEONGBUK-DO

DAESONGSAN 대송산

Behind Danyang is this wooded hill. There are shady walks under the fir trees, and exercise areas and artworks are scattered around the place.

Festivals

The usually sleepy town comes alive during the 10-day **Azalea Festival** in late May, which features concerts, fireworks, a funfair, outdoor films, sporting contests and stacks of stalls. A must-do is to hike up Birobong to admire the mountain azalea blooms.

Sleeping

Danyang lacks new motels, and the lakefront accommodation, like the town itself, is 20 years behind the times. Despite their Graeco-Roman façades, motel rooms are only average. Daemyung Resort is the best bet if you can obtain a special deal.

Rivertel (☎ 422 2619; www.erivertel.com; r W30,000; ⊠ ⬚) A variety of small, rather basic rooms are available here from owner Mr Kim, who speaks some English. Choose between a good view, a computer in the room or a larger room with a table and chairs.

Syanel Motel (☎ 423 0151; r W30,000; ⊠ ⬚) In this motel with a blue-and-white classical façade, rooms contain big TVs and a computer, and showers have firepower.

Seongsujang (☎ 421 2345; r W30,000; ⊠) Small but OK rooms – try for No 208, which has a balcony overlooking the lake and the artificial waterfall, and ask for some chairs.

Edelweiss Danyang Tourist Hotel (☎ 423 7070; www.danyanghotel.com; r W70,000; ⊠ ⬚) Out of town, but the price is reasonable for this tourist hotel with a lobby and rooms with light decor and lake views. The restaurant serves steak and oxtail soup. Prices rise to W99,000 on Saturday.

Daemyung Resort (☎ 420 8311; www.daemyung resort.com; package specials W98,000; ⊠) Special off-season deals that include two meals are usually possible in the studio apartments above Aquaworld.

Eating

Hanaro supermarket and Danyang market can supply self-caterers.

Jangdari Sikdang (meals W5000-15,000; ⏱ 10am-9pm) Order the speciality of this bright, clean restaurant, which is *pyunggang* (마늘솥밥정식), a garlic hotpot rice meal (W10,000). It includes a dish of real meat, soups, 15 other side dishes and the special hotpot rice that is cooked on a mega 24-hotpot electronic cooker. The bean-and-barley side dish makes a good dessert and the coffee is free.

Doljip Sikdang (meals W5000-15,000) With bonsai trees outside, this white-fronted restaurant offers diners their own private dining room. The foreigner-friendly food covers *bulgogi* (불고기), *galbi* (갈비) and hotpot rice meals with umpteen side dishes.

Getting There & Away

BOAT

From Danyang ferry terminal, boats leave for Janghoe (adult one way/return W6000/10,000) and continue along Chungju Lake to Cheongpung Resort (adult one way/return W10,000/17,000) and Chungju Dam Ferry Terminal (adult one way/return W18,000/30,000). The boat schedule varies and if the water level at Danyang is too low for the ferry boats, you can catch a bus to Janghoe and pick the ferry up there.

One excursion idea is to take a boat (or bus) to Janghoe, hike up Jebibong (5km, three hours return) in Woraksan National Park and then return to Danyang by bus.

BUS

Buses connect Danyang to the following destinations:

Destination	Price (W)	Duration	Frequency
Chungju	6200	1½hr	hourly
Daejeon	14,200	3hr	5 daily
Gu·insa	2600	30min	hourly
Seoul	11,700	3½hr	every 30min

TRAIN

Mugunghwa (W10,000, 2¾ hours, five daily) and *Saemaul* (express; W14,800, 2½ hours, two daily) services run to Cheongnyangni station in Seoul from the train station in old Danyang, 3km from the main town.

AROUND DANYANG
Nodong Donggul 노동동굴

Not as grand or as crowded as Gosu Donggul, this **cave** (adult/youth/child W4000/2500/1500; ⏱ 9am-5pm) also has stacks of limestone formations that have built up drip by drip over the centuries, and the steel staircases and catwalks give you a close-up view of them.

The cave has a poor bus service – local buses (W950, five minutes) leave from outside Danyang bus terminal at 9.25am and 2pm but return at 2.30pm and 5.50pm.

Cheon Donggul 천동굴

More of an adventure activity, this **cave** (☎ 422 2972; adult/youth/child W4000/2500/1500; ◷ 9am-5pm) requires visitors to squeeze through narrow clefts and crawl through low tunnels. It's only 470m long and was discovered in 1977.

The cave is a 10-minute walk from the nearby bus stop and a 15-minute walk from the entrance to Sobaeksan National Park. Buses (W950, 10 minutes, hourly) leave from outside Danyang bus terminal for Darian (Cheondong-ri).

Dodamsambong Sightseeing Boats 도담삼봉선착장

View more celebrated rocky scenery on these **boat trips** (☎ 422 3033; per trip W6000). Small, sightseeing boats take you on a short trip to view nearby rocky cliffs from the Namhangang (river).

SOBAEKSAN NATIONAL PARK 소백산국립공원

Sobaeksan (Little White Mountain; ☎ 423 0708; adult/youth/child W1600/600/300; ◷ 8am-6pm), one of Korea's largest parks, is rich in flora and offers good hiking trails through dense forests. The climbs are not particularly steep, but can still be hard work.

Birobong (1439m) is the highest peak in the park and is most easily reached from Darian/Cheondong-ni (three hours up and two hours down if you're reasonably fit). The route follows a picturesque 6.5km trail along the beautiful Cheondong valley. The peak is famous for azaleas, which bloom around late May.

Gu·insa 구인사

Deep in the mountains stands the isolated and impressive headquarters of the Cheontae sect of Korean Buddhism, which was reestablished by Sang·wol Won·gak in 1945. The **temple complex** (admission free) consists of 30 multistorey concrete buildings that line a narrow road and are connected by elevated walkways. The buildings are squeezed into a steep, narrow, thickly wooded valley. The opulence is obvious and building work is continuing at a hectic pace. Carry on past the buildings to reach the founder's tomb.

The temple has the atmosphere of a utopian community: the gardens are beautiful, everything is spotless, and the monks, nuns and lay members, dressed in loose-fitting grey trousers and shirts, appear to be uniformly quiet and polite. The communal kitchen serves hundreds of simple but free vegetarian meals three times a day and visitors are welcome.

Camping is available at Darian, Namcheolli and Huibang, and plenty of *minbak* charge from W20,000 at the park entrances.

Buses (W950, 10 minutes, hourly) leave from outside Danyang bus terminal for Darian. Direct buses (W2600, 30 minutes, hourly) leave Danyang bus terminal at 20 minutes past the hour for Gu·insa.

North Korea

Redefining the term rogue state through its isolationism, controversial nuclear weapons programme and missile testing, North Korea is probably the most mysterious country in the world today and one almost entirely untouched by tourism. Off the beaten path seems too slight a term for a nation that admits fewer than 2000 Westerners a year, and whose overwhelming attraction is its isolation and backwardness.

Here the Kim dynasty, which began life as a Soviet-sponsored communist government in the 1950s, has evolved into a hereditary dictatorship owing far more to Confucianism than Marxism. The founder of the state, Kim Il Sung, may have died in 1994, but he is still the president of the Democratic People's Republic of Korea (the name locals prefer for their country). His son, a man who has only ever uttered one sentence in public (it was 'Long Live the Victorious Korean People's Army' at a rally in Pyongyang in the early 1990s), continues to rule like a medieval monarch, an unknown quantity with nuclear weapons and a huge army at his beck and call, giving sleepless nights to governments in Seoul, Tokyo and Washington.

A trip to North Korea is strictly on its government's terms, and it's essential to accept that you'll have no independence during your trip – you'll be accompanied by two government-approved local guides at all times and only hear a very one-sided view of history throughout the trip. Those who can accept these terms will have a fascinating trip into another rather unsettling world. Simply to see a country where the Cold War is still being fought, where mobile phones and the internet are unknown, and where total obedience to the state is universally unquestioned is, for many, reason enough to visit. .

HIGHLIGHTS

- Marvel at the grotesque totalitarian architecture in **Pyongyang** (p358).
- Feel the full force of Cold War tensions with a visit to **Panmunjom** (p369) in the Demilitarized Zone, where an uneasy armistice holds
- Visit Pyongyang between August and October to see the incredible **Mass Games** (p355), a gymnastic spectacle featuring thousands of perfectly trained North Koreans
- Explore the remote far north and Korea's highest peak and holy mountain **Paekdusan** (p372)
- Enjoy pristine mountain walks in the stunning resort of **Kumgangsan** (p371)

Paekdusan ★

★ Pyongyang

★ Kumgangsan

★ Panmunjom

GETTING STARTED

Trips to North Korea usually run like clockwork. Two guides will accompany you everywhere you go outside the hotel and control what you see and the spiel you hear while seeing it. Forward planning is a must: almost everything you want to see needs to be approved before your arrival as ad hoc arrangements make the guides very nervous and thus less fun to be around. That said, itineraries are always provisional and some things are usually cancelled at the last moment for no discernable reason, although something else will always be substituted in its place.

The best option is to enjoy a positive relationship with your guides (who don't make the decisions; they simply enforce them and monitor you during your stay), as once they trust you, they'll help you make the most of your trip. Days are long in North Korean tourism – you'll see a surprising amount in just a four-day tour, and possibly be burned out on a full-week tour.

When to Go

The best time to plan a trip is during the Arirang Mass Games (mid-August until mid-October most years) or during a national holiday. Special performances, which have been rehearsed for months, can be included in the itinerary. During these periods train and plane tickets are harder to obtain, so ensure that you have booked well in advance. In general, the most pleasant months for a visit are April, May, June, September and October. July and August are often unpleasantly humid and overcast. Tours don't usually run in the winter: they finish in November, then start again in March. The month of February sees

the Great Leader's birthday and foreigners are particularly unwelcome at this time of year. Those finding themselves in North Korea in winter will find power shortages common (although not usually in hotels) and it's generally a cold and miserable time to visit.

Costs & Money

As a tourist, North Korea is no budget destination. Opportunities to cut costs by staying in youth hostels do not exist. As well as paying for your bed and board in advance, you will also have to pay for two guides and a driver, making group tourism one of the few measures that can save you money.

As a rough guide, solo travellers should bank on paying about €250 per day for guides, hotel and full board. This can be reduced to around €130 per day if you go as part of a group. Note that the euro and Chinese yuan are the accepted currency for visitors to use and that small change in both currencies (euro coins and yuan in denominations of under 50)

DON'T LEAVE HOME WITHOUT...

Anything medical or electrical that you will need during your stay; this includes simple everyday products such as painkillers, tampons and condoms. Everything from memory cards to batteries for your camera are best brought in too – such basic items are sometimes available, but their price and quality can be quite different from elsewhere. As most trips are no longer than a week, bringing fruit from China is a great idea for snacking between sights – even a bag of apples is a luxury item in Pyongyang. Small change in euros (€1 and 50c are especially useful) and yuan (10, 20 and 50 yuan notes) are a huge help, as there's never any change in the hotels and shops. Small token gifts for your guides are a good idea – pens, postcards of your hometown, cigarettes (for male guides only) or chocolates will always go down well. Just as important is what not to bring, as these rules are quite strict. Mobile phones and laptop computers are best left at home. Most of all, bring a sense of humour and an open mind – you'll need both to make North Korea enjoyable and rewarding.

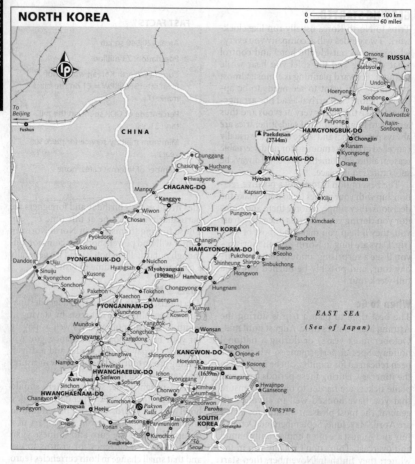

NORTH KOREA

is a huge advantage as most places can't change big notes.

Once in North Korea, the only major expenses will be the souvenirs and other gifts that are on sale at every tourist attraction. Apart from evening drinks and telephone/fax costs, there is little opportunity to spend your money elsewhere. It's customary to tip the guides at the end of each tour, so budget a minimum of €20 per guide for this.

Tours
Ryohaengsa (☎ +86-10-6437 6666/3133; fax 6436 9089; Korean International Travel Company, 2nd fl, Yanxiang, No A2 Jiangtai Rd, Chaoyang District, Qionghuating) Every visitor to North Korea must book all their accommodation, guides and transport with the government monolith, North Korea's version of Intourist for anyone lucky enough to have visited pre-*perestroika* Russia. Booking your tour through a travel agent will simply mean that they have the job of dealing with Ryohaengsa on your behalf. The advantage of this is that travel agents are IATA (International Air Transport Association) bonded and will return your money if your trip is cancelled, whereas Ryohaengsa will not. Moreover, dealing directly with the North Korean authorities is not most people's idea of fun.

Air Koryo (☎ 10-6501 1557/1559; fax 6501 2591; Swissotel Bldg, Hong Kong-Macau Center, Dongsi Shitau Lijiao, Beijing 100027) The main office in Beijing is the office most used to dealing with travellers and has Ryohaengsa staff working there.

The number of North Korean specialists is very limited, but those who run tours include:

Geographic Expeditions (☎ 1-415-922-0448; www .geoex.com; 1008 General Kennedy Avenue, PO Box 29902, San Francisco, CA 94129-0902) This upmarket American outfit was the first to pioneer US tourism to DPRK. While US citizens are allowed into North Korea only during the Mass Games, Geographic Expeditions have tours that include Paekdusan and Mt Chilbo as well as the DMZ and Kaesong. All-inclusive prices from the US (which include flights and accommodation in Beijing) start at around US$5000 for 11 nights, seven of which are in DPRK.

Koryo Tours (☎ 10-6416 7544; www.koryogroup.com; Room 43, Red House Hotel, 10 Tai Ping Zhuang, Chun Xiao Lu, Chun Xiu Lu, Dong Zhi Men Wai, Chaoyang District, 100027 Beijing) Nick Bonner's Beijing-based company has been offering DPRK tours for over a decade. Koryo are the undoubted specialists, having a very good relationship with Korea International Tourist Service (KITS) and doing a host of other things from producing film in DPRK to selling North Korean art in Beijing (www.pyongyangartstudio.com). Tours can be tailored to meet specialist interests and individual travel can also be arranged.

Its website is an excellent place to start for any tourist, as it is packed with information about all things DPRK. A standard five-night tour of North Korea is available for as little as €990 all inclusive from Beijing.

Regent Holidays (☎ 20-2921 1711; www.regent -holidays.co.uk; 15 John St, Bristol BS1 2HR) Specialists in obscure destinations, Regent have been taking groups into North Korea since the late 1980s. A fully inclusive nine-day tour including the

Mass Games costs £1295 (starting from Beijing). Longer tours including the charter flight to Paekdusan start at £1545 per person.

VNC Travel (☎ 030-23115001; www.vnc.nl; Catharijnesingel 70, Postbus 79, 3500 AB Utrecht) This Dutch company specialises in travel to Asia, and includes both group and individual tours to North Korea. A standard seven-day tour taking in Pyongyang, Kaesong, the DMZ and Mt Myohyang is €1034 (starting and ending in Beijing). Longer tours are also available.

Other operators that offer tours:

Bestway Tours & Safaris (☎ 1-604 2647378; www .bestway.com; Suite 206, 8678 Greenall Avenue, Burnaby, British Columbia, Canada V5J 3M6)

Explore (☎ 44-870 333 4001; www.explore.co.uk; Nelson House, 55 Victoria Rd, Farnborough, Hampshire GU14 7PA, UK)

Tin Bo Travel Services (☎ 1-613 238 7093; www.tinbo holidays.com; 2nd fl, 725 Somerset St W, Ottawa, Ontario K1R 6P7)

See (p378) for information about travelling on your own.

Travel Literature

The single best book to read if you're curious to know what a trip to DPRK is like is Guy Delisle's graphic novel *Pyongyang: A Journey in North Korea*. A French-Canadian cartoonist 'on the margins of the globalised world', Delisle was seconded to Pyongyang to work on cartoons, and his methodical documentation of all aspects of his trip is priceless. Highly recommended, even more so for any recent visitors who will find themselves laughing out loud in recognition.

SHOULD YOU VISIT?

North Korea is a police state with a human-rights record worse than anywhere else on earth. Concentration camps, executions, state-orchestrated terror and mass-control by a vast propaganda machine are a daily reality for millions here. All the revenue from your trip will go directly to the government, and during the Mass Games this is a sizable amount. So should you visit, and is it morally acceptable to do so?

The case against visiting, as outlined above, is strong. On the other hand, those who argue that you *should* visit point out that tourism is one of the few ways of encouraging openness in DPRK, of letting people see that the West is interested and, more importantly, friendly – not an insignificant fact for a population brought up on a relentless diet of anti-US propaganda. The one thing you should never do is come here to stir up trouble – your guides and any North Koreans having contact with your group will suffer very serious consequences and you'll achieve nothing more than a speedy deportation. If you do come, listen to the version of history given to you by the guides, accept that this is their version (however untrue) and leave serious criticism until you are back at your hotel.

North Korea Through the Looking Glass (Kong Dan Oh, Ralph C Hassig, Kongdan Oh) has established itself as a classic overview of DPRK politics and society, although it has the usual limitations of any work concerning one of the most secretive governments on earth: much is conjecture and cannot be adequately supported by documented evidence. For all that, it's still a fascinating introduction to the country.

Bruce Cummings has written over a dozen books about Korea, the division of the peninsula and its future. Highly recommended is *War and Television*, which recounts his experiences recording interviews in North Korea for a documentary on the Korean War. His other authoritative histories of the peninsula include *Korea's Place in the Sun*, one chapter of which gives an impressive analysis of the DPRK's political culture.

For a very readable, yet still substantial account of North-South relations since 1948, Don Oberdorfer's *The Two Koreas* is excellent. Oberdorfer puts the politics of both countries squarely in the context of constant efforts to reunify the peninsula, by peaceful means or otherwise.

Perhaps the closest North Korea has come to its own *Gulag Archipelago* is the horrific *The Aquariums of Pyongyang: Ten Years in the North Korean Gulag* by Kang Chol-hwan. This book describes the hell on earth that is life as a political prisoner here. Not for the faint-hearted, but definitely recommended for anyone seeking the whole picture.

Pyongyang: The Hidden History of the Hidden Capital, by Chris Springer, is a city guide that tells the stories behind the mysterious buildings, monuments and ministries of the capital, and is by far the most detailed guide to Pyongyang available.

North Korea by Robert Willoughby is the most comprehensive guidebook to the country, although much of it is irrelevant for travellers as most of the towns included are off-limits to non-NGO workers and diplomats.

Living With the Enemy: Inside North Korea, by Richard Saccone (2006), is a detailed diary of the author's year-long stay in the North in 2001, working on the now-aborted KEDO nuclear power project.

Internet Resources

The scarcity of information from North Korea has created a large web community of DPRK-watchers, and although every subject from annual grain production to Kim Jong Il jokes are covered, the bias of each website should always be borne in mind – few people are indifferent towards North Korea. The following sites offer the best coverage of events.

www.chosunjournal.com Maintained largely by Koreans living and studying in the United States. Its focus is on

TOP FIVE DPRK DOCUMENTARIES

The following documentaries are all highly recommended for a glimpse into DPRK, and are a great way for prospective visitors to get an idea of what to expect.

- *State of Mind* (www.astateofmind.co.uk) Unprecedented access to the lives of normal North Koreans is the hallmark of this beautiful documentary about two young Korean girls preparing for the Mass Games in Pyongyang.

- *Friends of Kim* (www.friendsofkim.com) A wry look at the pro-regime Korea Friendship Association's annual pilgrimage to North Korea and a wonderful portrait of the eccentrics who truly believe that the country is paradise on earth.

- *Seoul Train* (www.seoultrain.com) This superb documentary looks at the huge problems facing North Korean refugees, how they escape the North, survive in China and – if they're lucky – make it to South Korea.

- *The Game of Their Lives* (www.thegameoftheirlives.com) A fascinating look at the DPRK's proudest sporting moment, knocking Italy out of the 1966 World Cup. This charming film tracks down the surviving players in the North.

- *A High Level Delegation* (www.mk2.com) A Belgian parliamentary delegation comes off looking very helpless and buffoonish during a visit to DPRK, when faced with official intransigence and endless propaganda.

human rights abuse and the injustices of life in DPRK – essential reading.

www.koryogroup.com The Beijing-based North Korean travel specialists offer the best introduction to travelling around DPRK on their excellent website. Here you'll find everything from travel tips to itineraries and photos.

www.nautilus.org The website of a very highbrow US research fund called the Nautilus Institute for Security and Sustainability. Its stated mission is to 'solve interrelated critical global problems', putting North Korea at the top of the agenda.

www.nkzone.com An interactive site where people from all walks of life can post various DPRK-themed articles and start discussions on a wide range of topics.

www.stat.ualberta.ca/people/schmu/nk.html Lists the best selection of DPRK travelogues from the web.

SNAPSHOT

After a period of being pushed off the front pages by its one-time 'axis of evil' club members Iraq and Iran, North Korea stormed back into the world's consciousness in July 2006, when it launched seven missiles over the Sea of Japan in what was seen as an unprecedented act of provocation even by North Korea's standards. This was followed in October 2006 by the testing of a nuclear device, which sent shock waves around the world and completely changed the balance of power in East Asia.

The nuclear test and missile launches were generally seen as the culmination of a frustrating few years for the hermit kingdom – the days of Clinton administration engagement and the Sunshine Policy (see p42) of former South Korean President Kim Dae-jung having long since given way to the Bush Administration's insistence that North Korea give up its nuclear programme before it can have any direct negotiations with the US. At present the only contact North Korea has with the US is the six-party talks, which include China, Russia, South Korea and Japan, although North Korea had withdrawn from the talks at the time of writing.

The conventional wisdom during late 2006 was that Kim Jong Il had drastically overplayed his hand this time, and that, with the US in no mood for threats right now and Chinese anger at the North's apparent disregard for their advice, the DPRK might be destined for another bout of international isolation.

Domestically change remains glacial, but there have been some significant developments in openness in the past few years including the admission of both US and South Korean tourists previously banned from the country. Recovery from the famine of the late 1990s has been strong and people no longer look hungry on the streets. However, serious flooding in July 2006 provoked suggestions that much of North Korea's crops may have been washed away and the country could again slip back into starvation.

Outside Pyongyang rural poverty remains grinding. Cautious economic reforms initiated in 2002 have allowed a degree of free trade including private markets (totally off limits to tourists, sadly), where most North Koreans now shop. Yet there's still no sign of any real attempt to reform the country's lumbering, fuel-crippled economy, despite a private visit by Kim Jong Il to southern Chinese boom towns in 2006.

North Korea remains one of the most highly militarised societies on earth. Men and women in uniform are everywhere, particularly in Pyongyang. Both sexes are obliged to devote years of military service to the state and the army is the subject of most films, songs, books and art here.

After 50 years of total repression, there are no surviving networks of dissent. City streets are deserted after nightfall, as there is often no electricity to power the streetlights and, even more significantly, nothing to do. A standard North Korean evening will involve listening to TV or radio reports of joyful masses surpassing their grain quotas or the latest proclamation of the Great Leader.

Yet part of the excitement and fascination of the country is trying to divine the real from the fake and attempting to see past the ideology. While you may be horrified, amazed or awestruck by what you see in North Korea, you won't be able to help yourself seeing the world from a different perspective once you've been here.

HISTORY

For an overview of Korean history before the division of the peninsula, see p26.

Division of the Peninsula

The Japanese occupation of the Korean peninsula between 1910 and 1945 was one of the darkest periods in Korean history; the occupation forces press-ganged Koreans into slave labour teams to construct factories, mines and heavy industry – particularly in the north.

NORTH KOREA

TONY DOES THE DPRK *by Tony Wheeler*

I have a fascination with cities and countries that seem to exist at a 90-degree angle to reality. In the world today North Korea is undoubtedly the best example of this phenomenon, and when George W Bush – himself a denizen of a strange parallel universe – decided to skewer North Korea on his axis of evil, I simply had to go.

Unfortunately a solo visit to the hermit kingdom is really impossible – you can go by yourself, but it's still on an organised tour. But one glance at the group that assembled under tour guide Nicholas Bonner's watchful eye at the Beijing railway station was enough to confirm this would be no ordinary group tour.

Day 1 Our overnight train from Beijing arrived at the Chinese border town of Dondang in the early morning. Remarkably there's a giant Mao statue still standing in the square outside the railway station. That evening (the train is very slow) we arrived in Pyongyang and immediately went to pay homage to the Great Leader's Mansudae statue.

Day 2 Apart from our little group, Pyongyang International Airport was deserted. We flew up to the northwest corner of the country then took a bus along the beautiful coastline and in to the forested mountains of Outer Chilbo.

Day 3 Another flight took us to the Paekdu region where Lake Chon's icy surface crosses the border into China. It was here where Kim Jong Il was *said* to be born.

Day 4 Back in Pyongyang we go to the Arirang Mass Games in the 150,000-seat May Day Stadium, the world's biggest stadium. In the stands opposite 20,000 kids flip open card books with synchronised precision to make a steady stream of pictures, while tens of thousands more children, women, men and soldiers dance across the stadium floor. If wars are ever decided by whose army dances best, the North Koreans have it wrapped up.

Day 5 A day's solid sightseeing covers everything from the Victorious Fatherland Liberation War Museum (p364; see how North Korea almost single-handedly defeated the Japanese in WWII) to the Great People's Study Hall and the spy ship USS *Pueblo*, before we end the evening in the Egypt Palace Karaoke Bar in the hotel basement. For me the day's highlight was a chance to wander unescorted for 45 minutes in the shopping delights of Department Store No 1.

Day 6 A bus takes us across the peninsula to the port town of Wonsan. At our hotel, the restaurant staff have moved some dividers between our table and a tour group of well-lubricated Chinese who are singing loudly. Nick leaps from his seat and pulls the dividers aside, yelling in Chinese, 'We will have no divisions here!' A roar goes up and at their invitation we render our own drinking songs.

Day 7 After a visit to a collective farm and a park temple, we cross back over the peninsula to Pyongyang. We were all so knocked out by our visit to the Mass Games that we organise a second showing.

Day 8 We barrel down the six-lane (but extremely empty) highway to the somewhat inaccurately named DMZ – there's nothing very demilitarized about it. On the way back to Pyongyang we make an all too brief stop in the provincial town of Kaesong and at the beautiful hillside Kongmin mausoleums just outside the town.

Day 9 The airport is rather busier today when we fly out to Shenyang in China. Remarkably an Air Korea flight from Seoul taxis in right behind us; the bags from North and South are jumbled together on the luggage carousel.

Moreover, the use of Korean girls as 'comfort women' for Japanese soldiers – a euphemism for enforced prostitution – remains a huge cause of resentment today in both Koreas.

Most of the guerrilla warfare conducted against the Japanese police and army took place in the northern provinces of Korea and neighbouring Manchuria; northerners are still proud of having carried a disproportionate burden in the anti-Japan struggle. In fact, modern history books from Pyongyang imply that Kim Il Sung defeated the Japanese nearly single-handedly (with a bit of help from loyal comrades and his infant son).

While his feats have certainly been exaggerated, Kim Il Sung was a strong resistance leader, although not a strong enough force to rid Korea of the Japanese. This task was left to the Red Army, who, in the closing days of WWII, entered Manchuria and Northern Korea as the Japanese forces retreated. The United States suddenly realised that the strategic importance of the peninsula was too great for it to be left in Soviet hands. Despite an agreement at Yalta to give joint custodianship of Korea to the USSR, USA and China, no concrete plans had been made to this end, and the State Department assigned the division of the country to two young officers, who, working from a *National Geographic* map, divided Korea across the 38th parallel.

American forces gradually moved in from Japan, while Soviet forces kept to the dividing line. The intention to have democratic elections across the whole peninsula soon became hostage to Cold War tensions, and after the North refused to allow UN inspectors to cross the 38th parallel, the Republic of Korea was proclaimed in the South on 15 August 1948, while the North proclaimed the Democratic People's Republic just three weeks later on 9 September 1948.

The People's Republic

Stalin, it is rumoured, personally chose the 33-year-old Kim Il Sung to lead the new republic. The ambitious and fiercely nationalistic Kim was an unknown quantity, although Stalin is said to have favoured him due to his youth. He would have had no idea that Kim would outlive not only him and Mao Zedong, but communism itself, to become the world's longest serving head of state. As soon as Kim had assumed the leadership of North Korea, he applied to Stalin to sanction an invasion of the South. The man of steel refused Kim twice in 1949, but perhaps bolstered by Mao's victory over the nationalists in China the same year and the USSR's own A-bomb project, he gave Kim the green light a year later.

The brutal and pointless Korean War of 1950–53 saw a stunning North Korean advance into the South, where it almost drove US forces into the sea, followed by an equally impressive counter-attack by the United States and UN, which managed to occupy most of North Korea. As the situation began to look bleak, Kim advocated retreating to the hills and waging guerrilla warfare against the South, unaware that China's Mao Zedong had decided to covertly help the North by sending in the People's Liberation Army in the guise of 'volunteers'. Once the PLA moved in and the balance of powers stabilised again, the North pushed the front down to the original 38th parallel, and with two million dead, the original stalemate was more or less retained. The armistice agreement obliged both sides to withdraw 2000m from the ceasefire line, thus creating a huge nature reserve in the form of the Demilitarized Zone, still in existence today.

Despite the Chinese having alienated Kim by taking control of the war – Chinese commander Peng Dehuai apparently treated Kim as a subordinate, much to the future Great Lead-

er's anger – the Chinese remained in North Korea and helped with the massive task of rebuilding a nation all but razed to the ground by bombing.

Simultaneously, following his ill-fated attempt to reunite the nation, Kim Il Sung began a process of political consolidation and brutal repression. He executed his foreign minister and those he believed threatened him in an attempt to take overall control of the Korean Workers' Party. Following Khrushchev's 1956 denunciation of Stalin's personality cult, Central Committee member Yun Kong-hum stood up at one of its meetings and denounced Kim for similar crimes. Yun was never heard from again, and it was the death knell for North Korean democracy.

Unlike many communist leaders, Kim's outlandish personality cult was generated almost immediately – the sobriquet *suryong* or 'Great Leader' was employed in everyday conversation in the North by the 1960s – and the initial lip service paid to democracy and multiparty elections was soon forgotten.

The first decade under Kim Il Sung saw vast material improvements in the lives of workers and peasants. Literacy and full health care were soon followed by access to higher education and the full militarisation of the state. However, by the 1970s, North Korea slipped into recession, one from which it has never recovered. During this time, in which Kim Il Sung had been raised to a divine figure in North Korean society, an *éminence grise* referred to only as the 'party centre' in official-speak began to emerge from the grey anonymity of Kim's henchmen.

At the 1980 party congress this enigmatic figure, to which all kinds of wondrous deeds had been attributed, was revealed to be none other than the Great Leader's son, Kim Jong Il. He was awarded several important public posts, including a seat in the politburo, and even given the honorific title 'Dear Leader'. Mini-Me was designated hereditary successor to the Great Leader and in 1991 made supreme commander of the Korean Army, although he had never served a day in it. From 1989 until 1994, Kim father and son were almost always pictured together, praised in tandem and generally shown to be working in close proximity, preparing the North Korean people for a hereditary dynasty far more in keeping with Confucianism than communism.

Beyond Perestroika

It was during the late 1980s, as communism shattered throughout Eastern Europe, that North Korea's development began to differ strongly from that of other socialist nations. Its greatest sponsor, the Soviet Union, disintegrated in 1991, leaving the North at a loss for the subsidies it ironically needed to maintain its façade of autarky.

North Korea, having always played China and the USSR off against one another, turned to the Chinese, who have played godfather to the DPRK ever since. Quite why the People's Republic has done so has never been explicit. Chinese 'communism' has produced the fastest expanding economy in the world and any ideological ties with Maoism remain purely superficial, while China's increasingly close relationship to both the South and Japan also makes its reluctant support for the Kim regime all the more incongruous. Yet China remains the North's one trusted ally, although several times since the early nineties, Beijing has laid down the law to Pyongyang, even withholding oil deliveries to underscore its unhappiness at the North's continuous brinkmanship.

The regime's brinkmanship did pay off in 1994, however, when North Korea negotiated an agreement with the Clinton administration in which it agreed to cancel its controversial nuclear programme in return for US energy supplies in the short term. This was to be followed by an international consortium constructing two light-water reactors for North Korean energy needs in the long-term.

Midway through negotiations, Kim Il Sung, founding father of North Korea, gave way to a massive heart attack and died. He had spent the day personally inspecting the accommodation being prepared for the planned visit of South Korean president Kim Young-sam. This summit between the two leaders would have been the first ever meeting between the heads of state of the two nations, and Kim Il Sung's stance towards the South had noticeably changed in the last year of his life.

Kim's death rendered the North weaker and even less predictable than before. Optimistic Korea-watchers, including many within South Korea's government, expected the collapse of the regime to be imminent without its charismatic leader. In a move that was to further derail the reunification process, Kim Young-sam's government in Seoul did not therefore send condolences for Kim's death to the North – something even President Clinton felt obliged to do. This slight to a man considered (officially, at least) to be a living god was a miscalculation that set back any progress another five years.

While the expected collapse did not occur, neither did any visible sign of succession by the Dear Leader. North Korea was more mysterious than ever, and in the three years following Kim Il Sung's death, speculation was rampant that a military faction had taken control in Pyongyang, and that continuing power struggles between them and Kim Jong Il meant that there was no overall leader.

Kim Jong Il finally assumed the mantle of power in October 1997 after a three-year

---

THE GENERAL SHERMAN & USS PUEBLO

During the 'hermit kingdom' phase of the Joseon dynasty, one of Korea's first encounters with Westerners was the ill-fated attempt of the American ship, the *General Sherman*, to sail up the Taedong River to Pyongyang in 1866. It arrogantly ignored warnings to turn around and leave, and insisted on trade. When it ran aground on a sand bar just below Pyongyang, locals burnt it and killed all those on board including a Welsh missionary and the Chinese and Malay crew. An American military expedition later pressed the Seoul government for reparations for the loss, otherwise the incident was virtually forgotten in the South. However, northerners have always regarded it with great pride as being their first of many battles with, and victories over, the hated Yankee imperialist enemy.

Also of great pride to the North Koreans is the 'fact' that none other than the Great Leader's great-grandfather had participated in burning the ship. Today, all that is left of the *General Sherman* is a plaque. The site is overshadowed by the nearby ship the *Pueblo*, a US surveillance vessel that was seized by the North Koreans off the east coast of Korea in January 1968 during a heightening of tensions between the North and South. For a fee you can step aboard and hear another lecture on the violations of the ceasefire agreement by the US.

mourning period. Surprisingly, the presidency rested with the late Kim Il Sung, making him the world's only dead head of state, not to mention the longest serving – currently standing at 56 years – out-serving even Queen Elizabeth II. Kim Jong Il's power base is believed to be centred on his control of the military rather than his role in government. As supreme military commander and chairman of the National Defence Commission, he holds sway over the nation's all-powerful third estate.

However, the backdrop to Kim Jong Il's succession was horrific. While the North Korean economy had been contracting since the collapse of vital Soviet supplies and subsidies to the DPRK's ailing industrial infrastructure in the early 1990s, the terrible floods of 1995 led quickly to disaster. Breaking with a strict tradition of self-reliance (of course, one that had never reflected reality – aid had long been received secretly from both communist allies and even the South two months previously), the North appealed to the UN and the world community for urgent food aid.

So desperate was the Kim regime that it even acceded to unprecedented UN demands for access to the whole country for their own field workers, something that would have previously been unthinkable in North Korea's staunchly secretive military climate. Aid workers were horrified by what they saw – malnutrition everywhere, and the beginnings of starvation, which led over the next few years to the death of up to three million people.

Axis of Evil

Kim Jong Il's pragmatism and relative openness to change came to the fore in the years following the devastation, and a series of initiatives to promote reconciliation with both the South and the United States were implemented. These reached their height with a swiftly convened Pyongyang summit between the South's Kim Dae-jung and the Dear Leader in June 2000; the first ever meeting on such a level between the two countries. The two leaders, their countries ready at any second to launch holocaust against one another, held hands in the limousine from the airport to the guesthouse in an unprecedented gesture of solidarity. The summit paved the way for US Secretary of State Madeleine Albright's visit to Pyongyang later the same year. Kim Jong Il's aim was to have his country legitimised

through a visit from the American president himself. However, as Clinton's second term ended and George W Bush assumed power in Washington, the climate swiftly changed.

In his 2002 State of the Union address, President Bush labelled the North as part of an 'Axis of Evil', a phrase that has since passed into everyday language and haunted the DPRK leadership. The year that followed was to signal yet another low in the beleaguered nation's diplomatic endgame.

New lows were reached in 2002 when North Korea resumed its nuclear programme, claiming it had no choice due to American oil supplies being stopped and the two promised light-water reactors remaining incomplete. Frustrated at being ignored by the United States throughout the Bush presidency, North Korea test launched several missiles in July 2006, followed by the detonation of a nuclear device on its own soil three months later. Both actions caused international condemnation and failed to kick-start direct talks with Washington, which has been the North Korean goal throughout. However, following the speedy application of UN sanctions on North Korea following the tests, Pyongyang has said that it will return to the six-nation talks it had been boycotting.

Against all odds, North Korea has survived almost two decades since the end of the Cold War, and the Kim regime seems to be in full control of the country – once more going against the predictions of many Korea-watchers. How long the status quo can go on remains a mystery, but the fact that Kim Jong Il saw the country through its most devastating famine on record, complete international isolation and recurring energy crises suggests that the quick dissolution of the hermit state is far from certain.

THE CULTURE
The National Psyche

The North Koreans are a fiercely nationalistic and proud people. Most refugees confirm that the popular affection for Kim Il Sung was largely genuine, while Kim Jong Il has not endeared himself to the populace in the same way. While North Koreans will always be polite to foreigners, there remains a large amount of antipathy towards both the United States and Japan. Both due to propaganda and the very real international isolation they feel, North Koreans have a sense of being hemmed in on all sides – threatened particularly by the South and the United States, but also by Japan. The changes over the past decade in both China and Russia have also been cause for concern. These two big brothers who guaranteed survival and independence have both sought rapprochement with the South.

On a personal level, Koreans are very good humoured and hospitable, yet remain extremely socially conservative, the combination of centuries of Confucianism and decades of communism. By all means smile and say hello to people you see on the streets, as North Koreans have been instructed to give foreigners a warm welcome, but do not think about taking photos of people without the explicit permission of both your guide and subject. Similarly, giving gifts to ordinary people could result in very unpleasant consequences for them, so ask your guide at any point what is appropriate.

Kids are remarkably forthcoming and will wave back and smile ecstatically when they see a foreign tour group. Personal relationships with North Koreans who are not your tour guides or business colleagues will be impossible. Men should bear in mind that any physical contact with a Korean woman will be seen as unusual, so while shaking hands may be acceptable, do not greet a Korean female with a kiss in the European manner. Korea is still a very patriarchal society and despite the equality of women on an ideological level, this is not the case in day-to-day life.

Lifestyle

Trying to give a sense of day-to-day North Korean life is a challenge indeed. It's difficult

to overstate the ramifications of half a century of Stalinism – and it is no overstatement to say that North Korea is the most closed and secretive nation on earth. Facts meld with rumour about the real situation in the country; however, power cuts and food shortages are still everyday events in DPRK – although North Koreans are told to attribute both to American imperialism, leading to the comic tradition of Koreans shouting 'blame America!' whenever the lights go out. Food is now far more plentiful than it has been for years, although at the time of writing it was suggested that this may change again due to bad flooding in 2006. The 'arduous march' of the 1990s may not be over yet.

The system of political apartheid that exists in North Korea has effectively created a three-strata society. All people are divided up by *taedo* – a curious post-feudalist caste system – into loyal, neutral or hostile categories in relation to the regime. The hostile are deprived of everything and often end up in forced labour camps in entire family groups, maybe for nothing more than having South Korean relatives or for one family member being caught crossing into China. The neutral have little or nothing but are not persecuted, while the loyal enjoy everything from Pyongyang residency and desk jobs (at the lower levels) to Party membership and the privileges of the nomenclature. At the top of the tree, the Kim dynasty and its vast array of courtiers, security guards, staff and other flunkies are rumoured to enjoy great wealth and luxury.

It's hard to overstate the importance of the military in North Korean culture, as witnessed

---

TIME LINE

1392 The start of the Joseon dynasty, unsympathetic to northerners

1866 The *General Sherman* goes aground on the Taedong River; all on board are killed

1910 Japanese occupation begins

1948 Declaration of the Democratic People's Republic of Korea

1950 North Korean invasion of South Korea

1953 Korean War ends in stalemate

1980 Kim Jong Il anointed 'Dear Leader' and successor to his father

1983 Kim Il Sung bomb kills many South Korean cabinet members in Rangoon

1994 Kim Il Sung dies

1995 Floods devastate North Korea

2000 Kim Dae-jung and Kim Jong Il meet in an unprecedented summit in Pyongyang

2002 President George W Bush labels North Korea part of its 'Axis of Evil'

2006 North Korea test fires seven missiles and carries out a nuclear detonation leading to international condemnation and UN sanctions by the Military First campaign, which sees priorities in all fields going to the army. North Korea has the world's fifth-largest standing army and the social status of anyone in uniform is very high – rations increase in proportion to the individual's importance to the regime's survival.

North Korea is predictably austere. The six-day week (which even for office workers includes regular stints of backbreaking labour in the rice fields at planting and harvest time) makes for an exhausted populace, but this makes Sundays a real event and Koreans visibly beam as they relax, go on picnics, sing songs and drink in small groups all over the country. A glance at the showcase shops and department stores in Pyongyang confirms that there is only a small number of imported goods available to the general population, highly priced and of poor quality. Testimonies taken from North Korean refugees in China give a picture of daily life in the rural north of the country: many refugees tell tales of hair and teeth falling out due to malnourishment, and they tell stories of surviving on eating grass and rats during the famine years.

While in the 20 years following the Korean War it could genuinely be claimed that Kim Il Sung's government increased the standard of living in the North, bringing literacy and health care to every part of the country, the regression since the collapse of communism throughout the world has been just as spectacular, and people are now just as materially poor as their grandparents were in the early 1950s. Outside Pyongyang the standard of living is far worse, and this is visible on the street, although the carefully planned tour routes will never fully expose the poverty of the nation to the casual tourist. Still, glimpses of life in rural villages from the bus can be chilling.

Population

The current population of North Korea is anyone's guess. Officially it stands at 23 million, but the devastation wrought by the famine in the late 1990s has had untold effects on the country and its people. In a watershed announcement in 1999, the North Korean government shocked the world by admitting that as many as three million people had died of starvation since 1995. How closely this corresponds to the real figure is still completely unknown. Terrifyingly enough, some North Korean defectors in China have suggested that the population could have dropped to as little as 15 million over the past decade.

All of the 2.2 million inhabitants of Pyongyang are from backgrounds deemed to be loyal to the Kim regime. And with a complete lack of free movement in the country (all citizens need special permission to leave their town of residence), no visitor is likely to see those termed 'hostile' – anyway, most people in this unfortunate category are in hard-labour camps miles from anywhere. All North Korean citizens have been obliged to wear a 'loyalty' badge since 1970 featuring Kim Il Sung's portrait. Since the 1980s, Kim Jong Il badges have also been worn. You can be certain that anyone without one is a foreigner.

Sport

Soccer remains the most popular spectator sport, and seeing a match in Pyongyang is sometimes a possibility. These matches offer a chance to get as close to ordinary North Koreans as is generally possible for foreign visitors. North and South Korean national teams played each other for the first time in over a decade in 2002 in Seoul. With true diplomatic flair, the 'reunification game' ended in a 0-0 draw. The South's stellar display in the 2002 World Cup and less successful appearance in the 2006 event was sketchily reported in the North, a rare display of nationalism overcoming political differences.

The North's greatest sporting moment came at the 1966 World Cup in England, when they thrashed favourites Italy and stunned the world. They subsequently went out to Portugal in the quarterfinals. The story of the team is told in a strangely touching documentary – one of the few ever to be made by Western crews in DPRK – called The Game of Their Lives (www.thegameoftheirlives.com).

Weightlifting and martial arts are the only other sporting fields in which North Korea has created any international impact. One home-grown sporting phenomenon (for want of a more accurate term) that visitors should try to see is the Arirang Mass Games, held annually at the world's largest stadium, the May Day Stadium, in Pyongyang. These mass gymnastic displays involve over 100,000 soldiers, children and students holding up coloured placards to form enormous murals in praise of North Korea's achievements, truly an amazing sight.

Religion

In North Korea, all traditional religion is regarded, in accordance with Marxist theory, as an expression of a 'feudal mentality', an obsolete superstitious force opposing political revolution, social liberation, economic development and national independence. Therefore, it has been effectively proscribed since the 1950s. However, as the Kim regime became more and more deified in the 1990s, official propaganda against organised religion accordingly stopped. A number of Buddhist temples are on show to tourists, although they're always showpieces – you won't see locals or any real Buddhist community. However, in recent years three churches have been built in Pyongyang, suggesting that there is a surprising amount of religious freedom relative to other human rights.

TRADITIONAL RELIGIONS

The northern version of Korean shamanism was individualistic and ecstatic, while the southern style was hereditary and based on regularly scheduled community rituals. As far as is known, no shamanist activity is now practised in North Korea. Many northern shamans were transplanted to the South, chased out along with their enemies the Christians, and the popularity of the services they offer (fortune-telling, for instance) has endured there. Together with the near-destruction of southern shamanism by South Korea's relentless modernisation, we have the curious situation where the actual practice of northern Korean shamanism can only be witnessed in South Korea.

Northern Korea held many important centres of Korean Buddhism from the 3rd century through the Japanese occupation period. The Kumgangsan and Myohyangsan mountain areas, in particular, hosted large Zen-oriented (Jogye) temple-complexes left over from the Goryeo dynasty. Under the communists, Buddhism in the North (along with Confucianism and shamanism) suffered a fate identical to that of Christianity.

Some historically important Buddhist temples and shrines still exist, mostly in rural or mountainous areas. The most prominent among them are Pyohon Temple at Kumgangsan, Pyohon Temple at Myohyangsan, and the Confucian Shrine in the Songgyungwan Neo-Confucian College just outside of Kaesong (p369).

Arts

Largely due to Kim Jong Il's lifelong interest in celluloid, the North Korean film industry has had money pumped into it on a disproportionate scale. Kim Jong Il's input has been all encompassing and hands-on – he is listed as the executive producer of many films produced in the country, and is believed to have many actors, actresses and directors among his palace courtiers.

The only North Korean film that can be seen with ease in the West is Shin Sang-Ok's *Pulgasari*, a curious socialist version of *Godzilla* made by the kidnapped South Korean director, who escaped back to the South in 1986 (see p369).

The ongoing *Nation* and *Destiny* series of films is supposed to be a series of 100; so far 60 have been released. Far more interesting is the 1999 epic *Forever in Our Memory* that, surprisingly, tackles the mass starvation of the mid-1990s. The climax of the film sees a big flood threatening the harvest and soldiers and farmers standing on top of a dam to create a human dyke with their bodies, all the while screaming 'Long Live Kim Il Sung' and waving the North Korean flag.

You can request a visit to the Pyongyang Film Studios when booking your tour – and you may even be lucky enough to see an agit-prop classic in production.

North Korean literature has not profited from the Kim dynasty, which has done little to encourage original writing. Despite an initial artistic debate in the 1950s, all non-party-controlled forms of expression were quickly repressed.

Kim Il Sung was a fierce nationalist, relentlessly emphasising the superiority of Korean culture. Tourists with an interest in traditional arts can benefit – visits to performances of traditional Korean music, singing and dance can be arranged. Some even argue that in terms of traditional culture, the North is the 'real Korea', untainted by the Americanisation of the South. Exhibitions of traditional or modern pottery, sculpture, painting and architecture can be viewed on request, and it is highly recommended to include a visit to a cinema, a theatre or an opera performance. If one hasn't been pre-arranged, your guide should be able to organise a visit to a performance for a token extra charge, as long as you give some warning.

While the performances are unlikely to be cutting edge, or even comprehensible to the

NORTH KOREA SPEAK

It's a good idea to familiarise yourself with some of the linguistic and idiomatic quirks peculiar to the North, although your ever-zealous tour guide will be delighted to fill in any ideological gaps that become apparent.

Chollima Speed Nothing it seems, in North Korea, is capable of moving with anything other than Chollima Speed. Not simply a grand way of saying 'fast', Chollima Speed dazzles and amazes. Whether you feel like it or not, you too will be dazzled and amazed when various buildings, factories or monuments are described to you in terms of their amazingly brief construction periods. Chollima is an ancient Korean myth, a Pegasus who was capable of travelling 1000 *ri*, or 400km, in one day, and could not be tamed by any rider. The Chollima movement, launched in the shadow of China's equally disastrous Great Leap Forward, engaged the population in trying to over-fulfil already ridiculously ambitious production targets. While its results were impressive on paper, the reality was, of course, somewhat different. However, the myths, both ancient and modern, remain, and if you really want to please your guide, say *jongmal Chollima soktoimnida* ('that really is Chollima speed').

Juche Pronounced 'joo-chay', this is the cornerstone of North Korean philosophy, as witnessed by the Tower of the Juche Idea, the vast Pyongyang phallus designed by the Dear Leader himself. Juche encompasses many things – none of which are in any way related to DPRK's grim reality. Juche essentially stresses self-reliance and the individual's role in forging his/her own destiny, although no doubt it gets a cool reception at the concentration camps. Likewise, your guide will be delighted at your ideological progress if you say *Igosun Juchejog-imnida* ('It is Juche oriented').

The Great Leader This universally employed phrase describes Kim Il Sung (1912–94) who founded the DPRK and, over five decades in power, sought to apotheosise himself and his son.

The Dear Leader This reverential title refers to Kim Jong Il, the first person to lead a communist country by primogeniture. To confuse matters, since his father's death he has also been referred to as the 'Great Leader'. To make your guide's day, try to throw the phrase *widaehan ryongdoja Kim Jong Il tongji-ui mansumugang-ul samga chugwon hamnida* into the conversation ('I wish the Great Leader Comrade Kim Jong Il a long life in good health').

non-Korean speaker, Pyongyang does have a small opera and theatre scene. Again, it's a question of asking your guides and preferably your travel agent before you go, but it may be possible to spend the evening at one of Pyongyang's cultural institutes.

ENVIRONMENT

The one thing that strikes most visitors to North Korea is its squeaky-clean appearance. This is a function not just of the lack of consumer goods and their packaging but of determined policies that keep it that way. The streets are washed down twice a week, and before dawn each day street cleaners are out sweeping up any litter or leaves. You'd be hard pressed to find a single piece of paper on the streets, despite the absence of litterbins. Even in the countryside, locals are assigned a particular stretch of the main road to sweep – each and every day.

North Korea boasts a diverse range of plants and animals. The varying climatic regions have created environments that are home to

subarctic, alpine and even subtropical plant and tree species. Most of the country's fauna is contained within the limited nature reserves around the mountainous regions, as most of the lower plains have been converted to arable agricultural land. An energetic reforestation programme was carried out after the Korean War to replace many of the forests that were destroyed by the incessant bombing campaigns, notable exception being the area to the north of the DMZ, where defoliants are used to remove vegetation for security purposes. The comparatively low population has resulted in the preservation of most mountainous regions.

Only recently has the international community looked at assisting the North in assessing and monitoring the country's biodiversity. Three areas of particular focus are the DMZ, the wetlands of the Tumen River and the Paekdusan mountains. For those people interested in participating in a tour of North Korea with a greater emphasis on flora and fauna, then it is possible to organise an appropriate itinerary with your Korean tour company. Bird-watching endeavours to some of the wetland habitats of migratory birds are the most popular. These tours, however, often involve greater expenses, especially if a chartered flight is necessary.

Two particular flora species have attracted enormous attention from the North Koreans, and neither of them are native. In 1965 President Sukarno named a newly developed orchid after Kim Il Sung – kimilsungia – popular acclaim overcoming Kim's modest reluctance to accept such an honour. Kim Jong Il was presented with his namesake, kimjongilia, a begonia developed by a Japanese horticulturist, on his 46th birthday. The blooming of either flower is announced annually as a tribute to the two Great Leaders and visitors will notice their omnipresence throughout official tourist sites.

Environmental Issues

The main challenges to the environment are from problems that are harder to see. The devastating floods and economic slowdown during the 1990s wreaked havoc not only on property and agricultural land, but also on the environment. Fields were stripped of their topsoil, which, combined with fertiliser shortages, forced authorities to expand the arable land under cultivation. Unsustainable and unstable hillside areas, river banks and road edges were brought under cultivation, further exacerbating erosion, deforestation, fertiliser contamination of the land and rivers and the vulnerability of crops.

One advantage of its isolation is the pristine natural environment to be found in the mountains, untouched by commercialism or mass tourism. However, there has been substantial deforestation due to the famine. Fried leaves is a dish served very regularly in rural areas of DPRK – and some refugees have reported that their biggest surprise on finally reaching the South was to find that the hillsides were so lush and full of greenery. Due to food and fuel shortages, many areas of DPRK have simply been stripped of vegetation.

FOOD & DRINK
Staples & Specialities

While tour groups eat sumptuously by North Korean standards, the standard fare is fairly mediocre and varies depending on the food situation at the time. There is no danger of tourists going hungry, though, and you'll find you get by very well on a diet of kimchi, rice, soups, noodles and fried meat. Vegetarians will be catered for without a problem, but they may simply be given rice, egg and cucumber non-stop for the duration of their visit.

Drinks

In 2000, in a surprise move for a country with millions of malnourished children, North Korea purchased the Ushers brewery in Trowbridge, England, dismantled it, shipped it to Nampo and rebuilt it on the outskirts of Pyongyang. Pyongyang and Taedonggang beers are the most popular brands, although neither rival imported beers such as Heineken or Tiger.

Other drinks on offer include a pleasant range of North Korean fruit juices and sodas, and Coke and Fanta are also available now in some Pyongyang hotels and restaurants.

Soju (the local firewater) is drunk at dinners; It's rather strong stuff. Visitors might prefer Korean blueberry wine; the best is apparently made from Mount Paekdu blueberries. Blueberry wine comes in two forms: the gently alcoholic, which tastes like a soft drink, and the reinforced version, which could stun an elephant.

PYONGYANG

☎ 02 / pop 2.8 million / 200 sq km

Traffic has been increasing on the once-empty streets of this extraordinary capital. That said, little else has changed in Pyongyang ('flat land') over the last couple of decades. The city remains an eerie, unchanging place of wide streets, endless grey and white Soviet-style blocks, vast monuments to the party and an all-female team of fetishistically-clad traffic wardens manually directing traffic with domineering zeal.

In the best possible tradition of Minsk and Ashgabat, Pyongyang rose from the ashes of destruction and as such was a tabula rasa for the Kim dictatorship to impose its worldview on. Mysterious and grey, Pyongyang is definitely one of the world's strangest capitals, often wrapped in a thick mist and dominated by the immeasurably sinister and humungous pyramid of the unfinished Ryugyong Hotel.

Every visit focuses heavily on Pyongyang – this is after all a city built to impress with a population of approved, privileged citizens and a slew of awe-inspiring sights your guides are happy to show you. It's worth trying to get to know the city during your trip, as this is one of the few places you'll have a chance to get to know in North Korea.

The guides will be falling over themselves to show you a succession of monuments, towers, statues, and buildings that apotheosise the Juche idea and propagate the achievements of the Kim regime. These include the Tower of the Juche Idea, the Chollima Statue and the Mansudae Grand Monument, a vast rendering of the Great Leader in bronze, to which every visitor is expected to pay floral homage.

While these are all impressive, if surreal, the real delights of Pyongyang are to be had in the quieter moments when you can get glimpses of everyday life. If possible, suggest walking between sights rather than driving, which the guides prefer. A gentle stroll on Pyongyang's relatively relaxed Moran Hill, for example, will reveal that the locals have picnics, play music and idle away sunny afternoons. Despite the best attempts of the Korean Workers' Party, there is a semblance of normality surviving in the capital. You just have to look hard for it.

HISTORY

It seems incredible to think it, given its stark, thoroughly 20th-century appearance, but Pyongyang is ancient, stretching back to when the Goguryeo dynasty built its capital here in AD 427. By the 7th century the kingdom of Goguryeo had started to collapse under the strain of successive, massive attacks from Sui and Tang China. Cutting a deal with the Tang Chinese, the Shilla kingdom in the South was able to conquer Goguryeo in 668, creating the first unified Korea.

Later, during the Goryeo dynasty, Pyongyang became the kingdom's secondary capital. The city was completely destroyed by the Japanese in 1592 and then again by the Manchus at the beginning of the 17th century. Pyongyang thenceforth remained a relative backwater until the arrival of foreign missionaries, who constructed over 100 churches in the city. Pyongyang was once again destroyed during the Sino-Japanese War (1894–5) and remained neglected until the occupying Japanese developed industry in the region.

The US practically wiped Pyongyang out between 1950 and 1953, and yet as the capital of the DPRK under Kim Il Sung, modern Pyongyang rose from the ashes with inimitable 'Chollima speed'. Few historic buildings remain, but there are some in evidence, including a couple of temples and pavilions, the Taedong Gate and a few sections of the Goguryeo kingdom's inner and northern walls.

ORIENTATION

Pyongyang today is an imposing city. The regime has created a showpiece capital employing its own grandiose style of architecture, which borrows much from the Soviet model, and it's one that rarely fails to impress.

The larger part of the city is on the northern bank of the Taedong River, which curves gracefully off to the suburb of Mangyongdae to the west. The city is centred on Kim Il Sung Sq, which faces the Tower of the Juche Idea across the river. All the hotels where foreigners are put up are centrally located and not more than a few minutes' drive from the major sights of the city. Arriving by train, tourists will alight at Pyongyang station on Yokjon St, right in the city centre. From Sunan airport, due north of the city, it's a 20-minute ride into the centre.

Maps

Pyongyang maps are not detailed and rarely updated. However, as you will be accompanied everywhere by your guides, you hardly need to worry about getting lost; the basic map available will be plenty.

INFORMATION

There is no tourist office in Pyongyang, but there are numerous English-language publications designed for visitors detailing various aspects of North Korean life. An English-

---

PYONGYANG HIGHLIGHTS

- Ride the express lift to the top of the **Tower of the Juche Idea** (p362) for a magnificent view of the sprawling cityscape on a clear day

- Ride the spectacularly designed **Pyongyang metro** (p363)

- See where Kim Il Sung lies in state at the **Kumsusan Memorial Palace** (p362), which makes Lenin's mausoleum look like a shoebox – and can be visited by invitation only

- Escape the relentless grandeur of the city centre and have a walk on relaxed **Moran Hill** (p363)

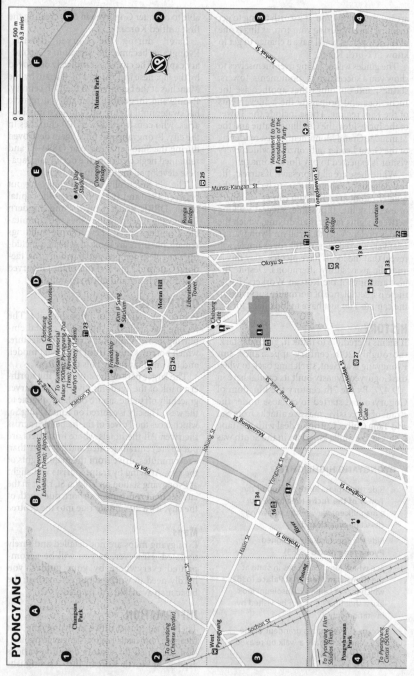

PYONGYANG

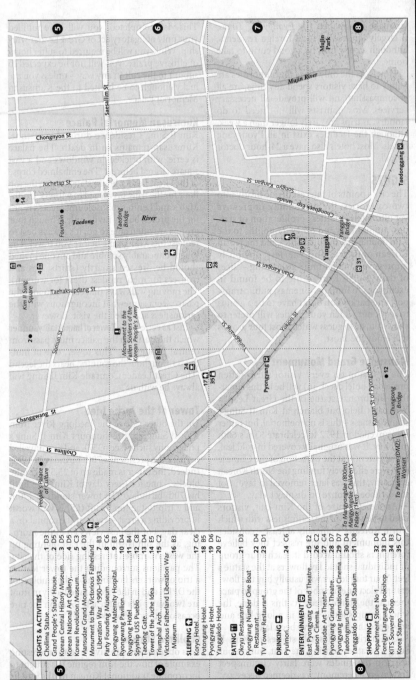

language newspaper, the *Pyongyang Times*, is largely ignored by local foreign residents, although a copy may be a good curio to take home.

Hotels, as the only place the authorities are happy to have visitors spend any time, are all encompassing and will provide all necessary services. Most tourists will not need to do laundry, as trips are rarely longer than a week, although the facilities exist in all Pyongyang hotels. Most hotels also have a 24-hour doctor on call.

SIGHTS

The city's points of interest divide neatly into two categories: the profoundly impressive yet ultimately pointless proliferation of statues, monuments and other monoliths to the Kim double-act, the Juche Idea and the North Korean military; and the less obviously impressive – but far more interesting – slices of daily North Korean life to be found in excursions to funfairs, cinemas, public transport and parks. You don't have to be a genius to work out which your guides will prefer to show you, or to guess which most tour groups will enjoy the most.

Mansudae Grand Monument

The first stop on every visitor's trip (often preceding hotel check-in) will be to this larger-than-life bronze statue of the Great Leader. You can't help but blanch at Kim Il Sung's shamelessness – this is no memorial, but rather was unveiled in 1972 to celebrate Kim's 60th birthday. It was originally covered in gold leaf, but apparently at the objection of the Chinese who were effectively funding the North Korean economy, this was later removed in favour of the scrubbed bronze on display today.

As the epicentre of the Kim cult, visitors need to be aware of the seriousness with which North Koreans – officially at least – consider this monument and the respect they believe foreigners should accord it. Each tour group or individual should lay flowers at the statue's feet. Your tour leader will usually buy the flowers and elect one member of the group to place them at the statue's feet. As this is done, the whole group should stand in a long line and bow once the flowers have been laid.

Ordinarily guides tell stories of Kim Il Sung's greatness during the visit, but on our last trip the guides were fairly circumspect and no great ceremony was deemed necessary.

This visit completed, you will have fulfilled your only obligatory act of Great Leader worship. While you will be required to suffer hours of effusive praise, you will not be expected to submit to the cult in any way – unless you are lucky enough to be invited to the Kumsusan Memorial Palace.

Kumsusan Memorial Palace

Kim Il Sung's residence during his lifetime, Kumsusan remains so in death. The palace is eerie, with bricked-in windows and a vast square cleared before it. The embalmed corpse of the Great Leader lies in state here on the top floor for the truly privileged to witness. Unlike Mao's and Lenin's mausoleums, access is not for the proles, but by invite only. Though tour groups are often able to go, it's always best to request this a long time before you travel. The tone is unbearably sombre and anyone invited should be dressed smartly (shirts, ties and trousers for men, modest dress for women). The moving walkways that carry you into the palace seem somewhat incongruous with the seriousness accorded the visit, however.

Just as eerie is the **Tower of Immortality**, under which the traffic to the palace must pass from central Pyongyang. This tower, one of hundreds throughout the country, bears the legend 'The Great Leader Comrade Kim Il Sung will always be with us'.

Tower of the Juche Idea

On the other side of the Taedong River from Kim Il Sung Sq, this honours Kim Il Sung's philosophy Juche (see p357), and was unveiled to mark the president's 70th birthday in 1982. Indeed, the tower is made up of 25,550 granite blocks – one for every day of Kim's life until his 70th birthday. The tower stands at 170m and a trip to the top by lift (€5) is well worth it, providing a great view over the capital on a clear day. For the best views go in the morning, as the sun is still in the east, lighting up the western, more interesting side of the city. The pavilions surrounding the tower feature a trio of workers holding aloft the emblem of the DPRK and in the river immediately in front are two water jets that reach 150m on the rare occasions they are working.

Chollima Statue

Less obviously impressive, but an interesting example of how the Kim regime has sought to incorporate traditional Korean myths into its socialist cult, is the bronze statue of the Korean Pegasus, the steed Chollima. According to legend, Chollima could cover hundreds of kilometres a day and was untameable (see North Korea Speak p357). Kim Il Sung appropriated the myth in the period of reconstruction following the Korean War so that the zeal of the North Korean workers to rebuild their shattered nation and construct vast and pointless monuments to the leadership became known as 'Chollima speed'. When North Korea broke through to the quarterfinals of the World Cup in 1966, it was apparently because Kim senior had urged them to play 'Chollima football'.

Triumphal Arch

Your guides will tell you with barely concealed glee that the Triumphal Arch is 3m higher than its cousin in Paris, making it the largest in the world.

The arch marks the site where Kim Il Sung first addressed the liberated Koreans after the end of Japanese occupation in 1945. The gloss you hear will omit the fact that the Soviets liberated Pyongyang, not Kim Il Sung's partisans, who themselves gave full credit to the Soviets at the time. A vast mural a short walk away details the event and pictures a young Kim addressing a wildly enthusiastic local population. Set back from the arch is the Kim Il Sung Stadium.

Kim Il Sung Square

This vast plaza would be the packed hub of any other world capital, but Pyongyang's central square and marching ground is strange in its emptiness, the open spaces seemingly cowed by the massive buildings surrounding it. Most impressive of these is the **Grand People's Study House**, the country's largest library and national centre of Juche studies. This is one of Pyongyang's most striking buildings, a socialist realist structure melded with traditional Korean architecture.

With over 30 million books, finding what you want is inevitably quite a challenge – and you will be proudly shown the incredible system of conveyer belts that can deliver books right to your desk. All foreign publications are viewable with special permission only, while even North Korean literature over 15 years old is proscribed to conceal the historical rewrites.

Other structures on the square include the **Korean National Art Gallery**, commonly included on tours, though it's frankly fairly dull, and the **Korean Central History Museum**, which is rarely visited by groups. There's a great view from the riverside bank across the Taedong to the Tower of the Juche Idea, where groups usually go to take photos.

Historic Pyongyang

To see something of Pyongyang's prewar history is a challenge. The **Taedong Gate** was the eastern gate to the original walled city of Pyongyang, and was built in the 6th century. The current gate was rebuilt in 1635, but is one of the oldest remaining structures in the city – a reminder that Pyongyang was once a traditional Asian city rather than the post-Soviet monolith it is today.

Nearby are the other major historical sites: the **Pyongyang Bell**, a bronze early-warning system for fire and invasion dating from 1726, and the beautiful **Ryongwang Pavilion**, originally built in 1111 and rebuilt in 1670.

Mangyongdae Children's Palace

This centre for extra-curricular activity – from martial arts to the playing of traditional instruments – makes for a great visit. Note the model of a 'North Korean' space shuttle at the entrance, a replica of the Soviet *Buran*. The palace visit will include displays of incredibly talented martial artists, gymnasts and musicians, all beaming at you as they perform. The tour usually culminates in the huge main auditorium with a stellar display of fantastically regimented youth. The grand finale is usually a loyalty song to Kim Jong Il.

Moran Hill

This is Pyongyang's top recreation ground for the masses. Couples wander, families picnic and there are people who even play musical instruments in an incongruously relaxed area of the capital. It's particularly busy on a Sunday and a lovely place to stroll and absorb something of daily life. Even the guides seem to relax more here and will often allow you more freedom to wander than elsewhere.

Pyongyang Metro

Finally, one other visit that is often included on a city tour is a trip on the impressive Pyongyang Metro. It's a good idea to request this in advance of travel, as it's definitely a highlight. The network, which is made up of two lines, has a simultaneous function as a nuclear bunker in the event of the long-awaited American invasion. Stations are deep below ground, and you can even see blast doors that will close if Pyongyang ever comes under nuclear bombardment (see below).

Museums

Pyongyang's museums unsurprisingly offer the regime's version of history. While one or two can be very interesting for a totally new perspective on events, the novelty can soon wear thin.

A visit to the **Korean Revolution Museum** is likely to be included on your itinerary. This shows the anti-Japanese struggle including numerous action exhibits depicting the fiercest of the battles.

The **Party Founding Museum** is located on the southern slope of Haebang Hill and is one of the least interesting museums. It originally housed the Central Committee of the Korean Workers' Party, as well as Kim Il Sung's office from where he 'led the building of a new democratic Korea'. Next door is the Great Leader's conspicuously modest residence, used after coming to power and presumably before the masses demanded he build himself numerous palaces.

Korean Central History Museum is all rather tedious and predictable – a large number of exhibits about the North's struggle against imperialism and oppression. On the other hand, the **Victorious Fatherland Liberation War Museum** is a fascinating place. The key battles of the Korean War are depicted vividly in dioramas, and there's some fascinating military hardware from war-damaged tanks and aircraft to torpedo boats used by both sides. These were all placed in the basement and the museum was then built around them.

Nearby, opposite the little Potong tributary of the Taedong, there is the impressive **Monument to the Victorious Fatherland Liberation War 1950–1953**, unveiled in 1993 to mark the 40th anniversary of the war's end. The sculptures reflect the different battles of the war; the Victory Sculpture is the centrepiece.

A rarely visited museum is the **Three Revolutions Exhibition**, North Korea's answer to America's Epcot Centre. The sprawling complex details the 'three revolutions' Kim Il Sung brought about in post-war Korea: ideological, technical and cultural. The six halls detail advances across the board in electronics, heavy industry, agriculture and technology (advances appear to be fairly slim, all the tech-

---

THE MYSTERY UNDERGROUND

There can be no better example of the Kim regime's prioritisation of the military-industrial complex than the fascinating Pyongyang metro. While two lines exist for civilian use, there are rumours of several government-only lines linking key ministries and military installations capable of withstanding a full-scale American bombardment. Since the system opened in 1973, each station has doubled as a nuclear bunker and there are frequent air-raid drills in Pyongyang, in which citizens make their way into the stations and the triple-blast doors shut behind them.

As tourists, visiting the Pyongyang metro will involve a one-stop trip between Puhung (Rehabilitation) and Yongwang (Glory) stations. All state visitors, from US Secretary of State Madeleine Albright to former South Korean President Kim Dae-jung, were given the same show trip, giving rise to a rumour that power cuts and lack of repair have meant that the rest of the system no longer functions on a day-to-day basis. In fact the whole system is used, although it's possible during the 1990s when North Korea was really on the skids that much of it was closed to make energy savings.

The entire system's construction was overseen by the Great Leader, who offered his 'on-the-spot guidance'. A guidebook to the Metro describes his wise words on opening the new network in 1973:

'The Great Leader President said to officials in a thoughtful tone "I think it is difficult to build the metro, but it is not to cut the tape." Hearing his words, which considered the trouble of builders first, the participants in the opening ceremony felt a lump in their throats and gave enthusiastic cheers, waving bundles of flowers.'

One of the deepest metros in the world, it is also one of the most elaborately decorated – marble platforms, vast chandeliers and impressive murals extolling the virtues of Juche and detailing yet more of the heroic activities of guess who…

nical exhibits looking more like a display of antiques). The world's weirdest planetarium can be found within the electronics industry hall, which looks like a silver replica of Saturn. There's also an interesting outdoor display of vehicles produced in North Korea.

Tomb of Tan'gun

History continues to evolve in North Korea, with new 'revolutionary discoveries' being made every year. While the government announced in 1993 that its archaeologists had discovered the tomb of Tan'gun, the founder of the first Korean kingdom, it wasn't until recently that North Korean historians made the incredible discovery that Tan'gun was in fact a member of the Kim clan.

During North Korea's more rational communist period, the government had agreed with most scholars of Korean history that Tan'gun was a mythical figure and that the kingdom of KoChoson (ancient Korea) with its capitals Pyongyang and Asadal was in fact located in Northeast China, if it indeed existed. However, it's been recently 'discovered' that KoChoson was in northern Korea and its capital was right where Pyongyang now stands. Tan'gun was a real man (and a Kim at that); archaeologists have also discovered his skeletal remains.

Those decayed bones (and those said to be of his wife) are on display at a grandly constructed, white, pyramid mausoleum just outside of Pyongyang. A small museum stands nearby, displaying 'artefacts' from Tan'gun's times, said to have been found in and around the tomb.

Pyongyang Film Studios

Some 20 films a year are still churned out by the county's main film studios located in the suburbs of Pyongyang. Kim Il Sung visited the complex around 20 times during his lifetime to provide invaluable on-the-spot guidance, while Kim Jr has been more than 600 times, such is his passionate interest in films.

Like all things North Korean, the two main focuses are the anti-Japanese struggle and the anti-American war. The main complex is a huge, propaganda-filled suite of office buildings where apparently post-production goes on, even though it feels eerily empty. A short uphill drive takes you to the large sets, however, which are far more fun. Here you'll find a generic ancient Korean town for historic films (you can even dress up as a king or queen and be photographed

sitting on a 'throne' carpeted in leopard skin), a 1930s Chinese street, a Japanese street, a South Korean street (look for the massage signs that illustrate their compatriots' moral laxity) and a fairly bizarre range of structures from a collection of 'European' buildings. Some groups have been lucky and seen films being made during their visit, although usually it's hauntingly empty.

Pyongyang Zoo

Rarely offered on standard tours, Pyongyang Zoo is worth a visit. It has a good aquarium and reptile house and a large array of animals, most of whom look pretty forlorn. Worst off are the big cats, nearly all gifts of long-dead communist big wigs around the world – the wonderful lions, tigers and leopards are kept in woefully inadequate compounds and many have lost the plot as a result. The zoo's two elephants and its hippo all look exceptionally lacklustre as well.

There's more fun to be had with the baboons and a collection of lemurs, while the oddest exhibit is the huge collection of domestic cats. It's very relaxed here; you'll find North Korean families on outings and this is one of the few environments where you can communicate with locals in a relatively carefree way.

Mangyongdae

The closest North Korea has to a Kim Il Sung Disney World is the suburb of Mangyongdae, one of the many cottage industries created by and simultaneously bolstering the ever-growing personality cult of Great Leaders one and two. Just 12km from the centre of Pyongyang, Mangyongdae has long been a destination for day trippers from the capital, due to its idyllic setting amid the gentle hills where the Sunhwa River flows into the Taedong. The suburb now houses the place of Kim Il Sung's birth – interesting to visit, as much to see the pretty setting, the fun fair and the relaxing Pyongyangites, as for the flourishing Kim cult.

Kim Il Sung's birthplace is a collection of traditional huts: a typical Korean peasant house with a thatched roof and a block of living rooms, as well as a small barn, most of which looks like it's been built in the past few decades. The emphasis is very much on the president's humble origins, and indeed, it's an open question as to whether Kim Il Sung was really born here at all.

The **Mangyongdae Revolutionary Museum**, located nearby, continues the theme of the Great Leader's childhood and makes the point that all his family members were Korean patriot revolutionaries of the humblest possible order.

You may also be lucky enough to visit the **Mangyongdae Revolutionary School**, where Pyongyang's elite sons are trained for the next generation of leadership. This is a fun tour through the various classrooms and gymnasiums, where children look at you with wonder.

To relax after the relentless propaganda, the **Mangyongdae Funfair** is a pleasant oasis built around the base of Song Hill, where you can relax with some day-trippers from the capital. You can throw a ball at American Imperialists at the coconut shy and take a ride on a North Korean rollercoaster.

Pyongyang Maternity Hospital

This smart hospital, designed apparently to look like a mother's outstretched arms about to embrace her child, is sometimes available for groups. Here all Pyongyang women give birth for the first time (whether they like it or not); after that it's the preserve of the privileged or the vulnerable. It's an impressive place, with relatively modern equipment and spotless floors. The tour typically includes patient rooms, treatment rooms and the incubators where you can see Pyongyang's newborns.

It's interesting that North Korean fathers have no contact with their children for five days after their birth for health reasons. In the meantime, the camera phone booths on the ground floor are where interaction is restricted to, although such technology simply underscores how much of a showpiece this place really is.

SLEEPING

Pyongyang has the largest range of hotels of any North Korean city. They are, like much of the city's architecture, built to impress, and while their façades are often striking, their interiors are all fairly uninspiring. The city's skyline is dominated by the fabulously impressive pyramidal Ryugyong Hotel – designed to be the world's largest luxury hotel in the 1980s. As you approach it, it becomes clear that it is a skeleton, with no windows or interiors. The project ran out of money and the vast structure now sits as a derelict monument to overly ambitious central planning, still dominating the city with its vast, sinister shape.

Yanggakdo Hotel (☎ 381 2134; fax 381 2930/1; s/d €175/290; ✗ ✑) This is where most tour groups stay, a massive mid '90s tower on its own island right in the middle of Pyongyang. The rooms are already showing their age, but they are at least spacious and comfortable, with great views from most. As well as a pool and sauna, there are numerous restaurants, a bowling alley, three pool tables, a karaoke lounge, several shops, a casino and a foreigners-only disco.

The advantage of the Yanggakdo is that you can wander around outside without your guides (although don't even think of crossing the bridge into the city), something you can't really do in other hotels in Pyongyang.

Koryo Hotel (☎ 381 4397; fax 318 4422; s/d €175/290; ✗ ✑) The city's other premier hotel, this 1985 orange-bronze structure is the preferred place to lodge UN functionaries and business people as well as some tour groups. Each of its twin towers has a revolving restaurant on top and its location is better than the Yanggakdo's, on the relative bustle of Changgwang St, a short walk from Pyongyang train station.

Potonggang Hotel (☎ 381 2229; fax 381 4428) Famously the only hotel in North Korea to get CNN, the Potonggang is owned by Unification Church leader Reverend Moon, who negotiated directly with Kim Il Sung in 1991 for its purchase. The hotel is situated by the small Pothong River, about 4km from the city centre and is often used for Japanese tourists. It's almost unheard of for Western groups to stay here.

There are many other hotels in Pyongyang, including the Sosan, the Pyongyang and Chongnyon, but it's not possible for Westerners to stay in them.

EATING & DRINKING

Pyongyang is by far the best place to eat in the country, offering both variety and decent fare. Almost all tour groups will eat out at least once a day, usually twice. Any restaurant outside your hotel that you are taken to is likely to be the exclusive preserve of foreigners and the party elite – there are popular local restaurants, such as those on Changgwang St, but foreign tour groups will not usually be taken there.

On tours all eating out will be included in your price, although there are extra charges for additional beers or specialties such as the local favourite, cold noodles.

Pyongyang Number One Duck Barbeque is one of the best places in town, and will often be where groups go on their last evening.

The **TV Tower** has a great restaurant at the top with some breathtaking views over the city. It's a popular lunchtime stop.

The **National Restaurant** is a camp and damp experience due to fake grass on the ceiling and a basement setting respectively. The food here is good, though, and there's a popular live show.

Pyongyang Number One Boat Restaurant is moored off Kim Il Sung Sq, and although we've heard stories of it cruising the Taedong for an hour during a meal, it's been stationary whenever we've eaten here. Eating is on a pleasant outdoor deck and it's very popular with tour groups and NGO staff.

The **Chongryu Restaurant** opposite the Romanian Embassy is usually included for groups. It's a pleasant place where you make your own hotpot dish on little individual gas stoves, although it's equally notable for its ropey Swiss rolls served as a dessert.

Okryu is one of the city's best-known restaurants, a huge monstrosity on the riverside that's famed for its cold noodles and very popular with locals. For this reason it's not usually on the schedule for groups, but you may be lucky. It was undergoing refurbishment at the time of research.

Pyulmori is a very exciting joint-venture coffee shop near to the Koryo Hotel. Run by a local charity supplying food to local orphanages, Pyulmori was the only place to get good coffee in North Korea at the time of writing. There is also a good selection of cakes and pies, and delightful staff.

Finally, the **Pyongyang Ostrich Farm** just outside the city has a restaurant serving (you guessed it) ostrich. It's a surreal spot for lunch if your group is on a trip there.

Nightlife in Pyongyang is almost nonexistent although hotel bars can be rowdy, especially at weekends. The large diplomatic and NGO presence in town means that there are some private clubs where foreigners can relax away from the strictures of everyday Pyongyang life.

The **Diplomatic Club** ('the diplo' to any self-respecting foreign resident) by the Juche Tower and the **Random Access Club** (RAC) in the diplomatic quarter of Munsudong are popular, but there's no way tourists can go to these, whatever diplomats may tell you.

ENTERTAINMENT

The nature of visiting North Korea is that the most mundane, everyday things become instantly fascinating. Given that contact with locals is kept to a minimum, while in Pyongyang you should take advantage of the relatively wide choice of evening entertainment to see how locals like to relax. Of course, what you will and won't be able to do depends on your guides, so let them know any requests as early on as possible, and of course, try to stay in their good books. There will often be a nominal charge of €10 for extra activities in the evening.

The **Pyongyang Circus** gets glowing reviews from visitors. It is mainly a human circus, and you may hear vicious rumours that during the famine many of the animals ended up on plates.

One suitably military pastime is a trip to the **Pyongyang shooting range** off Chongchun St, where all Pyongyang's sporting facilities are concentrated. It costs €1 for three bullets using a 2.2mm rifle or pistol. It makes a fun evening.

Cinema, theatre and opera trips are also possible (although rare), and while films, operas or plays aren't likely to be of a particularly gripping order, again, it's the experience that is interesting.

The main theatres are the **Pyongyang Grand Theatre**, the **East Pyongyang Grand Theatre** and the **Mansudae Art Theatre**, although spectacles vary little from one to the other. Musical 'classics' such as *The Flower Girl* and *A Daughter of the Party* are in constant rotation.

The **Pyongyang International Cinema** is a six-screen complex on Yanggak Island, near the Yanggakdo Hotel. The biennial **Pyongyang Film Festival** is held here every September in even-numbered years. Other cinemas include the **Taedongmun Cinema** (Sungri St) and the **Kaeson Cinema** (Moranbong Street) near the Triumphal Arch.

Soccer, a very popular local spectator sport, is a good way to spend an evening with ordinary Koreans. Ask if there are any matches on at Yanggakdo Football Stadium during your stay. For anyone interested in the surreal, a round at **Pyongyang Golf Course** (outside the Yanggakdo Hotel) will make a great anecdote for years to come – how many people can say they've played 18 holes in North Korea? Other sports are possible by prior arrangement. The **Olympic Pool** and the **Changgwang Health Complex** are both open to foreigners on Saturday.

Karaoke, pool and a visit to the **sauna** will remain your guide's preferred evening activity for you, and most hotels offer both. However, the Chinese sauna at the Yanggakdo is a 'special service' sauna for tired businessmen, so it's best to stick to the normal sauna, unless you are looking for more risqué activities.

SHOPPING

For a supposedly communist country, North Korea is littered with souvenir shops – every Pyongyang site has a small booth selling books, postcards and other trinkets. There are good book shops at both the Yanggakdo and Koryo Hotels and the Foreign Language Bookshop is the best in the city.

Next door to the Koryo Hotel is Korea Stamp (the sign is in English), and it's definitely worth your time to stop in, as North Korean stamps are spectacular propaganda pieces and T-shirts and postcards are also on sale.

KITS has opened a new souvenir shop opposite the Victorious Fatherland Liberation War Museum, although it's full of what KITS think foreigners want: twee souvenirs and traditional handicrafts that are unlikely to appeal to most.

Department stores can often be visited if the guides agree, and they can be a fascinating insight into what's available. You'll no doubt be taken to the most elite of stores, however, so don't expect to see many other shoppers.

Many tourists have expressed an interest in purchasing the metal badge with the Great Leader's picture printed on it that every North Korean wears; however, these are not for sale.

Insam (ginseng) is for sale in hotels, but prices seem ridiculously high. It claims to be from Paekdusan; *insam* from there has a high value for all Koreans. You may be able to pick up some more cheaply in Kaesong; ask your guide for advice. However, you can buy all grades of *insam* much more cheaply in the South.

GETTING AROUND

The usual restrictions exist with Pyongyang's network of buses, trams and metro trains: in theory you are free to use them all, providing your guides are with you. As a rule, they seem very reluctant to show you anything other than the two approved metro stations. Indeed, given that you will have a car or coach, they may think you mad to want to brave Pyongyang's

overcrowded mass-transit network. However, if they agree, the flat fare throughout the city is KPW5.

Both buses and trams have a substantial network throughout the city, but are overcrowded and slow. The metro is fast and convenient, but the network is limited.

Taxis are available outside all hotels for you to travel in with your guide, should the need arise. Reception can also book taxis for you if there are none outside the hotel.

AROUND NORTH KOREA

All tours begin and end in Pyongyang, but most also include a trip to other parts of the country. Almost everyone visits the DMZ at Panmunjom, as the government is very keen to show Westerners the net result of what they see as American imperialism. Visits to mountain resorts in the far-flung mountains in the country's northeast are also frequently included. Going into the countryside is the closest you can get to daily life in DPRK – Pyongyang simply isn't representative, and despite the best efforts of the government to take you to the country's most prosperous areas, the hardship of life outside the capital is evident to everyone.

KAESONG

pop 330,000

This bleak city is just a few miles from the DMZ and has the world's most concentrated build-up of military forces, although you wouldn't know it from looking around, as Kaesong is a fairly relaxed place just off the Reunification Highway from Pyongyang. The city itself is dominated by a massive statue of Kim Il Sung atop a large hill, while the city's main street runs from the hill to the highway, full of shops that (according to brief glances afforded from the bus) appear to be selling TVs and fans almost exclusively.

Once the capital of the Goryeo dynasty, Kaesong has an interesting old quarter as well as the country's most interesting hotel, but KITS are not inclined to spend much time here, and you are usually just billeted at the hotel for the night before returning to Pyongyang having seen the DMZ.

Despite Kaesong's history you won't see many relics of antiquity here due to three major wars, each leaving little but rubble. At least there is the **Songgyungwan Neo-Confucian College**, originally built in AD 992 and rebuilt after being destroyed in the 1592 Japanese invasion. Today it is host to the **Koryo Museum** of celadon pottery and other Buddhist relics; re-enactments of Confucian ceremonies are very occasionally held here. The buildings surround a wide courtyard dotted with ancient trees, and the surrounding grounds are very pleasant to walk around. It's a short drive northeast of town.

Kaesong may be your only chance while in the DPRK to see an authentic Korean royal tomb. The best one by far is the **Tomb of King Kongmin** (the 31st Goryeo king, who reigned between 1352 and 1374) and his queen. It is richly decorated with traditional granite facing and statuary. It's a very secluded site about 13km west of the city centre; there are splendid views over the surrounding tree-covered hills from a number of vantage points.

The third great tourist site is the 37m-high **Pakyon Falls**, one of the three most famous in North Korea. It's found in a beautiful natural setting some 24km north of town. Theoretically at least, some great hiking can be done around here: from the falls to the **Taehungsan Fortress**, to the mid-Goryeo **Kwanum Temple** (with cave) and the **Taehung Temple**.

Kaesong itself is a modern city with wide streets. It's of scant interest, though it does have an interesting older section consisting of traditional tile-roofed houses sandwiched

between the river and the main street. Within the town are a number of lesser tourist sights: the **Sonjuk Bridge**, a tiny clapper bridge built in 1216 and opposite, the **Songin Monument**, which honours Neo-Confucian hero Chong Mong-ju; the **Nammun** (South Gate), which dates from the 14th century and houses an old Buddhist bell; the **Sungyang Seowon** (Confucian academy); and **Chanamsan**, the hill from which Kim Il Sung's statue stares down at the city.

If you stay over here, you'll be based at the **Kaesong Folk Hotel**, a wonderful place consisting of 20 traditional Korean *yeogwan* (small, well-equipped en suite rooms) all off a courtyard, and featuring a charming stream running through it. Power cuts are common here, but some light in the evening and half an hour's hot water can usually be rustled up. It's basic (bring a pillow from your hotel in Pyongyang if you want – the rice pillows are distinctly hard!) but fascinating.

PANMUNJOM

Ironically the sad sight of a pointlessly divided nation remains a highlight of any trip to North Korea. While military history buffs will really be in their element, you don't have to be an expert to appreciate the weirdness of the site where the bloody Korean War ended in an unhappy truce. Seeing the situation from the North, facing off against US troops to the south is a unique chance to witness things from a new perspective.

KIDNAP VICTIMS

Nobody could accuse the North Korean government of lacking pragmatism. Need to teach spies Japanese? The simple solution is to kidnap Japanese civilians and employ them to do the job. By their own sheepish admission in 2002, the DPRK government kidnapped 13 Japanese nationals between 1977 and 1983, including couples enjoying romantic walks on desolate beaches and even tourists who were visiting Europe.

The Japanese government is unlikely to normalise relations with North Korea and pay billions of dollars in compensation for its colonial rule of the peninsula until the DPRK gives a fuller and more truthful account of the fate of its kidnap victims. As well as Japanese citizens, more than 400 South Koreans, mainly fishermen, have been abducted by the North and their fates remain unknown.

The most sensational kidnap of all was orchestrated by Kim Jong Il. The keen cineaste, appalled by the state of film production in the North, ordered that South Korean director Shin Sang-ok and his movie-star wife Choi Eun-hee be kidnapped and brought north to make films. After surviving four years in the gulag for attempting to escape, Shin and Choi were brought before Kim Jong Il who greeted them like old friends, explaining how much he needed them. Given unlimited funds and the elite lifestyle exclusive to the inner circle of Kim Jong Il, Shin made seven films before managing to escape with Choi during a visit to Vienna. His autobiography *Kingdom of Kim* makes for some chilling reading about life in North Korea's heart of darkness.

The eerily quiet drive down the six-lane Reunification Highway – the road is deserted save for military checkpoints – gives you a sense of what to expect. Just before you exit to the DMZ, the sign saying 'Seoul 70km' is a reminder of just how close and yet how far normality is.

There are several aspects to the DMZ visit. Your first stop will be at a **KPA post** just outside the DMZ. Here a soldier will show you a model of the entire site, pointing out South Korean as well as North Korean HQ and watchtowers. Then you'll be marched (single file!) through an anti-tank barrier to rejoin your bus, and you'll drive down a long concrete corridor. Look out for the huge slabs of concrete on either side, ready to be dropped into the road at any minute in the event of an invasion.

The next stop is the **Armistice Talks Hall**, about 1km into the DMZ. Here negotiations were held between the two sides from 1951 until the final armistice, which was signed here on 27 July 1953. You'll see two copies of the agreement on display in glass cases, along with the original North Korean and UN flags. Next door there's an exhibition of photos from the war, all presented in a typically one-sided manner. Outside, a plaque in red script best sums up the North Korean version of the ceasefire. It reads:

It was here on July 27, 1953 that the American imperialists got down on their knees before the heroic Chosun people to sign the ceasefire for the war they had provoked June 25, 1950.

From here you'll reboard the bus and drive to the demarcation line itself, and reminded in more than usually severe language about sticking together 'for your own safety'. The site consists of two sinister-looking headquarters staring at each other across the line (the North Korean is built to be the bigger of the two) and several huts built over the line for meetings. Amazingly, you can cross into South Korea a few meters within the huts, but the doors out to the south are closed and guarded by two soldiers.

Being at the very centre of the biggest military face-off on earth is rather like being at the eye of a storm – tension is in the air, but it is so peaceful as to make the very idea of imminent combat seem ridiculous. South Korean and American soldiers eyeball their northern

counterparts as they have done every day since 1953. Do not be fooled by the prevailing air of calm, though; any attempt to even approach the border proper will result in you being shot on the spot, possibly from both sides. In the 1980s, however, a Soviet tourist found a unique way to flee the communist bloc, and defected amid gunfire from both sides. Unless you are really short of time, this is not an advisable way to get to Seoul.

Throughout the 1970s and 1980s, the North Koreans tunnelled under the DMZ into South Korean territory. The largest was discovered in 1975, and US military experts estimated that 10,000 men per hour could pass through the tunnel into the South. The last tunnel was discovered in 1990 – and this persistent phenomenon gave the Pentagon such headaches that they allegedly hired psychics to help them find the tunnels.

The other interesting sight at the DMZ is the **Korean Wall**, a US-constructed antitank barrier that runs the length of the entire 248km border. It has been hijacked as an emotive propaganda weapon by the North, who since 1989 have been comparing it with the Berlin Wall. Indeed, the issue has proven an emotive one in the South as well, where students have demanded it be dismantled. You'll inspect the wall with binoculars and be shown a particularly hilarious North Korean propaganda video. Don't go here on a cloudy day, as it's a long and pointless drive.

MYOHYANGSAN

A trip to this pretty resort area, just 150km north of Pyongyang is often the first chance visitors will have to experience the pristine North Korean countryside, completely untouched by mass tourism. Mt Myohyang and the surrounding area of hills, mountain trails and waterfalls make for a charming trip, and if you begin to miss the relentless pomp and propaganda of Pyongyang, the **International Friendship Exhibition** (IFE) will remind you that you are still very much in North Korea.

Myohyangsan means 'mountain of mysterious fragrance' and it's certainly no misnomer. The scenery is quite wonderful, and in summer awash with flowers. The focus of all trips are, however, the two vast shrines that make up the IFE. The first one contains all the gifts presented to the eternal president Kim Il Sung. Before entering the vast traditional building, you will be asked to put on shoe covers in keeping with the reverential attitude shown by one and all. A member of your group may be honoured with the task of opening the vast doors that lead into the exhibit – after putting on ceremonial gloves to protect the polished door knob.

Kim Il Sung's gifts are very impressive. Particularly noteworthy is the beautiful armoured train carriage presented to him by Mao Zedong and a limousine sent to Kim by that great man of the people, Josef Stalin. The exhibits are arranged geographically, although you will thankfully only be shown the highlights of over 100,000 gifts spread over 120 rooms. Gifts from heads of state are displayed on red cloth, those from other officials on blue and gifts from individuals on brown. The undeniable highlight is a stuffed crocodile holding a tray of wooden glasses, presented to the Great Leader by the Sandinistas.

The tone of the visit is very strict and sombre, so avoid the very real temptation to ice-skate across the ridiculously over-polished floor in your foot covers. The most reverential and surreal part of the exhibit (quite an achievement) is the final room, in which there is a grinning life-sized waxwork of the Great Leader, to which you will be expected to bow your head before leaving respectfully. The waxwork itself was apparently a gift from the Chinese and Kim Il Sung is depicted standing against a 3D landscape of bucolic idyll, replete with birdsong, gentle breeze and elevator music. The tone is so remarkably odd that you'll have to concentrate not to get the giggles, especially when your guide insists on how serious it all is.

Next is Kim Jong Il's similarly spectacular warehouse. Since taking over as leader on his father's death, an incredible array of gifts have been showered upon the Dear Leader. They are housed in a vault built into the cave wall, recalling the secret lair of one of the Bond villains. There is a noticeable shift away from the grand fraternal gifts of fellow communist dictators that characterise Kim Il Sung's exhibit. Instead, Kim Jong Il's collection smacks of corporate and political gesture – characterising much of his reign since 1994. For example, where Kim Snr received gifts from Ceausescu and Honecker, Kim Jnr has gifts from Hyundai and CNN, as well as a good luck note from Jimmy Carter and a basketball from Madeleine Albright. Indeed, some parts of the exhibit look like any up-market electronics showroom – row after row of wide-screen televisions and stereo equipment donated by industrialists.

The highlight of Kim Jong Il's Friendship Exhibition is one of the only statues of the Dear Leader in the country. It depicts the Marshall seated benevolently, back-lit with pink soft-tone lighting.

Having completed a tour of both exhibits, the perfect way to unwind from the seriousness is with some walking on the beautiful mountain trails. Sangwon Valley is the most common place for a hike and is directly northeast of the IFE.

Don't miss **Pyohon Temple**, the most historically important Buddhist temple in western North Korea. The temple complex dates back to 1044, with numerous renovations over the centuries. It's just a short walk from the IFE, at the entrance to Sangwon Valley. It features several small pagodas and a large hall housing images of the Buddha, as well as a museum that sports a collection of wood blocks from the Buddhist scriptures the Tripitaka Koreana.

It is common for tours to visit the **Ryongmun Big Cave** either prior to or after a visit to Myohyangsan. This 6km-long limestone cave has some enormous caverns and a large number of stalactites. Enjoy sights like the Pool of Anti-Imperialist People's Struggle, the Juche Cavern and the Mountain Peak of the Great Leader.

Sleeping

Tourists are usually put up at the deluxe Hyangsan Hotel, a 15-storey pyramidal building that is now in a rather poor state of repair. In keeping with North Korean hotel tradition, there is a revolving restaurant on the top floor, complete with net curtains, from which absolutely nothing is visible in the evenings due to the hotel's isolated mountain location.

KUMGANGSAN

South of the port city of Wonsan on the east of the Korean peninsula, the most dramatic scenery in the entire country begins to rise. Kumgangsan (Diamond Mountains) have exerted a strange hold over people for centuries, including the notoriously insular Chinese who deigned to include Kumgangsan among the five most beautiful mountain ranges in the known world (the other four ranges were in China). Located just north of the 38th parallel, the area has also been annexed for very heavily controlled South Korean tourism by the Hyundai Corporation.

NORTH KOREAN REFUGEES IN CHINA

Since the early 1990s, there has been an increasing number of North Korean refugees making it across the heavily guarded border with China. The reasons are mainly economic: working for a few months in China can earn enough money to support a North Korean family through the winters by buying food from the private markets, and often refugees return to North Korea once they've saved some money in China.

In 2000, under pressure from the DPRK government, the Chinese authorities launched their harsh 'Strike Hard' campaign. The aim is to forcibly repatriate any North Koreans found in Northern China and send already malnourished individuals back to a country where at the very least they will be imprisoned, but perhaps executed. Even those lucky enough not to get caught often fall victim to people traffickers who force women into prostitution or marriage.

Those lucky enough to survive and make the journey to South Korea are forming refugee support networks, such as Life Funds for North Korean Refugees (www.northkoreanrefugees.com). These vital networks provide financial and emotional support for those who have managed to escape the 'worker's paradise'. For a first-hand account, read Soon Ok-Lee's incredible life story at www.soonoklee.com.

Kumgangsan is divided into Inner, Outer and Sea Kumgang regions. The main tourist activities (at least theoretically) are hiking, mountaineering, boating and sightseeing. The area is peppered with former Buddhist temples and hermitages, waterfalls, mineral springs, a pretty lagoon and a small museum. Maps of the area are provided by park officials to help you decide where you want to go among the dozens of excellent sites.

If your time here is limited, the best places to visit in the Outer Kumgang Region are the **Samil Lagoon** (try hiring a boat, then rest at Tanpung Restaurant); the **Manmulsang Area** (fantastically shaped crags); and the **Kuryong** and **Pibong Falls** (a 4.5km hike from the Mongnan Restaurant).

In the Inner Kumgang Region, it's worth visiting the impressively reconstructed **Pyohon Temple**, founded in AD 670 and one of old Korea's most important Zen monasteries. Hiking in the valleys around Pyohon Temple or, really, anywhere in the park would be rewarding and memorable. **Pirobong** (1639m) is the highest peak out of at least a hundred.

The usual route to Kumgangsan is by car from Pyongyang to Onjong-ri via Wonsan along the new highway (around 315km, a four-hour drive). Along the way to Wonsan, your car or bus will stop off at a teahouse by Sinpyeong Lake. From Wonsan, the road more or less follows the coastline south, and you'll get glimpses of the double-wired electric fence that runs the entire length of the east coast. There may also be a stop for tea at Shijung Lake.

Your final destination is the village of **Onjong-ri** and the first-class **Kumgangsan Hotel.** The hotel is quite a rambling affair consisting of a main building and several outer buildings that include chalets, a shop, a dance hall and bathhouse (fed by a hot spring). The food served here is good, especially the wild mountain vegetable dishes.

PAEKDUSAN

One of the most stunning sights on the Korean peninsula, Paekdusan (Mount Paekdu) straddles the Chinese–Korean border in the very far northeastern tip of DPRK. Apart from it being the highest mountain in the country at 2744m, and an amazing geological phenomenon (it's an extinct volcano now containing a vast crater lake at its centre), it is also of huge mythical importance to the Korean people.

Paekdusan is not included on most tours, as it involves chartering an internal flight to the city of Chongjin and then travelling into the mountains from there. However, if you have the time and money to include a visit on your trip, you will not be disappointed.

The natural beauty of the extinct volcano now containing one of the world's deepest lakes is made all the more magical by the mythology that surrounds the lake, both ancient and modern. The legend runs that Hwanung, the Lord of Heaven, descended onto the mountain in 2333 BC, and from here formed the nation of Choson – 'The Land of Morning Calm', or ancient Korea. It therefore only seems right and proper that four millennia later Kim Jong Il was born here 'and flying white horses were seen in the sky' according to official sources. In fact, Kim Jong Il was probably born in Khabarovsk, Russia, where his father was in exile at the time, but the necessity of maintaining the Kim myth supersedes such niggling facts.

Much like Myohyangsan, an area of spectacular natural beauty is further enhanced by revolutionary 'sights' such as **Jong Il peak** and the **Secret Camp** from where Kim Il Sung supposedly directed some of the key battles during the anti-Japanese campaigns of WWII, despite the fact that no historians outside DPRK have ever claimed that the area was a battle scene.

North Korea's current history books also claim that he established his guerrilla headquarters at Paekdusan in the 1920s, from where he defeated the Japanese. To prove this, you'll be shown declarations that the Great Leader and his comrades carved on the trees. More and more of these 'slogan-bearing trees' are being discovered every year, some so well preserved you'd think they were carved yesterday. The North Korean book *Kim Jong Il in His Young Days* describes the Dear Leader's difficult childhood during those days of ceaseless warfare at Paekdusan:

His childhood was replete with ordeals. The secret camp of the Korean People's Revolutionary Army was his home, and ammunition belts and magazines were his playthings. The raging blizzards and ceaseless gunshots were the first sounds to which he became accustomed. Day in and day out fierce battles went on and, during the breaks, there were military and political trainings. On the battlefield, there was no quilt to warmly wrap the new-born child. So women guerrillas gallantly tore cotton out of their own uniforms and each contributed pieces of cloth to make a patchwork quilt for the infant.

Visitors here will be shown the secret camp beneath Jong Il Peak, said to be the Dear Leader's birthplace, which features a log cabin, and plenty of monuments commemorating patriotic fighters and glorious battles. But the real reason to come here is the glories of nature: vast tracts of virgin forest, abundant wildlife, lonely granite crags, fresh springs, gushing streams and dramatic waterfalls – and, for those able to make the steep and treacherous climb, the astounding Jong Il peak, where heaven indeed seems close and the mundane world is so very far away. Few foreign travellers make it here at all, due to the formidable costs involved, and that is unlikely to change until a highway or train line is built.

Sleeping

Hotels in this area include the second-class Pegaebong Hotel located in the middle of the forest in Samjiyon County, a nice place built for mountain climbers in lodge style. Further away, you can also stay in the town of Hyesan, at the second-class Hyesan Hotel.

Getting There & Away

Paekdusan is only accessible from around late June to mid-September; at all other times it is forbiddingly cold and stormy. Access to the mountain is by air only, followed by car. There are charter flights available that can hold up to 30 people, for €4600 per round-trip flight. At €150 per person that isn't unreasonable, but it's a bit much for a solo trip. Unfortunately, this flight is currently the only transport offered to Paekdusan.

WONSAN

pop 300,000

The port city of Wonsan on the East Sea is not a huge tourist draw itself, but is an interesting stop en route to the Kumgangsan mountains. As it's not usually a destination, it reflects real North Korean life to a good extent. The city is an important port, a centre of learning with 10 universities and a popular holiday resort for Koreans, with beaches at nearby Lake Sijung and Lake Tongjong. An overnight stop can be pleasantly rewarding.

The city, 200km east of Pyongyang, is surrounded by verdant mountains. It is modern with high-rise buildings, but also pleasantly attractive, especially during the summer months. The two main tourist hotels are the Songdowon Tourist Hotel and the Tomgmyong Hotel, both second class.

The nicest part of Wonsan is the suburb of Songdowon on the northwestern shore. There is a clean sandy beach here set among pines where the Jokchon Stream runs into the East Sea, and a small zoo and botanical garden, both pleasant enough to walk in.

NAMPO

pop 730,000

On the Taedong delta, 55km southwest of Pyongyang is Nampo, North Korea's most important port and centre of industry. Nampo has made its name for being the 'birthplace of the Chollima movement', after the workers at the local steel plant supposedly 'took the lead in bringing about an upswing in socialist construction' according to local tourist pamphlets. Sadly there's nothing much to see in the town itself.

The reason tourists come here (usually on an overnight stop en route to Kaesong) is to see the **West Sea Barrage**, a classic piece of socialist tourism, built across an 8km estuary of the Taedong, which solved the irrigation and drinking water problems in the area. The impressive structure, built during the early 1980s and opened in 1986, is nevertheless rather a dull visit. You'll drive across it, then up to a hill at the far end from where you'll get good views and enjoy a quick (hilarious) video at the visitor centre. You'll then (if all is running to plan) drive down to the sluice gates and watch them open – the purported highlight of the trip.

It's now common to include Nampo in an overnight trip from Pyongyang, where your group will sleep some way outside the city at the **Ryonggang Hot Spring House**, a former government guest house now open to tourists. It's a fairly unique place – some 20 well-appointed villas containing several bedrooms each are spread out in the sprawling grounds, each room containing its own spa bath where you can take the waters in your room for a maximum of 15 minutes at a time – it's not clear what will happen if you stay in for longer than 15 minutes, but the guides make it clear that it would be bad.

On the other side of the West Sea Barrage, there are nice **beaches** about 20km from Nampo. Here, if you are lucky enough to go, you will see the locals enjoying volleyball and swimming.

SINCHON

This small, nondescript place is often visited between Nampo and Kaesong. It's interesting to stop here, as this is a small North Korean town and it's easy to get a sense of daily life from passing through.

The reason you're here, though, is to visit the **Sinchon Museum**, which details the US atrocities committed in the town against civilians during the Korean War. That US atrocities were committed here and in other places is not in question (both sides frequently violated the Geneva Convention), but the typically hyperbolic portrayal of these sad events does nothing for the victims save making them into a propaganda tool.

On arrival the museum director brings tourists into the administration building and gives a long, deeply bigoted lecture about how Americans 'never change' and how the bloodthirsty US soldiers enjoyed carrying out the murder of some 35,000 people here.

The museum itself is a disgrace to 'history' with its paintings of American brutality (people having their heads sawn open, a man being pulled in two by two cows attached to either arm, people being burned at the stake) – the entire place will make your blood boil with its sheer one-sidedness.

Following the museum, the standard tour includes laying a wreath at a memorial next door and then travelling to the site of two barns where children and mothers were burned alive by the US Army. The guide is a survivor of the atrocity and you're expected to be shocked and ashamed (even if you aren't American!). Sinchon basically demonstrates the North's lack of will to move on from the horror of the past, as well as its dogged determination to extract every drop of propaganda from its dead. There is no hotel in Sinchon, but from here it's a three-hour drive to Kaesong.

CHILBO

The area around Mount Chilbo is one of the most beautiful places in North Korea. It's also incredibly remote – the only way to get here is to charter a flight from Pyongyang to Chongjin Orang (€4,000 return), which is done quite often with bigger tour groups. The World Tourism Organisation has pioneered a homestay programme and an ecotourism zone here. There's also the **Waechilbo Hotel** for when the homestay isn't functioning.

There's very little to do here save enjoy the spectacular scenery, but this is a unique experience which allows visitors to get as close as possible to every day life in North Korea. The **Kaesim Buddhist Temple** is one visit you shouldn't miss. The temple dates from the 9th century and the scenery surrounding it is wonderful, with waterfalls, lakes, dense forest and views to the Chilbo Sea.

RAJIN-SONBONG

This eccentric corner of North Korea, right on the border with China and Russia has been designated a 'free trade zone' since 1991, but it's a total joke as there's very, very little going on. The two towns of Rajin and Sonbong (sometimes referred to collectively as Rason) are both unremarkable industrial ports surrounded by attractive hills, wetlands and forest.

There's very little to see or do. The Chinese-owned five-star **Emperor Hotel** (possibly the country's best) is here, although its casino has closed (the main attraction for many Chinese to come) so it's even quieter than usual. Rajin-Sonbong also boasts what must be the world's worst **zoo**: on a recent visit it contained three ducks, an exceptionally large turkey, some foxes we couldn't see, a picture of a monkey, three bears – one of which was missing an arm – and a cow tied to a fence (we couldn't decide whether the cow was part of the display or just passing through).

Despite the lack of things to do, Rajin-Sonbong is uniquely beautiful, with its rocky cliffs, lakes and sandy coastline, but it feels like the end of the universe, and it's very unusual to come here these days. There are two guesthouses for tourists who don't stay at the Emperor.

NORTH KOREA DIRECTORY

ACCOMMODATION

All accommodation in North Korea is in state-run hotels, all of which are perfectly fine – particularly those in Pyongyang. You won't have any control over where you stay, but you can always make requests. All hotels have the basics of life: a restaurant, a shop (although bring everything you need outside of Pyongyang) and usually some form of entertainment, from the ubiquitous karaoke to pool tables and a bar.

A new homestay scheme in Chilbo was being pioneered in 2006, although we were unable to stay there during research for this guide. If you'd like to experience a homestay, ask your tour operator.

While most hotel rooms are probably bugged, there's only a very small chance that

anyone's listening. In any case, save anything truly controversial for until after you get back to China.

CHILDREN

While North Koreans love children and often spoil them rotten, a DPRK tour is not suitable for kids. The long, exhausting days and endless sightseeing may tire out even diehard Kimophiles, and they are likely to bore a child to tears. Equally, the lack of creature comforts and facilities for foreign children would make residents think twice before bringing their families.

CUSTOMS

North Korean customs procedures vary in severity from general polite inquiries to thorough goings over. This book and other North Korea guides are fine to bring in, although any other books about the country and its politics or history should be left in China. There are, however, some very strict rules about bringing other items into the country, most importantly modems and mobile phones. If you are entering and exiting at the same point, you can hand them over for storage and collect them on exit – this seems to be perfectly safe. Video cameras have on occasion been confiscated, although they are not officially proscribed. The following, however, are proscribed:

- telescopes and magnifiers with over x6 magnification
- wireless apparatus and parts, including mobile phones, camcorders or video cameras and transistor radios
- tobacco seeds, leaf tobacco and other seeds
- publications, video tapes, recording tapes, films, photos and other materials that are 'hostile to the North Korean socialist system or harmful to the North Korean political, economic and cultural development and disturb the maintenance of social order'

Note that they are very serious about the last of these prohibitions, which may include any foreign-printed information you have about either North or South Korea, although guidebooks are not a problem.

DANGERS & ANNOYANCES

As a foreigner you will be both conspicuous and unfathomably wealthy compared to the average local. Be as vigilant as you would be anywhere else, but realistically, your chances of being a victim of crime are very low. Pyongyang's Sunan airport seems to be one place where petty theft could be a problem.

The major potential for disaster is thoughtless visitors openly criticising the regime while in the country. In 2002, according to rumours, an American aid worker was incarcerated for two months after asking why Kim Jong Il was so plump while ordinary North Koreans were so skinny. It is to be hoped that most readers would have more sense than to make such a remark. If in doubt, bite your tongue – be similarly discreet on the phone, by fax and in your hotel room, all of which can be monitored.

Likewise, spare a thought for both your guides and the few locals you will come in contact with. Despite being the official representatives of a brutal Stalinist regime, your tour guides are vulnerable to persecution themselves. Running away from them, disobeying them or otherwise going against the grain will be far more dangerous for them than for you.

When meeting North Koreans in the street, take your lead from the guides. Ask before you take photographs, do not give them any gifts that could incriminate them in imperialist flunkeyism and generally proceed with caution.

EMBASSIES & CONSULATES

North Korea now enjoys full diplomatic relations with most EU countries, although many do not maintain embassies in Pyongyang. In theory, North Korean embassies can all process visa applications abroad, but in reality they are largely useless for the average tourist. The Beijing Embassy remains the most useful, as well as being the only embassy used to dealing with tourists.

North Korean Embassies & Consulates

Canada (☎ 613 232 1715; 151 Slater St, 6th fl, Ottawa K1P5H3)
China (☎ 10-6532 1186/1189, visa section ☎ 6532 4148/6639; fax 6532 6056; Ritan Beilu, Jianguomenwai, Chaoyang District, Beijing) This is the most useful embassy in the list. Ryohaengsa travel usually has a worker (☎ 6532 4862) within the consular and visa section of the embassy. The entrance to the consular section is on the east side of the building at the northern end of the fruit-and-vegetable stalls.

France (☎ 0417475385; fax 0417476141; 47 rue du Chaveau, 92200 Neuilly-sur-Seine)
Germany (☎ 229 3189/3181; fax 229 3191; Glinka str 5-7, D-10117 Berlin)
Hong Kong (☎ 2803 4447; Consulate General of DPRK, 20/F Chinachem Century Tower, 178 Gloucester Rd, Wanchai)
Russia Moscow (☎ 495-143 6249/9063; ulitsa Mosfilmovskaya 72, RF-117192); Nakhodka Consulate (☎ 423-665 5210; ulitsa Vladivostokskaya 1)
Sweden (☎ 7673836; fax 7673835; Norra Kungsvägen 39, 181 31 Lindingö)
Switzerland (☎ 31 951 6621; Pourtalèsstrasse 43, 3074 Muri)
UK (☎ 20-8992 4965; fax 8992 2053; 73 Gunnersbury Ave, London W5 4LP)
USA (Permanent Representative of the DPRK to the UN; ☎ 212-972 3105; fax 972 3154 820; 2nd Ave, New York, NY 10017) The USA and the DPRK have no diplomatic relations, but North Korea does maintain an office in New York for the UN.

Embassies & Consulates in North Korea

The few embassies that might be of help to travellers are listed following.

The UK Embassy represents the interests of Australians, New Zealanders and Canadians, while the Swedish legation looks after US citizens and EU citizens whose own country does not have representation in Pyongyang. Most embassies are located in the Munsudong diplomatic quarter.

China (☎ 381 3133, 381 3116; fax 381 3425)
Germany (☎ 381 7385; fax 381 7397)
India (☎ 381 7215, 381 7274; fax 381 7619)
Russia (☎ 381 3101/2; fax 381 3427)
Sweden (☎ 381 7904/7485, 382 7908; fax 381 7258)
UK (☎ 382 7980, 381 7980; fax 381 7985)

In recent times, Italy, Australia and Canada have established diplomatic relations with Pyongyang, but at the time of writing were operating through their Beijing embassies with the exception of Canada, whose Seoul office is responsible for the DPRK. Contact details:

Australia (☎ 10-5140 4111; www.austemb.org.cn; 21 Dongzhimenwai Dajie, Sanlitun, Beijing 100600)
Canada (☎ 82 2 3455 6000; www.korea.gc.ca; 19th & 10th Floors, Kolon Bldg, 45 Mugyo-Dong, Chung-Ku, Seoul 100-170)
Italy (☎ 10-6532 2131/2/3/4/5; www.italianembassy.org .cn; San Li Tun 2, Dong Er Jie, Beijing 100600)
USA (☎ 10-6532 3831; www.usembassy-china.org.cn; 3 Xiu Shui Bei Jie, Beijing, 100600)

HOLIDAYS

New Year's Day 1 January
Kim Jong Il's birthday 16 February
Kim Il Sung's birthday 15 April
Armed Forces Day 25 April
May Day 1 May
The Death of Kim Il Sung 8 July
Victory in the Fatherland Liberation War 27 July
National Liberation (from Japan) Day 15 August
National Foundation Day 9 September
Korean Workers' Party Foundation Day 10 October
Constitution Day 27 December

Note that North Korea does not celebrate Christmas or the Lunar New Year, or many of South Korea's major traditional holidays.

Foreign tourists are usually not welcome, unless by special invitation, around the birthdays of the Kims (16 February and 15 April). By all means, try to be in Pyongyang during May Day or Liberation Day. Both holidays are celebrated with huge extravaganzas featuring military-style parades that rank among North Korea's most memorable sights.

INTERNET ACCESS

There is no internet access to be had in DPRK for tourists, but you can send an email and even receive a reply via the communication centre at the Yanggakdo Hotel in Pyongyang, where you'll pay €2 per 125KB (roughly half a page of text).

Intranet (ie a closed internet with no connections to the wider web) is being developed in quite a few places in the country, but obviously this remains entirely government controlled.

LEGAL MATTERS

It is extremely unlikely that a tourist will experience legal problems with the North Korean authorities, but if this does occur, stay calm and ask to speak to your country's diplomatic representative in North Korea. Usually, tourists who break the law in North Korea are deported immediately. Breaking the law here is a particularly stupid thing to do.

MAPS

You do not need a map of anywhere in North Korea, due to the unique hand-holding arrangement with the guides. However, Pyongyang maps are available at most hotels and shops in the capital and can be helpful for getting to grips with its layout. Elsewhere maps aren't really needed, nor are they available. There are few good-quality maps of North Korea available outside the country; the best on offer from travel specialists is the general map of Korea published by Nelles Maps.

MONEY

The unit of currency is the North Korean won (KPW). Bank notes come in denominations of one, five, 10, 50, 100, 500, 1000 and 5000. However, visitors do not usually deal with the won: everything can be paid for with euro or Chinese yuan (but do bring small change of both; big notes are almost impossible to change). While you are unlikely to use the won, it may be possible to get some from your guides as a souvenir (although it's officially illegal to take it out of the country, so hide it in your luggage well).

Credit cards not issued by American banks can be used to pay for hotels and for cash advances in Pyongyang. However, it makes best sense to carry all the cash you will need with you in euros or yuan, as the situation can change at any time. Travellers cheques are more trouble than they are worth.

PHOTOGRAPHY & VIDEO
Film & Equipment

You can buy colour-print film at reasonable prices from the hard-currency gift shops, but everything else is expensive, so bring what you need. There are modern photo-processing facilities on the 2nd floor at the Koryo Hotel, but you'd probably be better off waiting until you return to China or back home. Memory cards could not be bought in North Korea at the time of writing, so bring as many as you can to store pictures on.

Restrictions

Always ask first before taking photos and obey the reply. North Koreans are especially sensitive about foreigners taking photos of them without their permission. Not only are Koreans camera shy, they are acutely aware of the political power of an image in the Western press. Your guides are familiar with the issue of tourists taking photos that end up in a newspaper article that contains anti-DPRK content. The repercussions of such an event could be serious for your guides and the tour company that is sponsoring you. Avoid taking photos of soldiers or any military facilities, although you're encouraged to do so at the DMZ.

Video

If you are able to get a video camera into North Korea, the restrictions are similar to those with a camera. But, as a number of journalists have made video documentaries about the country in the guise of simply filming tourist sights, the guides and customs officers have become far stricter about their use. Although there is no blanket ban as such, if you are unlucky customs may confiscate your video camera.

POST

Like all other means of communication, the post is monitored. It is, however, generally reliable and the colourful North Korean stamps, featuring everything from tributes to the Great Leader to Princess Diana commemoratives, make great souvenirs. Sending postcards anywhere in the world costs €1. Some people have suggested that postcards arrive more quickly, as they do not need to be opened by censors. In either medium, keep any negative thoughts about the country to yourself to ensure your letter gets through.

SOLO TRAVELLERS

The concept of 'solo traveller' in North Korea is somewhat redundant, as even when 'alone' you are with two official guides, which can be intense. With the fairly constant deification of the Great and Dear Leaders, solo travellers can find long trips in North Korea trying without a group of foreigners to raise eyebrows at. However, if you want your own itinerary or need to travel when there are no tours, travelling solo is your only option. Most travel agencies offering group tours to DPRK, such as those listed on p346, will also be happy to negotiate tailor-made itineraries for individuals via Ryohaengsa.

TELEPHONE & FAX

Pyongyang has recently seen the mass-installation of new public telephones and their massive popularity (there are often queues to use them) suggests that a high proportion of the capital have telephones at home, although this is clearly not the case in the countryside. North Korean telephone numbers are divided into 381 numbers (international) and 382 (local). It is not possible to call a 381 number from a 382 number or vice versa. International calls start at €2.50 per minute to China and €8 to Europe. To dial North Korea, the country code is 850. Nearly all numbers you dial from abroad will be Pyongyang numbers, so dial +850-2-381 and then the local number.

Mobile phones are not used by the public, but a network has been established in Pyongyang for the party elite. You won't be able to use your phone here, and if you bring it in, be sure to declare it and it will be wrapped to put it beyond use until you leave the country (it will remain in your custody throughout your stay).

Faxing is still popular in a land without email. From Pyongyang hotels it's not exactly cheap though – one page to China will cost you €4.50, while a page to Europe will set you back €13! Following pages are slightly less expensive.

TIME

The time in Korea is Greenwich Mean Time plus nine hours. When it is noon in Korea it is 1pm in Sydney or Melbourne, 3am in London, 10pm the previous day in New York and 7pm the previous day in Los Angeles or San Francisco.

You will also see years such as Juche 8 (1919) or Juche 93 (2004). Three years after the death of Kim Il Sung, the government adopted a new system of recording years, starting from Juche 1 (1912) when Kim No 1 was born. Despite the wide use of these dates internally, they are always clarified with 'normal' years.

TOILETS

In Pyongyang and around frequently visited tourist sites, toilet facilities are basic but sanitary. There are regular cuts in the water supply outside Pyongyang, and often a bucket of water will be left in your hotel room for this eventuality. A straw poll of tour operators reveals the worst toilet in North Korea to be at the rest stop on the Pyongyang–Wonsan highway. Toilet paper is supplied in hotels, but it's always a good idea to carry tissues for emergencies, especially as diarrhoea is a common problem for visitors.

TRAVELLERS WITH DISABILITIES

North Korean culture places great emphasis on caring for the disabled, especially as the Korean War left such a brutal legacy among young recruits. Popular songs such as *I Love an Unmarried Disabled Soldier* encourage marrying the war-wounded, and so disabled visitors need not fear a lack of local understanding. Facilities are basic, but manageable, and even in situations where disabled access is a problem, the guides are likely to find some locals to help out.

VISAS

People of all nationalities need a visa to visit North Korea. Traditionally visas have not been issued to US or South Korean travellers, but nationals of both countries can now visit under certain conditions.

Restrictions have relaxed somewhat across the board. Until recently it was necessary to supply a full CV listing all your previous employment as well as to provide a letter from your employer detailing the duties of your current job. As this still didn't prevent journalists entering the country in the guise of tourists, this practice seems to have stopped, and now you just have to supply the name of your employer and your job. Ensure that if you work in any field of the media that you do not put this. Try to do something innocuous instead.

Each visa needs approval from Pyongyang, so apply as far before your trip as you can (preferably allow two months, although one month should be fine). Your travel agency will handle the application for you, and in most cases the visa is a formality if you travel with a well-known agency.

Tour groups usually have visas issued in Beijing the day before travel, so don't worry about leaving home without your visa. It does mean that you need to spend 24 hours in Beijing before going on to Pyongyang, though. Individual visas can usually be issued at any North Korean Embassy.

The embassy visa charges are included in nearly all packages. North Korean visas are not put into passports, but are separate documents taken from you when you exit the country. If you want a souvenir, make a photocopy. No stamp of any kind will be made in your passport.

WOMEN TRAVELLERS

While communist ideology dictates equality of the sexes, this is still far from everyday reality in a traditionally patriarchal society. However, women travellers will have no problem at all in the country, as no North Korean would be foolhardy enough to get themselves in trouble for harassing a foreigner. There are an increasing number of female guides being employed by Ryohaengsa and it is possible to request them for individual travel.

TRANSPORT

GETTING THERE & AWAY

Beijing is now the only real transport hub for people entering North Korea, offering both regular trains and flights to Pyongyang. Traffic entering through Russia from Vladivostok – which is still a theoretical possibility – has fallen off to a trickle. This situation is exacerbated by the fact that tourists are often obliged to pick up their visas in Beijing, thus making the use of other routes impossible.

Entering the Country

Immigration is rather severe, but straightforward, as the major hurdle is getting the visa in the first place. Your guides will take your passports for the duration of your stay in North Korea. This is totally routine, so do not worry about them being lost.

AIR

The national airline Air Koryo, running a fleet of old Soviet Tupolevs, flies to Beijing, Shenyang and Vladivostok. The most popular route is from Beijing, from where flying time to Pyongyang is just over an hour. There are three flights per week on Tuesday, Thursday and Saturday in each direction, and a return flight costs €300. The international flight codes are JS151 and JS152. The weekly flight from Vladivostok is the second most popular, going in both directions every Thursday, while there's a flight to/from Shenyang on both Wednesday and Saturday. China Southern Airlines has also recently restarted flights from Beijing, currently on Mondays, Wednesday and Fridays. Pyongyang's airport code is FNJ.

Air Koryo (☎ 10-6501 1557/1559; fax 6501 2591; Swissotel Bldg, Hong Kong-Macau Center, Dongsi Shitau Lijiao, Beijing 100027) This building adjoins the Swissotel, but the entrance is around the back. You must have a visa before you can pick up your ticket, or Korea International Travel Company (KITC) can pick it up for you (it charges 10% commission).

TRAIN

There are four trains each week in either direction between Beijing and Pyongyang via Dandong and Sinuiju, the border towns of China and DPRK respectively. They run Monday, Wednesday, Thursday and Saturday. On each day, train No 27 leaves Beijing at 5.48pm and arrives at Pyongyang the next day at 6.05pm (about 23 hours). Going the other way, train No 26 departs from Pyongyang at 10.10am arriving in Beijing at 9am. The fare each way is €75 for a soft sleeper. In contrast to the plane, it's possible to pick up your train tickets to Pyongyang without a DPRK visa.

The North Korean train is actually just two carriages attached to the main Beijing–Dandong train, which are detached at Dandong (Chinese side) and then taken across the Yalu River Bridge to Sinuiju (Korean side), where more carriages are added for local people. Non-Koreans remain in their original carriages.

The trains usually spend about four hours at the border for customs and immigration – two hours at Dandong and two hours at Sinuiju. You may wander around the stations and take photos, but ask permission first and obey the directives of signs and officials about going outside.

Sinuiju station will be your first introduction to North Korea and the contrasts with China will be quite marked. Everything is squeaky-clean and there are no vendors plying their goods. A portrait of the Great Leader looks down from the top of the station, and at all other train stations in North Korea.

Soon after departing Sinuiju, you'll be served lunch. The food is excellent and the service is fine. Make sure you have some small denomination euro notes to pay for the meal (about €5), as this is not usually included in tours. There are no facilities for changing money at Sinuiju or on the train. The dining car is for the use of non-Koreans only.

Your guide will meet you on arrival at Pyongyang train station and accompany you to your hotel. Likewise, when you leave North Korea, your guide will bid you farewell at Pyongyang train station or the airport and you then travel to China unaccompanied. Be very careful taking pictures from the train in North Korea. While you'll get some great opportunities to snap everyday DPRK scenes, do not take pictures in stations as this will cause big trouble if you are caught.

When leaving North Korea, you can link up with the *Trans-Siberian* at Dandong, China. To make this connection you need to reserve your tickets with CITS (China International Travel Company) or KITC in Beijing beforehand.

Leaving the Country

If you are departing by air, your guide will accompany you to the airport. You must pay an airport departure tax of €15 at the airport, while there is no departure tax for the train. Similarly your guides will leave you at Pyongyang station if you are taking the train out.

GETTING AROUND

All accommodation, guides and transport must be booked through the government-run Ryohaengsa. You can also book through a travel agent (p346) and they will then deal with Ryohaengsa on your behalf.

The main office of **Ryohaengsa** (☎ +86-10-6437 6666/3133; fax 6436 9089; Korean International Travel Company, 2nd fl, Yanxiang, No A2 Jiangtai Rd, Chaoyang District, Qionghuating) is in Beijing, and there are also branches in Dandong, Liaoning Province and in Yanji in Jilin.

Directory

ACCOMMODATION
Expect to pay W15,000 for a dormitory or room in a *yeoinsuk* (small, family-run budget hotel with shared bathroom); W25,000 for a *yeogwan* (motel with small en suite) or basic countryside *minbak* (private home with rooms for rent); W30,000 for a motel; W50,000 for a *pension* (upmarket rural retreat) or smart *minbak*; at least W90,000 for an upper midrange hotel; and W200,000 upwards for top-end luxury. Upper midrange and top-end hotels add 21% tax and service to the bill, but this has been included in all the prices quoted in this guidebook. If the accommodation has internet access it will invariably be broadband.

Modern motels, often clustered around bus terminals, offer the best deal. Tip: look for the newest motel building and stay there.

Accommodation is normally charged per room, so solo travellers receive little or no discount. Still it's always worth asking. If you're staying a few days or it's off season (outside July and August on the coast or outside July, August, October and November in National parks), you can always try for discount.

Only staff in Seoul guesthouses and upper midrange and top-end hotels are likely to speak any English. An extra bed or *yo* (mattress or futon on the floor) is usually available. Check-out time is generally noon. Prices can rise on Friday and Saturday and at peak times (July and August near beaches or national parks, and October and November near national parks).

Laundry is a problem – bring lots of clothes or else many travellers wash their clothes every night and hang them up in their room to dry, or lay it on the *ondol*-heated floor in winter. Launderettes are virtually extinct and *yeogwan* and motels rarely offer laundry services.

In general, booking accommodation is unnecessary and is difficult in the case of motels as staff very rarely speak any English.

Budget accommodation is defined as rooms that cost W39,000 or less, midrange is rooms from W40,000 to W150,000, and top end is anything over W150,000.

Backpacker Guesthouses
Seoul has a dozen small guesthouses, ideal for budget-minded foreign tourists, where the staff are friendly and speak English, and

---

BOOK ACCOMMODATION ONLINE

For more accommodation reviews and recommendations by Lonely Planet authors, check out the online booking service at www.lonelyplanet.com. You'll find the true, insider lowdown on the best places to stay. Reviews are thorough and independent. Best of all, you can book online.

it's easy to meet other travellers and pester them with questions. The guesthouses offer dormitories (W15,000 per night) and double rooms (W35,000), some of which are en suite. Communal facilities include toilets, showers, satellite TV, a kitchen and washing machine. Free internet and breakfast is also provided. Sadly they hardly exist outside Seoul.

Camping & Mountain Huts
Nature lovers can camp at beaches and at the entrances to some national and provincial parks. The cost is only W3000, but facilities are very basic and they are only open in July and August. *Sanjang* (mountain huts) cost the same although the better, newer ones cost W5000.

In general, *yeogwan*, motel and *minbak* accommodation at the national-park entrances are reasonably priced, and only a few major hikes in Seoraksan and Jirisan National Parks require overnighting in a mountain hut. Huts and camping grounds can be fully booked at weekends and peak times – log on to www.npa.or.kr to make a reservation.

Hanok
Staying in a *hanok* – a traditional *yangban* (aristocrat) wooden house – is a unique experience. Rooms are very small and grouped around a courtyard, and guests usually sleep on a *yo* on an *ondol*-heated floor. Seoul and Jeonju in Jeollabuk-do are just about the only places to experience a *hanok* stay as few have

survived the Korean War and the postwar bulldozers.

Homestays
View www.labostay.or.kr or www.homestaykorea.com to contact Korean families willing to offer rooms in their homes to foreigners. Guests often receive royal hospitality, and the cost is around US$35 (single) or US$50 (double) for bed and breakfast. Rates are greatly reduced for long stays. It's your best opportunity to experience the local lifestyle at first hand. Book online at least two weeks before you arrive.

Hotels
Luxury hotels are scarce outside of major cities and Jejudo. They are world class in terms of communal facilities, but rooms and bathrooms can be on the small side with some imperfections – showers above baths are common as are marked carpets. The lobbies, fitness centres and restaurants are often their strong points. Hotels generally quote rack rates which then have 21% tax and service added on top, but discounts or packages are nearly always available.

Websites that offer discounted prices and special deals include www.koreahotels.net and www.khrc.com. Always check if discounted prices include the 21% service and tax. The discounts look good but may be less than you could obtain direct, and some hotels claim that the best rates are obtainable from their own websites.

Minbak & Pension

Most *minbak* provide basic accommodation (and usually meals) on islands, near ski resorts, in rural areas and near beaches and national parks. Expect to pay W25,000 for a room but double that in peak seasons. You sleep on a *yo* on an *ondol*-heated floor with only a TV and a heater or fan in the room. Facilities are usually en suite. Lots of people can squeeze into one room – an extra person usually costs W10,000. Nowadays there are more upmarket *minbak*, which are similar to *pension* and cost W50,000 or more, and provide smart, stylish rooms with beds and kitchenettes. *Pension* are more luxurious than most *minbak* and cost W50,000 to W70,000 with spacious rooms, often with stylish furniture, balconies, kitchens and great views.

Motels

They started out as love motels, and rooms can still be rented by the hour, but nowadays the modern motels also provide the best-deal accommodation for touring Korea. In general you don't need to worry about where to stay in Korea – motels are so numerous that there's no need to book ahead. How they all make money is a mystery. Invariably priced at W30,000 (but allow up to W10,000 extra for special facilities like a waterbed, Jacuzzi or a computer), the newest ones provide a mid-range style of room at a budget price. Most motel rooms are just regular rooms, although you might find large mirrors, mood lighting and maybe round beds or a free packet of condoms. It's unusual to come across erotic art, and you'll never see bondage gear or whips in the corner!

In modern motels, rooms and bathrooms are reasonably sized, with a high standard of fittings, furnishing and décor, a comfortable double bed, a large TV, video player (free videos available), air-con, a fridge with free soft drinks, a water dispenser, small towels, a hairdryer, shampoo, lotions and even hair brushes and toothbrushes. TVs have satellite or cable links and can pick up 50 or so channels including an X-rated one. Windows are double (or triple) glazed for quietness. Modern high-rise motels have 30 or so rooms and an elevator, but usually no English is spoken, no staff are employed to help with bags, and there is no coffee shop, laundry, restaurant, bar or communal facility. You just get a clean, facility-filled room.

Every city, small town and tourist area has batches of motels, usually surrounding the bus terminal or train station. Some look like Disneyland castles, while others are metal clad or have big neon signs on the roof. Staff rarely understand any English so write '방을 좀 볼 수 있을까요?' (Can I see a room please?) on a piece of paper and hand it over to the receptionist, who is usually hidden away behind a small glass window.

As with *yeogwan*, twin beds are not usually available, but you can ask for an *ondol* room (sleeping on padded quilts on the floor), or ask for a *yo* to be put in a room with a double bed. Any extra person usually costs W10,000. Don't be mislead by the name 'motel' – some *yeogwan* call themselves a motel, but the exterior usually gives it away.

Rental Accommodation

Many expat workers live in accommodation supplied by their employers, but a few live in a guesthouse, homestay or *yeogwan* on a monthly basis and negotiate a reduced daily cost. Serviced apartments and apartment sharing are other options in Seoul, although spare rooms are difficult to find – try the notice boards on the Seoul government or newspaper websites, such as www.koreah-erald.co.kr.

Renting an apartment is tricky because of the traditional payment system and because prices in Seoul keep going up. *Chonsei* is when you loan from W50 million to W200 million (or more) to the landlord and get it all back at the end of the rental period. *Wolse* is when you pay a smaller returnable deposit of W3 million to W10 million plus a monthly rental fee. However some accommodation is available to foreigners on the Western system, with a small refundable deposit and a monthly rent.

If you are looking to rent, take note that real estate is measured in *pyeong* (1 *pyeong* is 3.3 sq metres). A large apartment is 50 *pyeong* and medium-sized is about 30 *pyeong*, though smaller budget ones of 15 *pyeong* to 20 *pyeong* do exist.

Sauna Dormitories

Saunas and *jjimjilbang* (luxury saunas) nearly all have a dormitory or napping room. They are not really meant for overnight sleepers, but they can be used for that purpose. Pay the entry fee (usually under W10,000), use the facilities and then head for the dormitory. Don't expect much in the way of bedding, and the pillow may be a block of wood.

Serviced Apartments

More than 20 serviced apartments have sprung up in recent years in Seoul as an alternative to small hotel rooms and the hassle of finding and renting an apartment. Known locally as residences or suites, prices range from W75,000 to W250,000 a day with a reduction for month-long stays.

Temple Stays

Overnight stays in Buddhist temples (www .templestaykorea.net) are a unique experience and cost around W50,000. Guests are given Buddhist robes to wear and stay in their own room or single-sex dormitory-style accommodation, sleeping on a padded quilt on the floor. Don't go to bed too late as guests are asked to get up around 3.30am the next day to join the monks at dawn prayers. Remember to take your shoes off before entering Buddhist shrines, and to use the side door. As you might expect, alcohol and cigarettes are not allowed.

Sweeping paths, making stone rubbings and hiking in the mountains could also be on the programme, as well as meditation and a tea ceremony. Simple vegetarian meals are provided. Temple stays are an enlightening experience, providing genuine insights into the daily lifestyle and beliefs of Korean monks.

Yeogwan & Yeoinsuk

Yeogwan provide old-fashioned budget rooms, but are only W5000 to W10,000 cheaper than the much better modern motels. Rooms (and bathrooms) are smallish but are fully equipped with satellite or cable TV, a fan, air-con, heating, a fridge, bed and sometimes a table and chairs. The drawbacks

---

BUDDHIST PRAYER BEFORE EATING A MEAL

Now we take our meal that caused no harm to any sentient beings.
Let us consider whether our behaviour deserves this meal.
Let us cultivate our minds away from greed, anger and foolishness.
We eat this meal to become enlightened.

---

are that furnishings and fixtures are dated, rooms and corridors are usually gloomy, and bedding is often quilts rather than sheets. Quilts are usually aired rather than washed so you may want to bring a pair of sheets with you. 'Adequate but shabby' sums up most *yeogwan*.

Few *yeoinsuk* (family-run budget hotels) have made it into this guide despite their bargain W15,000 to W20,000 price tag because most are too grotty to recommend. Facilities are usually shared, and rooms are tiny, bare cells furnished with just a TV and fan, and none too clean. The ancient proprietors may be unwilling to accept foreigners, and guests are usually Korean single males down on their luck. Youth hostel or sauna dormitories provide a much more pleasant budget option.

Youth Hostels

Sixty large youth hostels (www.HIhostels. com) are spread around the country. Modern and clean, the dormitories offer the best deal for solo travellers at W11,000 to W15,000 a night (W22,000 in Seoul). Family rooms cost as much as motel rooms and are not as good. Not many foreigners stay in these hostels, perhaps because they are rather institutional and soulless, can be inconveniently located and are sometimes full of screaming children on a school trip. Membership costs W25,000 for adults, W18,000 for youths.

ACTIVITIES

See the Korea Outdoors chapter for hiking (p74), cycling and mountain biking (p73), diving (p75), winter sports (p77) and hot spring spas (p76).

Martial Arts

Korean martial arts are attracting worldwide interest. Taekwondo is now an Olympic sport, but there are other lesser-known ones. English-speaking martial art groups advertise in the *Korea Herald* Bulletin Board on Thursdays. The World Martial Arts Festival, held every October in Chungju (p337), includes obscure martial arts from many countries.

GICHEON

Gicheon (www.gicheon.org) is an indigenous and ancient Korean martial art that is so little known that most Koreans have never heard of it. The mind/body discipline is based on six body postures and special exercises are designed to promote joint flexibility and free up the *gi* energy paths. See the website for courses, contacts and more information.

HAPKIDO
This gentle martial art uses deep breathing to achieve focus, and practitioners are taught to make use of their opponent's aggression and weak points to achieve victory.

SUNMUDO
This Zen Buddhist practice focuses on breathing as an aid to attaining enlightenment. To watch demonstrations or take part in Sunmudo training, head to the mountain temple at Golgulsa (p203).

TAEKWONDO
Millions of Korean children learn taekwondo in private academies, and you can often see them in local neighbourhoods heading to evening classes in their taekwondo outfits. All trainee soldiers in Korea also learn taekwondo, a Korean martial art with a global following that is based on *taekkyon*, a martial art which is thousands of years old and features on ancient Goryeo tomb murals. *Taekkyon* is a defensive art that teaches movement, while taekwondo is known for its high kicks.

The **World Taekwondo Federation** (Map pp96-7; www .kukkiwon.co.kr), based at Kukkiwon, has regular competitions and training sessions in the main *dojang* (hall), as well as a small museum.

Pool & Four Ball
There are pool halls all over the country that cost around W7000 an hour. Look for the obvious 'billiard cues and balls' signs outside. They often have pool (called 'pocketball' in Korea) and tables for games of 'four ball', which is similar to billiards, but there are no pockets and players must hit cannons. Two red balls and two white ones are used. The players (any number) hit the white balls in turn. The object of the game is to hit both of the red balls in one shot without hitting the other white ball. It sounds easy but it isn't.

You score minus one if you are successful, and you also get to take another turn. You score nothing if you hit just one red, and you score plus one if you hit the other white ball or miss everything. Beginners start with a score of three points and when you improve you start with five points, then eight and so on. When your score reaches zero, to finish

you must do a more difficult shot – hit one red and two side-cushions or two reds and one side-cushion without hitting the other white ball.

Ssireum
Korea has its own unique and traditional style of wrestling called *ssireum*, which is more similar to Mongolian wrestling than Japanese sumo. Wrestlers grab each other's *satba* (a cloth tied round the waist) and try to throw their opponent to the ground. Matches usually last seconds rather than minutes.

BUSINESS HOURS
For most government and private offices, business hours are from 9am to 6pm Monday to Friday. From November to February government offices may close an hour earlier. Tourist information centres are usually open from 9am to 6pm daily while national parks are open daily from sunrise to sunset. Keep in mind that many (but not all) government-run museums and tourist sites close on Mondays.

Banking hours are from 9.30am to 4pm Monday to Friday. The hours that ATMs are available vary and are written on the machine, but they are not generally open 24 hours. Post offices are generally open from 9am to 6pm Monday to Friday, but some are open longer hours.

Department stores traditionally open from 10.30am to 7.30pm six days a week. Nowadays some open every day and a few open until late evening. New youth-oriented shopping malls tend to stay open until 10pm. Small general stores often stay open until midnight even in suburban areas, and many convenience stores are open 24 hours. Shops are generally open from 10am to around 9pm every day, but the trend towards more days off means that some do now close on Sunday. Travel agents may take Saturday afternoon off as well as Sunday.

Restaurants usually open from 10am to 10pm every day. Cinemas traditionally open at 11am, with the last show ending just before midnight, but a few run later. In big cities, midnight showings and even all-night movies are becoming a more popular option.

Pubs and bars open daily from 6pm to midnight but they close later on Friday and Saturday. Some open at noon for the thirsty early birds.

DIRECTORY

There is plenty for night owls to do in Korean cities as some saunas, restaurants, PC *bang* (internet rooms), DVD *bang* (room for watching DVDs), *noraebang* (karaoke rooms), convenience stores, bars and nightclubs stay open all night.

CHILDREN

Lonely Planet's *Travel with Children* is recommended reading. Foreigners travelling with young children are a novelty in Korea, but once they've got over their surprise, expect the locals to be particularly helpful and intrigued. View www.travelwithyourkids .com for general advice and a first-hand report on Seoul for kids, which gives the city a thumbs up.

Only luxury hotels are likely to be able to organise a cot, but you could always ask for a *yo*. Bring your own car safety seat and bicycle helmets as they are rare. Few restaurants have high chairs. Nappy-changing facilities are more common in Seoul toilets than in the provinces. Bring your own baby food unless you can decipher *Han·geul* (Korean phonetic alphabet) labels. Baby-sitting services are almost non-existent, except in Lotte World Hotel in Seoul.

The good news is that zoos, funfairs and parks can be found in most cities along with cinemas, DVD rooms, internet rooms, video game arcades, ten-pin bowling alleys, *noraebang*, pool tables and board-game cafés. Children will rarely be more than 100m away from an ice cream, a cake or a fast-food outlet. In winter hit the ski slopes, and in summer head for the water parks or beaches. To keep kids happy in Seoul see p118.

CLIMATE CHARTS

Korea has four very distinct seasons: spring from mid-March to the end of May; summer from June to August; autumn September to November; and winter from December to mid-March. Of course the actual weather doesn't always fit these neat categories.

Temperatures vary hugely between midsummer and mid-winter, with August being very hot and sticky, while December and January are literally freezing. Winters in the north are colder than in the more southerly Busan or Jejudo. Heavy rainfall always arrives with the summer monsoon season (late June to mid-July). See p14 for advice about the best times to visit.

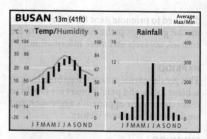

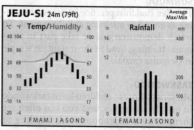

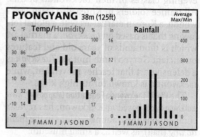

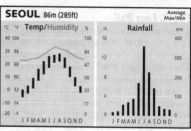

COURSES

Bullish for *bulgogi* or keen on *kimchi*? Check out Han's Culinary Academy (p118) in Seoul for Korean cooking classes in English.

Untangle *Han·geul* at Korean language classes in Seoul (p118).

CUSTOMS

All plants, fresh fruit and vegetables that you bring into Korea must be declared. You are not allowed to bring in meat. If you have more than US$10,000 in cash and travellers cheques, this should be declared and you have to fill in a form. Gifts worth more than US$400 should also be declared.

When leaving the country, the duty-free allowance is not generous: 1 litre of alcohol, 200 cigarettes and 59ml (2oz) of perfume. Antiques of national importance are not allowed to be exported, so if you are thinking of buying a very expensive, genuine antique, check with the **Cultural Properties Appraisal Office** (☎ 662 0106). View www.customs.go.kr for further information.

DANGERS & ANNOYANCES

Drivers routinely jump red lights, so take extra care on pedestrian crossings even if they are protected by lights. Drivers almost never stop for pedestrian crossings that are not protected by traffic lights, so they are useless. Motorcyclists often drive along pavements and pedestrian crossings, particularly in Seoul. Cars also find pavements and pedestrian crossings a convenient place to park.

The lack of street names, signs and numbers can make navigation around cities difficult. This guidebook adds a street name to reviews where one exists and is signed, but don't expect taxi drivers, passers-by and even shopkeepers to know it. Tip: the small number signs on some buildings have the street name underneath, although only in *Han·geul*.

SMOKING OR NONSMOKING?

Many Koreans smoke and they used to be allowed to smoke anywhere they wanted. This has all changed recently, but the smoking rules (like the driving rules)* are not always enforced. In theory smoking is banned in schools and hospitals and on public transport, and restricted to designated smoking areas in other public places. The nonsmokers are winning the war but hard-core smokers still light up in restaurants, cafés, bars and PC *bang*. It's not too common and so isn't usually a problem. However the nonsmoking icon has not been used in this guide book because many places that claim to be nonsmoking don't strictly enforce nonsmoking rules.

DISCOUNT CARDS

Bring your student or pensioner card to Korea if you have one, although benefits are fairly limited. A youth-hostel membership card provides a few discounts. Trains and subways are discounted for seniors, and other transport operators and government-run tourist attractions often offer discounts or free entry to anyone aged over 65 years old. Other organisations may restrict discounts to local residents, but it is always worth a try so just ask.

EMBASSIES & CONSULATES
South Korean Embassies & Consulates
Australia (☎ 06-270 4100; 113 Empire Circuit, Yarralumla, ACT 2600)
Canada (☎ 613-244 5010; www.emb-korea.ottawa .on.ca; 150 Boteler St, Ottawa, ONT K1N 5A6)
China (☎ 1-532 6775; www.koreaemb.org.cn; 4th Ave East, Sanlitun, Chaoyang District, Beijing 100600)
France (☎ 01 4753 0101; 125 rue de Grenelle, Paris 75007)
Germany (☎ 30-260 65432; www.koreaemb.de; Kurfurstenstrasse 72-74, Berlin 10787)
Hong Kong (☎ 2529 4141; 5th fl, Far East Finance Centre, 16 Harcourt Rd, Central)
Ireland (☎ 01-660 8800; 15 Clyde Rd, Ballsbridge, Dublin 4)
Japan (☎ 03-3452 7611; 1-2-5 Minami-Azabu, Minato-ku, Tokyo)
Netherlands (☎ 070-358 6076; Verlengde Tolweg 8, the Hague 2517 JV)
New Zealand (☎ 04-473 9073; 11th fl, ASB Bank Tower Bldg, 2 Hunter St, Wellington)
Philippines (☎ 02-811 6139; 10th fl, Pacific Star Bldg, Makati Ave, Makati, Metro Manila)
Russia (☎ 095-956 1474; 14 Spiridonovka St, Moscow)
Singapore (☎ 65-6258 0789; www.koreaembassy.org .sg; 47 Scotts Rd, 05-01 Goldbell Towers, Singapore 228233)
Taiwan (visa office ☎ 02-2758 8320; Room 1506, 333 Keelung Rd, Section 1, Taipei)
Thailand (☎ 02-247 7537; 23 Thiramruammit Rd, Ratchadapisek, Huay Kwang, Bangkok 10320)
UK (☎ 020-7227 5500; 60 Buckingham Gate, London SW1E 6AJ)
USA (☎ 202-939 5600; www.koreaembassyusa.org; 2450 Massachusetts Ave NW, Washington DC 20008)

Embassies & Consulates in South Korea
Go to www.embassyworld.com or www .embassiesabroad.com for contact details on embassies. Embassies in Seoul include:
Australia (Map pp88-9; ☎ 2003 0100; www.australia.or .kr; 11th fl, Kyobo Bldg, Jongno 1-ga, Jongno-gu)

YOUR OWN EMBASSY

It's important to realise what the embassy of the country of which you are a citizen can and can't do to help you if you strike trouble. Generally speaking, it won't be much help in emergencies if the trouble is remotely your own fault. Remember that you are bound by the laws of the country you are in. Your embassy will not be sympathetic if you end up in jail after committing a crime locally, even if such actions are legal in your own country.

In genuine emergencies you might get some assistance, but only if other channels have been exhausted. If you need to get home urgently, a free ticket home is very unlikely – the embassy would expect you to have insurance. If you have all your money and documents stolen, it might assist with getting a new passport, but a loan for onward travel is out of the question.

Some embassies used to keep letters for travellers or have a small reading room with home newspapers, but these days a mail-holding service is rare and newspapers generally tend to be out of date.

Canada (Map pp92-3; ☎ 3455 6000; www.korea.gc.ca; 9th fl, Kolon Bldg, 45 Mugyo-dong, Jung-gu)

China (Map pp88-9; ☎ 738-1038; www.chinaemb.or.kr; 54 Hyoja-dong, Jongno-gu)

France (Map pp86-7; ☎ 3149 4300; 30 Hap-dong, Seodaemun-gu)

Germany (Map pp88-9; ☎ 748 4114; www.gembassy.or .kr; 308-5 Dongbinggo-dong, Yongsan-gu)

Ireland (Map pp92-3; ☎ 774 6455; www.irelandhouse -korea.com; 15th fl, Daehan Fire & Marine Insurance Bldg, 51-1 Namchang-dong, Jung-gu)

Japan (Map pp88-9; ☎ 2170 5200; www.kr.emb-japan .go.jp; 18-11 Junghak-dong, Jongno-gu)

New Zealand (Map pp88-9; ☎ 730 7794; www.nzembassy .com/korea; 18th fl, Kyobo Bldg, Jongno 1-ga, Jongno-gu)

Russia (Map pp98-9; ☎ 752 0630; http://seoul.rus embassy.org; 34-16 Jeong-dong, Jung-gu)

Singapore (Map p000; ☎ 779 2464; www.mfa.gov .sg/seoul; 28th fl, Seoul Finance Centre, 84 Taepyeongno 1-ga, Jung-gu)

Taiwan (Map pp88-9; ☎ 399 2767; 6th fl, Gwanghwa-mun Bldg, 211 Sejongno, Jongno-gu)

UK (Map pp92-3; ☎ 3210 5500; www.britishembassy .or.kr; 4 Jeong-dong, Jung-gu)

USA (Map pp88-9; ☎ 397 4114; http://seoul.usembassy. state.gov; 32 Sejongno, Jongno-gu)

FESTIVALS & EVENTS

Festival dates alter, so check before you go.

Snow Festivals (January) Held in Taebaeksan and other mountain areas. Expect giant ice sculptures, sledding fun and igloo restaurants.

Cherry Blossoms (April) Every region has streets and parks where people go to enjoy the blossoms.

World Ceramics Biennale (April to June) Korea's top bash for people potty about pottery is held in odd-num-bered years in Icheon (p148), just south of Seoul.

Buddha's Birthday Parade (May) Held in Seoul starting at 7pm on the Sunday evening before Buddha's birthday. It's the country's biggest and most joyful street parade.

Modern Dance Festival (May) International dance groups strut their stuff in Daehangno, Seoul.

International Mime Festival (May) The lakeside city of Chuncheon hosts street performers, magicians, acrobats and quirky shows such as a soap- bubble opera.

Dano Festival (May or June) Held according to the lunar calendar, this traditional festival (p176) features shamanist rituals, mask dances and market stalls.

Mud Festival (July) Held on Daecheon Beach with stacks of muddy fun and games (p320).

Gwangju Biennale (September to November) Korea's leading international art show (p254) is a two-month carnival of the avant garde. It is held in even-numbered years.

Pusan Film Festival (September/October) Korea's top international film festival (www.piff.org) is held in Busan (p234). Don't let Pusan/Busan fool you – the film festival has retained the old spelling.

Mask Dance Festival (late September/early October) A well-established 10-day festival that brings together more than 20 traditional dance troupes in Andong (p219).

World Martial Arts Festival (October) See all sorts of unusual martial arts in Chungju (p337).

Baekje Festival (October) This major festival (p315), packed with events, is held in Buyeo in even-numbered years and in Gongju in odd-numbered years.

FOOD

Exploring Korea's unique and diverse cuisine is one of the pleasures of any visit — see p62. Western, Japanese, Chinese and fast food is also widely available. Price categories for the eating listings in this book are:

Budget Most meals under W7000.

Midrange Most meals in the W7000 to W18,000 range.

Top end Most meals cost more than W18,000.

GAY & LESBIAN TRAVELLERS

Korea has never passed any laws that overtly discriminate against homosexuals, but this should not be taken as a sign of tolerance or acceptance. Korean law does not mention homosexuality because it is considered so bizarre and unnatural as to be unmentionable in public. Many older Koreans share the outlook of conservative American Christian fundamentalists. Younger people are less prejudiced than their parents, so some progress is being made, although only one celebrity so far has outed himself.

Virtually all Korean gays and lesbians keep their sexual orientation a secret from their extended family, work colleagues and friends, although the closet door is inching open. Major cities have a handful of gay clubs, bars and saunas, although they maintain a low profile. Despite increasing discussion of the issue in the media, it is generally a taboo topic, especially for the older generation. Gay and lesbian travellers who publicise their preferences can expect some shocked and hostile reactions. But if you don't raise the issue it's unlikely that anyone else will.

Male to male (and female to female) touching is more common in Korea than in the more uptight Western nations, but is simply a sign of friendship, nothing more.

View www.chingusai.net for news of a gay men's activist group, www.seoulsisters.com to link up with mainly expat lesbians, and www.utopia-asia.com for the latest news on gay

and lesbian issues plus listings of bars and events in Korea's bigger cities. See p131 for information on the gay scene in Itaewon, Seoul, where Koreans and foreigners mix and mingle.

HOLIDAYS
Public Holidays

Eight Korean public holidays are set according to the solar calendar and three according to the lunar calendar, meaning that they fall on different days each year. Restaurants, shops and tourist sights stay open during most holidays, but may close over the three-day Lunar New Year and Chuseok (Thanksgiving) holidays. School holidays don't cause any particular problems for tourists, although beaches can be busy in August, but school trips in May can overcrowd museums and tourist sights.

New Year's Day (1 January) Bells ring out at midnight.

Lunar New Year (7 February 2008, 26 January 2009, 14 January 2010, 3 February 2111, 23 January 2012) Korea grinds to a halt during this three-day holiday when everybody returns to their hometown, visits relatives, bows to their elders and eats rice cakes. Trains and planes are booked up months ahead and expressways are one long traffic jam.

Independence Movement Day (1 March) The anniversary of the day in 1919 when nationwide protests against Japanese colonial rule began.

Children's Day (5 May) Take the darlings out for the day and load them up with gifts.

Buddha's Birthday (24 May 2007, 12 May 2008, 2 May 2009, 21 May 2010, 10 May 2111, 28 May 2112) Baby Buddha is ceremoniously washed, and colourful lanterns decorate all the Buddhist temples and overflow into the streets.

Memorial Day (6 June) Honours those who died fighting for their country.

Constitution Day (17 July) Commemorates the founding of the Republic of South Korea in 1948.

Liberation Day (15 August) Celebrates the day the Japanese surrendered to Allied forces in 1945, marking the end of their 35-year rule of Korea.

Chuseok (Thanksgiving; 25 September 2007, 14 September 2008, 30 October 2009, 22 September 2010, 12 September 2111, 30 September 2012) The Harvest Moon Festival is a three-day holiday when families get together, eat crescent-shaped rice cakes and visit their ancestors' graves. Avoid travelling at this time.

National Foundation Day (3 October) Dan-gun, the legendary founder of the Korean nation, was supposedly born on this day in 2333 BC.

Christmas Day (25 December) Grandfather Santa hands out presents.

UNUSUAL FESTIVALS

Korea's many oddball festivals include:

- Gangneung's **Cuttlefish Festival** – has a tricky catch-a-cuttlefish-by-hand competition

- Chodang's **Uncurdled Tofu Festival** – only exciting for vegetarians

- Jeong-eup's **Bullfighting Festival** – more pushing and shoving than actual fighting

- Muju's **Firefly Festival** – the tiniest festival theme

- Gimje's **Horizon Festival** – because all the other festival topics have been taken.

Visit www.tour2korea.com for more festival information.

DIRECTORY

INSURANCE

A policy covering theft, loss, medical expenses and compensation for cancellation or delays in your travel arrangements is highly recommended. If items are lost or stolen, make sure you obtain a police report straightaway – otherwise your insurer might not pay up. There is a wide variety of policies available, but always check the small print. See p404 for health insurance and p402 for car insurance.

Worldwide coverage to travellers from over 44 countries is available online at www.lonely planet.com/travel_services.

INTERNET ACCESS

Internet rooms (all with high-speed access) are on almost every street in the country, mainly serving youthful computer game addicts playing Starcraft or Lineage. They charge W1000 to W2000 per hour – look out for the 'PC 방' signs. Many post offices and some tourist information centres, cafés and other establishments provide free internet access, as do guesthouses in Seoul. Some motels and nearly all hotels provide computers with broadband access. Internet Service Providers (ISPs) can offer you an English-language home page and continuous broadband access for around W25,000 a month. See p393 for useful regional tourism websites.

LEGAL MATTERS

Most tourists' legal problems involve visa violations or illegal drugs. In the case of visa transgressions, the penalty is normally a fine and possible expulsion from the country. As for using or selling narcotics, think twice: you could spend a few years researching the living conditions in a South Korean prison.

MAPS

The Korean Tourism Organisation (KTO) and tourist information centres in every prov-

ince and city hand out free tourist maps in English, which are good enough for most purposes. Ask at the ticket booths at national and provincial parks for good-quality hiking maps which usually contain some English.

MONEY

The South Korean unit of currency is the won (W), which comes in W10, W50, W100 and W500 coins. Notes come in denominations of W1000, W5000 and W10,000. The highest-value note was worth about US$10 at the time of research, so be prepared to carry around a thick wad of notes. See p15 for the cost of everyday items, and the inside front cover for exchange rates at the time of printing. Go to www.keb.co.kr for current exchange rates.

Banks in most high streets offer foreign exchange services (look for a 'Foreign Exchange' or currency sign), although changing money can take some time. Tourist shops and hotels exchange money, but compare their rates and commissions with the banks before using their services. US dollars are the easiest to exchange but any major currency is accepted. Travellers cheques have a slightly better exchange rate than cash.

Don't forget to reconvert any surplus won into another currency before you leave the country, as exchanging won outside Korea can be difficult or impossible. If you reconvert more than US$2000 worth of won at Incheon airport, you will have to show bank receipts to prove that you exchanged the money legally.

ATMS

Korean ATMs are a little strange. If you have a foreign credit card, you need to find an ATM with a 'Global' sign or the logo of your credit card company. NICE ATMs often accept foreign cards. Most Global ATMs have basic instructions in English and operate in units of W10,000. ATMs can be found outside banks and post offices and inside deluxe hotels, subway stations and department stores. Restrictions on the amount of money you can withdraw vary from machine to machine; it can be below W300,000 per day, but many ATMs have a W700,000 limit. Another problem is that ATMs have time restrictions and most only operate between 9am and 10pm. If you can't find one, Itaewon subway station (Line 6) has a Global ATM that has instructions in English, is open 24 hours and has a withdrawal limit of W300,000.

LEGAL AGES

Women can get married at 16 but men have to wait until they are 18, while the age of consent for sex (outside marriage) is 18. To drive a car you must be 20 years old, but you can now vote at 19. Anyone under 20 is not allowed to buy or drink alcohol nor to buy or smoke cigarettes.

Credit Cards

More and more motels, hotels, shops and restaurants in cities and tourist areas accept foreign credit cards, but there are still plenty of *yeogwan,* restaurants and small businesses that don't. Be prepared to carry around plenty of cash, especially if you are touring around outside the main cities.

PHOTOGRAPHY & VIDEO

Korea is more than up to date with all the latest digital equipment and services. Due to the arrival of the Digital Age, photographic shops are not as numerous as they once were, but they can burn your memory-stick photos onto a CD (W3000). All the major camera and video brands are available including the local ones, such as Samsung, which are challenging the Japanese manufacturers. Yongsan Electronics Market and Techno Mart in Seoul (p135) are the best places to buy the latest camera and video equipment.

Most people do not mind being photographed, but monks, market traders, riot police and *haenyeo* (female divers) in Jejudo are among those who may not want to be photographed, so always ask first. Never take photographs inside Buddhist shrines or of shamanist ceremonies without asking permission first. In the Demilitarized Zone (DMZ) you can take photos, but always follow the advice of your tour guide or you might spark off a second Korean War. For professional hints on how to improve your pictures, purchase Lonely Planet's *Travel Photography.*

POST

Korean postal services (www.koreapost.go.kr) are reliable and reasonably cheap, and post offices often have free internet access. Domestic postal rates are W190 for a postcard, W220 for a letter and W2700 for a package weighing 2kg. Local mail is usually delivered in two days or so, but letters with the address in English can take a day or two longer.

Postcards are W350 and aerograms W400 to any country, but international letter and parcel rates vary according to the destination. Airmail letters (20g) cost W650 (for zone three: North America, Europe, Australia and New Zealand). For zone three, airmail rates are W18,000 for a 2kg packet, W86,200 for a 10kg parcel and W133,000 for 20kg. Surface rates are W12,000 (2kg), W28,000 (10kg) and W48,000 (20kg).

Don't seal your package if you want to take advantage of the lower rate that applies to sending printed papers only. Larger post offices have a packing service that costs from W2000 to W5500.

SHOPPING

Bustling traditional markets that sell everything under the sun can still be found in most cities and towns, while modern high-rise fashion malls, ritzy departments stores packed with brand-name shops, and chain stores cling together in semi-pedestrianised streets that fill up with people in the evenings. Korean craft shops abound and souvenir shops are mixed in with restaurants in the tourist villages that have grown up at the entrances to national and provincial parks. In Seoul, specialist markets (p135) cover everything from fashion, fish and flowers to electronics, embroidery and eel-skin bags.

Global Refund (☎ 02-776 2170; www.globalrefund .com) and **Korea Refund** (☎ 02-537 1755) offer a partial refund of the 10% VAT (between 5% and 7%). Spend more than W30,000 or W50,000 in any participating shop and the retailer gives you a special receipt, which you must show to a customs officer at Incheon International Airport. Go to a Customs Declaration Desk (near check-in counters D and J) before checking in your luggage, as the customs officer will want to see the items before stamping your receipt. After you go through immigration, show your stamped receipt at the refund desk to receive your won refund in cash or by cheque.

SOLO TRAVELLERS

Solo travellers are at a disadvantage in Korea because few motels and hotels have single rooms, and singles pay the same or almost the same as a couple. When touring solo around the country, budget travellers could consider staying in youth-hostel dormitories, although motels are a better option if you don't mind paying W30,000 a night.

Some traditional Korean meals are for sharing and are not available in single portions, so find a companion if you want to enjoy *hanjeongsik* (Korean-style banquet), *jjimdak* (steamed chicken in a hot sauce) or a barbecue meal.

On the plus side, lone travellers in particular can expect locals to go out of their way to help or act as a tourist guide.

TELEPHONE & FAX

Fax

If you want to send a fax, first ask at your guesthouse, motel or hotel, but if they can't help you, try the nearest stationery store or photocopy shop. Deluxe hotels have business centres which are usually helpful.

Mobile Phones

Korean mobile phones operate on the CDMA system, which few countries other than Japan and Korea use, but you can rent mobile phones at Incheon International Airport from one of the three main providers, SK, KTF or LG. They offer similar but not identical schemes. Charges at present are W3000 a day. Incoming calls are free while outgoing domestic calls cost W660 a minute, or W750 to W1000 a minute to the US for example, depending on the international access code used. Other countries cost more – up to W1700 a minute. Local text messages are usually free. A SIM card can be rented for W1300 a day. Check that prices quoted include the 10% VAT, and since the industry is in constant flux, don't be surprised if things have changed. A couple of deluxe hotels in Seoul offer rent-free mobile phones to their guests.

Phone Codes

Korea's nine provinces and seven largest cities have their own area codes. It's easy to forget that the major cities have their own codes – thus Gwangju City's code (☎ 062) is one digit different to the surrounding province of Jeollanam-do (☎ 061). South Korea's country code is ☎ 82. Do not dial the first zero of the area codes if you are calling from outside Korea. Phone numbers that begin with a four-figure number starting with 15 do not have an area code.

Province/City	Code
Busan	☎ 051
Chungcheongbuk-do	☎ 043
Chungcheongnam-do	☎ 041
Daegu	☎ 053
Daejeon	☎ 042
Gang-won-do	☎ 033
Gwangju	☎ 062
Gyeonggi-do	☎ 031
Gyeongsangbuk-do	☎ 054
Gyeongsangnam-do	☎ 055
Incheon	☎ 032
Jeju-do	☎ 064
Jeollabuk-do	☎ 063
Jeollanam-do	☎ 061
Seoul	☎ 02
Ulsan	☎ 052

Phonecards

Telephone cards usually give you a 10% bonus and can be bought at convenience stores and many small shops. There are two types of cards so if your card does not fit in one type of phone, try a different-looking phone. The more squat phone accepts the thin cards. A few phones accept credit cards. Local calls cost W140 for three minutes.

Dial KT (☎ 001), Dacom (☎ 002) or Onse (☎ 008) to call abroad, and you can make international calls from many phone booths. Much cheaper international rates (up to 380 minutes to the US for W15,000) are offered by other providers whose call-back telephone cards are on sale in Itaewon and Dongdaemun in Seoul. Some cards are discounted on their face value. Internet phones are even cheaper.

TIME

South Korea has one time zone, Greenwich Mean Time (GMT) plus nine hours. When it is noon in Seoul it is 1pm in Sydney, 3am in London, 10pm the previous day in New York and 7pm the previous day in San Francisco. See the time-zone world map at the back of this book. Korea does not have a daylight-saving period.

TOILETS

Korea's *hwajangsil* (public toilets) have greatly improved and there are more and more clean, modern and well-signposted ones. Virtually all toilets are free of charge, some are decorated with flowers and pictures and cleaning staff generally do an excellent job. But always carry paper tissue around with you as few restrooms supply toilet paper. If there is toilet paper it's usually somewhere outside the cubicles.

All tourist attractions, parks, subway stations, train stations and bus terminals have public toilets. It's quite okay to use toilets in office blocks or anywhere else if the need arises. Even when you go hiking in the mountains there are lots of toilets although some are very basic. Asian-style squat toilets are losing their battle with European-style ones with seats, but there are still a few around. Face the hooded end when you squat.

TOURIST INFORMATION

In Seoul the excellent **KTO tourist information centre** (KTO; Map pp88-9; ☎ 729 9496; www.tour2korea .com; ⏰ 9am-6pm) has stacks of brochures on every region as well as helpful and well-informed staff. They can book hotels for you and advise you about almost anything.

A very useful **tourist phone number** (☎ 1330; ⏰ 24hr) connects you with English-speaking tourist information staff. They can also act as interpreters if someone can't understand you and you have a mobile phone. Dial ☎ 02-1330 if you're on a mobile phone. If you want to contact a tourist information centre outside Seoul, dial the provincial or metropolitan code first – so for information on Gang·won·do, dial 033-1330.

Many tourist areas throughout the country have their own tourist information centres, so it's not a problem to find one.

For tourist information on the provinces and metropolitan areas check the following websites:

Busan www.pusanweb.com
Chungcheongbuk-do http://foreign.cb21.net/english
Chungcheongnam-do www.chungnam.net
Daegu www.thedaeguguide.com
Daejeon www.daejeon.go.kr
Gang·won·do http://eng/gwd.go.kr
Gwangju www.gwangju.go.kr
Gyeonggi-do www.gg.go.kr
Gyeongsangbuk-do www.gyeongbuk.go.kr
Gyeongsangnam-do http://english.gsnd.net
Incheon http://english.incheon.go.kr
Jeju-do http://tour2jeju.net
Jeollabuk-do www.provin.jeonbuk.kr
Jeollanam-do www.jeonnam.go.kr
Seoul www.seoul.go.kr
Ulsan www.ulsan.go.kr and www.theulsanweb.com

TOURS

Hyundai Asan (☎ 02 3669 3000, 02 773 2122) operates tours to Geumgangsan in North Korea that run by bus across the DMZ, using the east coast road north of Sokcho in Gang·won·do. Geumgangsan (spelled 'Kumgangsan' in North Korea) is a famous scenic area of towering mountain peaks, granite pinnacles and waterfalls (p371). No visas are required. If you share a dormitory (six people) a three-day/two-night tour costs W230,000, while the same tour costs W350,000 per person if you share a double room at Haegeumgang Hotel. Hiking, a hot spa bath, a circus and shopping are available on the tour. The North Korean government sometimes cancels tours for political or other reasons. Other tours of the North may become available (to Kaesong for example).

See p119 for tours around South Korea.

TRAVELLERS WITH DISABILITIES

In the past, Korea did not cater for disabled travellers as Koreans with disabilities tended to stay at home and there were very few disabled foreign tourists. But in Seoul and some other cities this is changing, although promised improvements have been slow to arrive. Most subway stations in Seoul now have stair lifts, elevators and toilets with wheelchair access and handrails. Tourist attractions, especially government-run ones, offer generous discounts or even free entry for disabled people and a helper. More information is available on www.easyaccess.or.kr.

VISAS

With a confirmed onward ticket, visitors from nearly all West European countries, New Zealand, Australia and around 30 other countries receive 90-day permits on arrival. Visitors from the USA and a handful of countries receive 30-day permits, citizens of Italy and Portugal receive 60-day permits, and Canadians receive a six-month permit.

Around 20 countries, including the Russian Federation, China, India, the Philippines and Nigeria, do not qualify for visa exemptions. Citizens from these countries must apply for a tourist visa, which allows a stay of 90 days. You cannot extend your stay beyond 90 days except in rare cases such as a medical emergency; if you overstay the fine starts at W100,000. Log on to www.moj.go.kr or www .mofat.go.kr to find out more.

Applications for a work visa can be made inside Korea, but you must leave the country to pick up the visa. Most applicants fly (or take the Busan ferry) to Fukuoka in Japan, where it usually takes two days to process the visa. You can also apply for a one-year work visa before entering Korea but it can take a few weeks to process. Note that the visa authorities wil want to see originals (not photocopies' your educational qualifications. This guard against fake degree certifica

You don't need to leave Ko work visa as long as you car the same employer. But i ers you must normall pick it up outside

If you don't want to forfeit your work or study visa, you must apply at your local immigration office for a re-entry permit before making any trips outside South Korea. The fee is W30,000 for a single re-entry or W50,000 for multiple re-entry, but permits are free for some nationalities.

If you are working or studying in Korea on a long-term visa, it is necessary to apply for an alien registration card within 90 days of arrival, which costs W10,000. This is done at your local immigration office.

VOLUNTEERING

Volunteers are always needed to teach English and entertain children who live in orphanages. Around 26,000 children are stuck in the orphanage system with little chance of escape as Koreans are very reluctant to adopt children, partly because of the huge educational costs and partly because of the traditional emphasis on blood lines. Contact the **Y-Heesun Volunteer Support Group** (www.yheesun.com) for more information.

Willing Workers on Organic Farms (WWOOF; ☎ 02 723 4458; www.wwoofkorea.com) has 50 farms that welcome volunteer workers who work a few hours a day in return for free board and lodging. For a W50,000 joining fee you'll receive a booklet with contact details.

WOMEN TRAVELLERS

Korea is a relatively crime-free country for all tourists including women, but the usual precautions should be taken. Korea is a very male-dominated society, although it is becoming less so.

WORK

South Korea is a deservedly popular place for English-language teachers to find work. Recently salaries have been rising and native English teachers [...] -year contract can expect [...] or more a month, [...] nt, return flights, [...] 0-days paid holi- [...] letion bonus all [...] ome tax is very [...] 4.5% pension [...] ome nationali- [...] ders can save [...] ble appetite

for studying English so finding an English-teaching job should not be too difficult. New teachers in Seoul should check out p131.

Most English teachers work in a *hagwon* (private language school) but some are employed by universities or government schools. Private tutoring, company classes, English camps and even teaching via the telephone are also possible. Teaching hours in a *hagwon* are usually around 30 hours a week and are likely to involve split shifts, and evening and Saturday classes. Overtime (around W20,000 an hour) is often possible if you want it.

A degree in any subject is sufficient as long as English is your native language. However it's a good idea to obtain some kind of English-teaching certificate before you arrive, as this increases your options and you should be able to find (and do) a better job. Conversation classes are easy enough, but you never know when a student might fire a tricky grammar question at you. Just what is the difference between 'I have eaten *kimchi*' and 'I ate *kimchi*'?

Some *hagwon* owners are less than ideal employers and don't pay all that they promise, so check out the warnings on the websites below before committing yourself. Ask any prospective employer for the email addresses of foreign English teachers working at the *hagwon*, and contact them for their opinion and advice. One important point to keep in mind is that if you change employers, you will usually need to obtain a new work visa, which requires you to leave the country and fly or take a ferry to Fukuoka in Japan to pick up your new visa. That is likely to cost over W300,000, although your new employer may pick up all or at least part of the tab.

The English-language newspapers have very few job advertisements, but hundreds of English-teaching vacancies are advertised on the following websites:

www.englishspectrum.com Has stacks of job offers (job seekers can advertise too) and a bulletin board with accommodation options.

www.eslcafé.com A dozen new job postings daily and useful forums on working and living in Korea.

www.eslcity.com Offers lesson ideas as well as job vacancies.

www.eslhub.com Contains full- and part-time teaching jobs and other classifieds.

www.pusanweb.com Has jobs in Busan and elsewhere.

Transport

CONTENTS

GETTING THERE & AWAY

ENTERING THE COUNTRY

Disembarkation in Korea is a straightforward affair, but you have an extra form to fill in if you are carrying more than US$10,000 in cash and traveller's cheques.

Passport

There are no restrictions when it comes to citizens of foreign countries entering Korea. Most visitors don't need a visa, but if your country is not on the visa-free list, you will need one (p393).

THINGS CHANGE...

The information in this chapter is particularly vulnerable to change. Check directly with the airline or a travel agent to make sure you understand how a fare (and ticket you may buy) works and be aware of the security requirements for international travel. Shop carefully. The details given in this chapter should be regarded as pointers and are not a substitute for your own careful, up-to-date research.

AIR
Airports & Airlines

Most international flights leave from Incheon International Airport, which is at least an hour from Seoul by bus, and there are six regional airports that provide international flights, mainly to China and Japan. The two major ones are Gimhae International Airport (which serves Busan, Korea's second-largest city) and Jejudo International Airport on Korea's southern holiday island. View www.airport.co.kr for information on all the airports. Eight flights a day travel between the small international terminal at Seoul's Gimpo airport and Haneda airport in Tokyo (both airports are nearer their respective cities' downtown areas than Incheon and Narita).

Korea's own carriers are Korean Air and Asiana Airlines. Many airlines serve Korea including:

Aeroflot (airline code SU; ☎ 02-551 0321, airport 032-744 8672; www.aeroflot.com) Hub Moscow.

Air Canada (airline code AC; ☎ 02-3788 0100, airport 032-744 0898; www.aircanada.ca) Hub Pearson International Airport, Toronto.

Air China (airline code CA; ☎ 02-774 6886, airport 032-744 3256; www.air-china.com) Hub Beijing.

Air France (airline code AF; ☎ 02-3483 1033, airport 032-744 4900; www.airfrance.com) Hub Charles de Gaulle International Airport, Paris.

All Nippon Airways (airline code NH; ☎ 02-752 5500, airport 032-744 3200; www.fly-ana.com) Hub Narita Airport, Tokyo.

Asiana Airlines (airline code OZ; ☎ 1588 8000, airport 032-744 2134; www.flyasiana.com) Hub Incheon International Airport, Seoul.

Cathay Pacific Airways (airline code CX; ☎ 02-311 2800, airport 032-744 6777; www.cathaypacific.com) Hub Hong Kong International Airport.

China Eastern Airlines (airline code MU; ☎ 02-518 0330, airport 032-744 3780; www.ce-air.com) Hub Shanghai.

China Southern Airlines (airline code CZ; ☎ 02-3455 1600, airport 032-744 3270; www.cs-air.com) Hub Guangzhou.

Garuda Indonesia Airways (airline code GA; ☎ 02-773 2092, airport 032-744 1990; www.garuda-indonesia.com) Hub Soekarno-Hatta International Airport, Jakarta.

Japan Airlines (airline code JL; ☎ 02-757 1711, airport 032-744 3601; www.japanair.com) Hub Narita Airport, Tokyo.

TRANSPORT

CLIMATE CHANGE & TRAVEL

Climate change is a serious threat to the ecosystems that humans rely upon, and air travel is the fastest-growing contributor to the problem. Lonely Planet regards travel, overall, as a global benefit, but believes we all have a responsibility to limit our personal impact on global warming.

Flying & Climate Change

Pretty much every form of motor transport generates CO_2 (the main cause of human-induced climate change) but planes are far and away the worst offenders, not just because of the sheer distances they allow us to travel, but because they release greenhouse gases high into the atmosphere. The statistics are frightening: two people taking a return flight between Europe and the US will contribute as much to climate change as an average household's gas and electricity consumption over a whole year.

Carbon Offset Schemes

Climatecare.org and other websites use 'carbon calculators' that allow travellers to offset the greenhouse gases they are responsible for with contributions to energy-saving projects and other climate-friendly initiatives in the developing world including projects in India, Honduras, Kazakhstan and Uganda.

Lonely Planet, together with Rough Guides and other concerned partners in the travel industry, supports the carbon offset scheme run by climatecare.org. Lonely Planet offsets all of its staff and author travel.

For more information check out our website: www.lonelyplanet.com.

KLM Royal Dutch Airlines (airline code KL; ☎ 02-2011 5500, airport 032-744 6700; www.klm.nl) Hub Schiphol Airport, Amsterdam.

Korean Air (airline code KE; ☎ 1588 2001, airport 032-744 5132; www.koreanair.com) Hub Incheon International Airport, Seoul.

Lufthansa Airlines (airline code LH; ☎ 02-3420 0400, airport 032-744 3400; www.lufthansa.com) Hub Frankfurt Airport.

Malaysia Airlines (airline code MH; ☎ 02-777 7761, airport 032-744 3501; www.malaysiaairlines.com) Hub Kuala Lumpur International Airport.

Northwest Airlines (airline code NW; ☎ 02-732 1700, airport 032-744 6300; www.nwa.com) Hub Detroit Metro Airport.

Philippine Airlines (airline code PR; ☎ 02-744 3581, airport 032-744 3720; www.philippineair.com) Hub Manila Airport.

Qantas Airways (airline code QF; ☎ 02-777 6871, airport 032-744 3283; www.qantas.com.au) Hub Kingsford-Smith Airport, Sydney.

Singapore Airlines (airline code SQ; ☎ 02-755 1226, airport 032-744 6500; www.singaporeairlines.com) Hub Changi International Airport.

Thai Airways International (airline code TG; ☎ 02-3707 0011, airport 032-744 3571; www.thaiair.com) Hub Bangkok International Airport.

United Airlines (airline code UA; ☎ 02-757 1691, airport 032-744 6666; www.ual.com) Hub Los Angeles International Airport.

Tickets

Be sure you research all the options carefully to make sure you get the deal that best suits your circumstances and requirements. The internet is a useful resource for researching airline prices.

Automated online ticket sales work well if you're doing a simple one-way or return trip on specified dates, but are no substitute for a travel agent with the low-down on special deals, strategies for avoiding layovers and other useful advice.

Paying by credit card offers some protection if you unwittingly end up dealing with a rogue fly-by-night travel agency, as most card issuers provide refunds if you can prove you didn't receive what you paid for. Alternatively, buy a ticket from a bonded agent, such as one covered by the **Air Travel Organisers' Licensing** (ATOL; www.atol.org.uk) scheme in the UK. If you have doubts about the service provider, at the very least call the airline and confirm that your booking has been made.

The following websites can search for air fares to Korea when booking online or researching prices prior to visiting your travel agent:

www.airbrokers.com American round-the-world ticket specialists who can include Korea.

www.cheapestflights.co.uk Cheap worldwide flights from the UK.

www.cheapflight.com Excellent American site with fast access to fares to Korea.
www.expedia.com Microsoft's travel site with access to worldwide fares.
www.travelocity.com Search fares quickly and easily from virtually anywhere to anywhere.

Korean airport departure taxes are included in the ticket price.

Ticket prices have not been listed as they vary so much and change so quickly, depending on the airline, the season, the amount of competition, the level of demand and so on. Ever-increasing security, fuel and other surcharges add another element of uncertainty. Prices of flights from Korea can increase 50% in July and August, and special offers are less common during holiday periods. The peak of the peak for outbound flights is August, when it can be difficult or even impossible to find a seat.

INTERCONTINENTAL TICKETS & AIR PASSES

These round-the-world tickets can provide a good deal if you want to visit other countries besides Korea. A typical ticket could include India, Southeast Asia, Europe and America as well as Korea.

From America or Canada, the Cathay Pacific **All Asia Pass** (www.cathaypacific.com) is worth considering if your time is limited. The basic deal is up to 18 cities in Asia including Seoul, in three weeks (extendable to 30 or 90 days if you pay extra).

From Australia

For flights from Sydney, Melbourne or Brisbane to Incheon airport, try Cathay Pacific or Malaysian Airlines, which may have special deals.

Two of the best-known travel agents in Australia are **Flight Centre** (☎ 133 133; www.flight centre.com.au) and **STA Travel** (☎ 1300 733 035; www .statravel.com.au), which have offices all round the country.

Off-season special offers can reduce the price of return flights from Incheon airport to Australia.

From Canada

Look out for special offers on return flights from Toronto or Vancouver to Incheon airport – try United Airlines or Air Canada for a start.

Travel Cuts (☎ 1-866-246 9762; www.travelcuts.com) is one of the largest student and discount travel

agents in Canada, with offices in cities right across the country.

Return flights from Incheon airport to Toronto and Vancouver can double in price in July and especially August. Prices to destinations like Winnipeg are expensive even in the low season.

From China

Keep an eye out for Air China specials (try www.easetravels.com) between Beijing and Incheon airport. These days Incheon airport is linked to more than 20 Chinese cities as tourism and trade between the two countries is booming. Some regional Korean airports, such as Busan, Daegu, Gwangju and Jeju, also have flights to Chinese cities.

Return flights from Incheon airport to China used to be very rarely discounted, but this began to change in 2006 with some price-war skirmishing among the airlines. Ferries from Incheon port provide an alternative to flying.

From Continental Europe

The cheapest return flights from different cities in Continental Europe to Incheon airport are usually similar, although ultra specials are sometimes available – for starters try Aeroflot, KLM or Lufthansa.

In Germany check out **STA Travel** (☎ 03-0311 0950; www.statravel.de) for up-to-date fare details.

In France contact **Usit Connect Voyages** (☎ 01-4329 6950; www.usitconnections.fr), **OTU Voyages** (☎ 08-9268 8363; www.vdm.com) and **Nouvelles Frontieres** (☎ 08-2500 0825; www.nouvelles-frontieres.fr) for reliable travel agencies with branches nationwide.

In Holland call **NBBS Reizen** (☎ 020 620 5071; www.nbbs.nl) or **Holland International** (☎ 070 307 6307; www.hollandinternational.nl) for the latest flight information.

Special offers on return flights from Incheon airport to Continental Europe can save you up to W100,000. Book early (for instance on Thai Air or Singapore Airlines) for the best deals on summer trips to Europe. Taxes, surcharges and landing charges can be high, so check that quotes include them.

From Hong Kong

To book flights, contact **Phoenix Travel Services** (☎ 2722 7378; fax 2369 8884) in the Tsimshatsui district of Hong Kong, which receives good reviews from travellers. **Tiglion Travel** (www.tiglion .com) is another option, while **STA Travel** (☎ 852 2736 1618; www.hkst.com.hk/statravel) has six branches

TRANSPORT

in Hong Kong and Macau. Check the classifieds in the English-language newspapers for a guide to current prices and discount offers, although they may not tell the whole story.

Return flights from Incheon airport to Hong Kong are sometimes discounted.

From Japan

Japanese tourists make up the majority of foreign visitors to Korea, and increasing numbers of Koreans are flying to Japanese cities, sometimes just for the weekend. There are direct nonstop flights from 26 Japanese cities to Incheon, but flights from Tokyo are usually the cheapest – try United or Northwest Airlines. Fares go up and down with the seasons, and fares in Golden Week (April and May) and August cost up to twice the price of low-season fares. Flights are also available from Japan to airports in Busan, Daegu and Jejudo. Fast ferry boats from Japan to Busan are another option.

Across Traveller's Bureau (☎ 03-5795 4727; www.across-travel.com) has three branches in Tokyo. **STA Travel** (☎ 03-5391 2922; www.statravel.co.jp) and **Just Travel** (☎ 03-3207 8311) have English-speaking staff who can help you find discounted fares. Also check classified advertisements in the **Japan Times** (www.japantimes.co.jp) or on its website, which operates an online travel service, as well as in the **Tokyo Journal** (www.tokyo.to), a monthly magazine for expats.

Special offers on return flights from Incheon airport to Tokyo and Osaka, usually on United Airlines, can save you some hard-earned money.

From New Zealand

Airlines seem to take it in turns to offer the lowest fare, but try Malaysian Airlines as a starting point. Korean Air may have a reasonable fare if you are continuing on to Europe.

Flight Centre (☎ 0800-243 544; www.flightcentre.co.nz) and **STA Travel** (☎ 0508-782 872; www.statravel.co.nz) are two of the largest travel agents with offices in the main cities.

Return flights from Incheon airport to New Zealand are rarely discounted (due to plenty of Koreans visiting, studying and even emigrating to NZ), but you can always ask.

From Singapore

Cut-price youth fares can slash the cost of return flights from Singapore to Incheon airport.

STA Travel (☎ 6737 7188; www.statravel.com.sg) and **Four Seas Travel** (☎ 2200 7848; www.fourseastravel.com) have offices in Singapore, and other travel agents advertise special offers in the classified columns of the *Straits Times*.

Return flights from Incheon airport to Singapore are rarely discounted.

From the UK

The UK has an endless number of worldwide discount flights, so it's always worthwhile to do a thorough check before buying a ticket. From Heathrow or Gatwick (both near London) try Emirates via Dubai or direct flights on Korean Air. Off-season specials are always likely.

London has hundreds of discount travel agents including **Trailfinders** (☎ 020-7938 3939; www.trailfinders.co.uk), which has offices in nine cities, and **STA Travel** (☎ 0870 160 0599; www.statravel.co.uk).

From Korea, buy tickets as early as you can or go via Southeast Asia to reduce the cost of flights. In July and August every flight can be booked out.

From the USA

From New York and Los Angeles, there are usually return-flight specials to Incheon airport – try United, NorthWest or Malaysian Airlines. Taxes, fuel, security surcharges and all the rest of it can add substantially to the fare.

Check out **STA Travel** (☎ 800-781 4040; www.statravel.com) for discounted fares. Prices of return flights from Incheon airport to New York and Los Angeles double in July and August, and you'll be lucky to find a ticket.

LAND

Having North Korea as a hostile neighbour for over 50 years has turned South Korea into a virtual island. However, if North Korea does ever relax its isolationist policies, the South could quickly be linked by road and rail through North Korea to China, Russia and beyond. It's an exciting prospect but unlikely to happen any time soon.

SEA

International ferries are worth considering if you're travelling around North Asia. You can catch a ferry to Incheon in South Korea from a number of Chinese ports, travel around South Korea, and then leave on a fast ferry from Busan to Japan. Another ferry option is travelling to or from Russia via Sokcho in Gang-won-do.

To/From China

Ferries link 10 Chinese ports with Incheon. Some are crowded with petty traders, but they provide a cheaper option than flying. The cheapest fares offer a thin mattress on a dormitory floor, while the more expensive fares give you a small cabin with a bunk bed and TV. Child fares are usually half the adult fare, and some ferry companies offer students a 20% discount. Prices listed are for one-way tickets and sailing times are subject to variation. Most ferries leave Incheon from Yeonan Pier, but the larger boats depart from International Terminal 2.

A ferry-and-train package is available from cities in Korea to Beijing, Shanghai, Hangzhou or Shenyang in China via the Incheon-Tianjin ferry – see www.korail.go.kr for details.

Ferries (☎ 063 2171 6411; W105,000–220,000) also leave Gunsan in Jeollabuk-do for Qindao in China three times a week and take 18 hours. The international ferry terminal is a W7500 taxi ride from Gunsan bus terminal.

Four Season Cruise (☎ 243 6633; W125,000) runs twice a week between Mokpo in Jeollanam-do and Shanghai in China.

To/From Japan

First-floor booths in the international ferry terminal near Jungang subway station in Busan sell tickets for overnight ferries to three Japanese cities: Fukuoka (round trip W152,000, departs 10.30pm, arrives 6am), Shimonoseki (round trip W161,000 to W608,000, departs 8pm, arrives 8am) and Osaka (round trip W237,000, departs 4pm, arrives 10am).

For a quick trip to Fukuoka on the Kobe or Beetle hydrofoils, walk upstairs to the 2nd floor. There are five daily departures (round trip W171,000, three hours, departs 8.45am, 10am, 2pm, 3pm, 3.45pm) plus one additional departure on Friday morning (9.30am).

Other destinations are Hitakatsu (round trip W130,000, one hour 40 minutes) and Izuhara (round trip W130,000, two hours 40 minutes).

Add a W2600 departure tax for these international trips.

To/From Russia

Dongchun (☎ 033-639 2632) operates a ferry twice a week (Mondays and Thursdays) from Zarubino and Vladivostok in Russia to Sokcho in Gang-won-do. With the cheaper fares (Zarubino one way/return W144,000/244,800, Vladivostok one way/return W168,000/285,000), you sleep on the floor and share facilities. The more expensive fares entitle you to a cabin for two or four people with your own bed, TV and bathroom. You can connect to the Trans-Siberian railway, although most passengers are Korean and on a package tour to Paekdusan on the Chinese–North Korean border. These package tours cost from W549,000 for seven days (1 March to 31 May) or from W710,000 (1 June to 30 September).

KOREA–CHINA FERRIES FROM INCHEON

Ferries leaving from Incheon's **Yeonan Pier** (☎ 032 891 2030):

Destination	Phone	Price (W)	Departures	Duration
Dalian	032-891 7100	115,000–230,000	4.30pm Tue & Thu, 6pm Sat	17hr
Dandong	032-891 3322	115,000–210,000	6pm Mon, Wed & Fri	16hr
Qinhuangdao	032-891 9600	115,000–250,000	7pm Mon, noon Fri	23hr
Shidao	032-891 8877	105,000–200,000	6pm Mon, Wed & Fri	14hr
Yantai	032-891 8880	110,000–336,000	7pm Tue, Thu & Sat	14hr
Yingkou	032-891 5555	115,000–220,000	7pm Tue, noon Sat	24hr

Ferries leaving from Incheon's **International Terminal 2** (☎ 032 781 3068):

Destination	Phone	Price (W)	Departures	Duration
Lianyungang	032-770 3700	120,000–350,000	7pm Tue, 3pm Sat	24hr
Qingdao	032-777 0490	110,000–160,000	5pm Tue, Thu & Sat	15hr
Tianjin	032-777 8260	115,000–250,000	1pm Tue, 7pm Fri	24hr
Weihai	032-777 0490	110,000–200,000	7pm Mon, Wed & Sat	14hr

TRANSPORT

GETTING AROUND

South Korea is a public-transport dream come true with everything reasonably priced. Planes, trains and express buses link major cities, intercity buses link cities and towns large and small, while local buses provide a surprisingly good service to national and provincial parks and villages in outlying rural areas. Car ferries ply numerous routes to offshore islands. Local urban buses, subways and taxis make getting around cities and towns easy. All transport works on the Korean *ppallippalli* (hurry hurry) system, so buses and trains leave on time, and buses and taxis tend to be driven fast with little regard to road rules.

Comparing the three forms of transport, Seoul to Busan (444km) costs W19,300 by ordinary bus and W28,800 by deluxe bus, which take 5½ hours and run at least every 30 minutes. The train options are KTX (high-speed, W44,800, three hours, every 30 minutes), *Saemaul* (express W36,800, 4½ hours, every 45 minutes) and *Mugunghwa* (semi express, W24,800, 5½ hours, every 45 minutes), most of which are faster and more comfortable than the buses. Flying costs W58,000 and only takes an hour, but travelling to and from the airports takes another 1½ hours.

As in other countries, rising fuel prices are pushing up the price of transport, so in 2007 expect KTX train fares to rise 3%, *Saemaul* train prices to increase 12%, and bus fares to go up between 7% and 10%.

AIR
Airlines in Korea
South Korea has only two major domestic carriers – **Korean Air** (☎ 1588 2001; www.koreanair .com) and **Asiana Airlines** (☎ 1588 8000; www.flyasiana .com) – but a new low-cost operator, **Jeju Air** (www.jejuair.com), started up in June 2006. Initially flying between Jejudo and Gimpo, Seoul (p274), and undercutting the prices of the other two airlines, the plan is to expand the number of routes.

Both the major domestic airlines provide flights to and from a dozen local airports, and charge virtually identical but very reasonable fares – less than US$100 even for the longest domestic flights. Gimpo International Airport handles nearly all of Seoul's domestic flights, but Incheon International Airport handles a handful of domestic flights to Busan, Daegu

and Jejudo. The longest flight time is just over an hour between Seoul Gimpo and Jejudo. Fares are 15% cheaper from Monday to Thursday when seats are easier to obtain. Flights on public holidays have a surcharge and are often booked out. Students and children receive discounts, and foreigners should always carry their passports on domestic flights for ID purposes.

BICYCLE
Cycling around Korea is not recommended due to the local driving habits, but hiring a bike for short trips in areas with bike paths or little traffic is a good idea – see p73 and individual destination chapters for recommended cycling trips. Bicycle hire is usually W2000 an hour, but try for a discount for a day's hire. You'll have to leave your passport or negotiate some other ID or deposit. Helmets are not available and you may need your own padlock.

BOAT
Korea has a very extensive network of ferries that connects hundreds of offshore islands to each other and to the mainland. The large southern island of Jejudo can be reached by ferry from Mokpo or Wando in Jeollanamdo or on longer boat trips from Busan and Incheon, although most people fly these days. On the west coast, ferries from Incheon's Yeonan Pier service a dozen nearby and more distant islands, while other west-coast islands further south can be reached from Daecheon harbour and Gunsan. Mokpo, Wando, Yeosu and Busan provide access to countless islands strung along the south coast. Remote Ulleungdo off the east coast can be reached by ferry from Pohang or Donghae. Inland ferries run along a couple of large scenic lakes – Soyang Lake in Gang·won-do and Chungju Lake in Chungcheongbuk-do. See the provincial chapters for details on all these floating excursions.

BUS
Thousands of long-distance buses whiz to every nook and cranny of the country, every 15 minutes between major cities and towns, and at least hourly to small towns, villages, temples and national and provincial parks. Only a selection of bus destinations are given in the transport sections of each city, town or tourist site covered. All the bus frequencies given are approximate, as buses don't usually run on a regular timetable and times vary

DOMESTIC AIR FARES – SOUTH KOREA

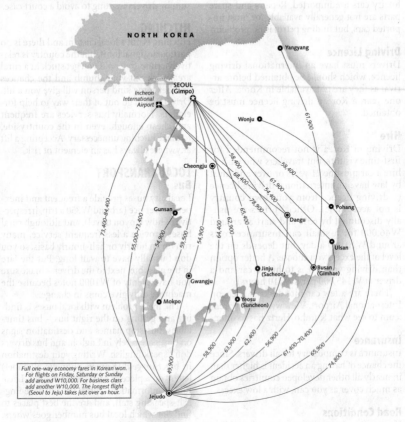

NORTH KOREA

Yangyang

Incheon International Airport ✈

SEOUL (Gimpo) ☆

Wonju ●

61,900

Cheongju ◉

58,400
58,400
68,400
61,900
54,400
78,900

Pohang ●

Gunsan ●

73,400–84,400
55,000–73,400
54,900
59,500
54,900
64,400
62,900
65,400
63,900

Daegu ●

Ulsan ●

Jinju (Sacheon) ●
Busan (Gimhae) ◉

Gwangju ◉

Mokpo ●

Yeosu (Suncheon) ●

49,900
58,900
63,900
62,400
56,900
61,400–70,400
65,900
74,800

TRANSPORT

Full one-way economy fares in Korean won. For flights on Friday, Saturday or Sunday add around W10,000. For business class add another W10,000. The longest flight (Seoul to Jeju) takes just over an hour.

Jejudo

throughout the day. Bus terminals have staff on hand to ensure that everyone boards the right bus, so help is always available. Buses don't have toilets on board, but on long journeys drivers take a 10-minute rest at a refreshment stop every few hours.

Express buses link major cities, while intercity buses stop more often and serve smaller cities and towns. The buses are similar, but they use separate (often neighbouring) terminals. Expressways have a special bus lane that operates at weekends and reduces delays due to heavy traffic. Buses always leave on time (or even early!) and go to far more places than trains, but are not as comfortable or smooth, so for travelling long distances trains can be the better option.

Udeung (superior-class express buses) have three seats per row instead of four, but cost 50% more than *ilban* (standard buses). Buses that travel after 10pm have a 10% surcharge and are generally superior class.

Expect to pay around W4000 for an hour-long journey on a standard bus.

Buses are so frequent that it's not necessary to buy a ticket in advance except perhaps on holidays and weekends. Buy tickets at the bus terminals.

CAR & MOTORCYCLE
Bring Your Own Vehicle

Contact **customs** (www.customs.go.kr) for information on regulations concerning importing your own car. The vast majority of cars running in the country are Korean-made, although a few luxury cars are imported. Repairs and spare parts are not generally available for most imported cars, but finding petrol is no problem.

Driving Licence

Drivers must have an international driving licence, which should be obtained before arrival as they are not available in Korea. After one year, a Korean driving licence must be obtained.

Hire

Driving in Korea is not recommended for first-time visitors, but travellers who wish to hire a car must be 21 years or over and must by law have an international driving licence (a driving licence from your own country is not acceptable). Official prices are usually discounted by 65% and start at around W46,000 for a small car. Insurance costs around W10,000 a day, but depends on the level of the excess you choose. A better option than driving yourself is to hire a car and a driver at W145,000 per day (10 hours).

There are a few car-hire desks at Incheon International Airport. View www.kumhorent .com to see what Kumho-Hertz has to offer.

Insurance

Insurance is compulsory for all drivers. Since the chance of having an accident is higher than in nearly all other developed countries obtain as much cover as you can, with a low excess.

Road Conditions

Korea has about the worst road-accident record among the 29 OECD countries, and foreign drivers in large cities are likely to spend most of their time lost, stuck in traffic jams, looking for a parking space or taking evasive action. Impatient and careless drivers are a major hazard and traffic rules are frequently ignored. Driving in rural areas or on Jejudo is more feasible, but public transport is so good that few visitors feel the urge to sit down behind a steering wheel.

Speed cameras are ubiquitous, and your credit card may be debited for a speeding fine even after you've handed the car back.

Road Rules

Vehicles drive on the right side of the road. The driver and front-seat passengers must wear seatbelts, drunk drivers receive heavy fines and victims of road accidents are often paid a big sum by drivers wanting to avoid a court case.

HITCHING

Hitching is not a local custom and there is no particular signal for it, but the country is relatively crime-free, so if you get stuck in a rural area, stick out your thumb and the chances are that some kind person will give you a lift. Drivers often go out of their way to help foreigners. Normally bus services are frequent and cheap enough, even in the countryside, to make hitching unnecessary. Accepting a lift anywhere always has an element of risk.

LOCAL TRANSPORT
Bus

Local city buses provide a frequent and inexpensive service (around W850 a trip, irrespective of how far you travel), and although rural buses provide a less-frequent service, many run on an hourly or half-hourly basis, so you don't usually have to wait long. Put the fare in the glass box next to the driver – make sure you have plenty of W1000 notes because the machines only give coins in change.

The main problem with local buses is finding and getting on the right bus – bus timetables, bus-stop names and destination signs on buses are rarely in English, and bus drivers don't speak English. Writing your destination in big *Han·geul* (Korean phonetic alphabet) letters on a piece of card can be helpful. Local tourist information centres usually have English-speaking staff, and are the best places to find out which local bus number goes where, and where to pick it up.

Subway

Six cities now have a subway system: Seoul, Busan, Daejeon, Daegu, Gwangju and Incheon. The subway is a cheap and convenient way of getting around these major cities, and since signs and station names are in English as well as Korean, the systems are foreigner-friendly and easy to use.

Taxi

Taxis are numerous almost everywhere and are so cheap that even high-school students use them. Fares vary only slightly in different areas. Every taxi has a meter that works on a distance basis but switches to a time basis when the vehicle is stuck in a traffic jam. Tipping is not a local custom and is not expected or necessary.

Ilban (regular taxis) cost around W1800 for the first 2km, while the *mobeom* (deluxe taxis) that exist in some cities cost around W4000 for the first 3km.

Since very few taxi drivers speak any English, plan beforehand how to communicate your destination to the driver. Ask to be dropped off at a nearby landmark if the driver doesn't understand what you're saying or doesn't know where it is. It can be useful to write down your destination or a nearby landmark in *Han·geul* letters on a piece of paper.

Any expressway tolls are added to the fare. In the countryside check the fare first as there are local quirks, such as surcharges or a fixed rate to out-of-the-way places with little prospect of a return fare.

TRAIN

South Korea has an excellent but not comprehensive train network operated by **Korea National Railroad** (☎ 1544 7788; www.korail.go.kr), connecting most major cities and the towns along the way. Trains are clean, comfortable and punctual, and just about every station has a sign in Korean and English. Trains are the best option for long-distance travel, although buying a ticket in advance is a good idea, especially at the weekends. Go to the website, click on 'online reservation' and then 'inquiry/reservation' to access all the train schedules and fares.

Talks about reopening rail links between North and South Korea are continuing, but this depends on the agreement of the North Korean government. If the rail link ever started running, it would open the way to the development of a Seoul–London and even a Seoul–Singapore rail link, but this is probably a very distant dream.

Classes

There are four classes of trains. Developed in Korea, the new high-speed KTX trains, introduced in 2004, can travel at over 300km/h. At present the high-speed track extends from Seoul to Daejeon, which KTX trains reach in an hour or less, and is being extended to Busan on the east coast. The next fastest and most luxurious are *Saemaul* trains, which also stop only in major cities. *Mugunghwa* trains stop more often and are almost as comfortable and fast as *Saemaul* trains. *Tonggeun*

(commuter) trains are the cheapest and stop at every station, but only run infrequently on certain routes and are a dying breed. Some trains have a dining car, while others have *gimbap* (Korean sushi) lunch boxes and a snack trolley.

Costs

KTX trains are 40% more expensive than *Saemaul* trains (and KTX 1st class is another 40%). *Saemaul* 1st class is 22% more than the standard *Saemaul* fare. *Saemaul* standard fares are 50% more than *Mugunghwa* class, which is 80% more expensive than *tonggeun* (commuter) class. KTX tickets are discounted 7% to 20% if you buy seven to 60 days before departure. Tickets are discounted 15% from Tuesday to Thursday, and *ipseokpyo* (standing tickets) are discounted 15% to 30% depending on the length of the journey; with a standing ticket, you are allowed to sit on any unoccupied seats. Children travel for half price and seniors receive a 25% discount. The full range of discounts is complicated and confusing. For fares and schedules see the website.

Reservations

The railway ticketing system is computerised and you can buy tickets up to two months in advance at railway stations and some travel agents including **Hanjin Travel Service** (☎ 02 729 2680), inside the KTO tourist information centre (Map pp88–9) in Seoul. There are far fewer trains than buses, so seat reservations are sensible and necessary on weekends, holidays and other busy times.

Train Passes

Foreigners can buy a KR Pass at overseas travel agents or from the website of **Korea National Railroad** (www.korail.go.kr). The KR Pass offers unlimited rail travel (including KTX services) for three/five/seven/10 consecutive days at a cost of US$76/114/144/166. Children (four to 12 years) receive a 50% discount, and youths (13 to 25 years old) receive a 20% discount.

Are they worth it? The problem is that distances in Korea are not great, trains don't go everywhere, and the pass is unlikely to save you much if any money. Using a flexible combination of buses, trains and planes is the best way to see the country.

Health

CONTENTS

Health issues and the quality of medical care vary significantly depending on whether you stay in cities or venture further out into rural areas.

Travellers tend to worry about contracting infectious diseases while abroad, but infections are a rare cause of serious illness or death while overseas. Accidental injury (especially traffic accidents) and pre-existing medical conditions such as heart disease account for most life-threatening problems. Becoming ill in some way, however, is relatively common. Fortunately most common illnesses can either be prevented with some common-sense behaviour or be treated easily with a well-stocked traveller's medical kit.

HEALTH ADVISORIES

It's usually a good idea to consult your government's travel-health website before departure, if one is available:
Australia (www.dfat.gov.au/travel)
Canada (www.travelhealth.gc.ca)
New Zealand (mfat.govt.nz/travel)
South Africa (www.dfa.gov.za/travelling)
UK (www.doh.gov.uk/traveladvice)
US (www.cdc.gov/travel)

The following advice is a general guide only and does not replace the advice of a doctor trained in travel medicine.

BEFORE YOU GO

Pack medications in their original, clearly labelled containers. A signed and dated letter from your physician describing your medical conditions and regular medications (use generic names) is also a good idea. If carrying syringes or needles, be sure to have a physician's letter documenting their medical necessity. If you have a heart condition bring a copy of your ECG taken just prior to travelling.

If you take any regular medication, bring double your needs in case of loss. In Korea you need a local doctor's prescription to buy medication, and it may be difficult to obtain particular branded medications available in Western countries.

INSURANCE

Even if you are fit and healthy, don't travel without health insurance – accidents do happen. Declare any existing medical conditions you have; the insurance company will check if your problem is pre-existing and will not cover you if it is undeclared. You may require extra cover for adventure activities. If your health insurance doesn't cover you for medical expenses abroad, consider getting extra insurance. If you're uninsured, emergency evacuation is expensive; bills of over US$100,000 are not uncommon.

Find out in advance if your insurance plan will make payments directly to providers or reimburse you later for overseas health expenses; in many countries doctors expect payment in cash. Some policies offer lower and higher medical-expense options; the higher ones are chiefly for countries that have extremely high medical costs, such as the USA. You may prefer a policy that pays doctors or hospitals directly, rather than you having to pay on the spot and claim later. If you have to claim later, make sure you keep all documentation.

Some policies ask you to call back (reverse charges) to a centre in your home country where an immediate assessment of your problem is made.

RECOMMENDED VACCINATIONS

No special vaccinations are required or recommended for South Korea, but check the latest situation with your tour company before visiting the North.

INTERNET RESOURCES

There is a wealth of travel health advice on the internet. For further information, **Lonely Planet** (www.lonelyplanet.com) is a good place to start. The **World Health Organization** (WHO; www.who.int/ith) publishes a superb book called *International Travel & Health*, revised annually and available online at no cost. Another website of general interest is **MD Travel Health** (www.mdtravel health.com), which provides complete travel-health recommendations for every country and is updated daily. The **Centers for Disease Control and Prevention** (CDC; www.cdc.gov) website also has good general information.

FURTHER READING

Pick up a copy of Lonely Planet's *Healthy Travel Asia & India*. Other recommended references include Traveller's Health by Dr Richard Dawood and *Travelling Well* by Dr Deborah Mills (www.travellingwell.com.au).

MEDICAL CHECKLIST

The following are recommended items for personal medical kits:

- antifungal cream (eg Clotrimazole)
- antibacterial cream (eg Muciprocin)
- antibiotics if you are planning on visiting rural areas: one for skin infections (eg Amoxicillin/Clavulanate or Cephalexin) and another for diarrhoea (eg Norfloxacin or Ciprofloxacin)
- antihistamine – there are many options (eg Cetrizine for daytime and Promethazine for night)
- antiseptic (eg Betadine)
- anti-spasmodic for stomach cramps (eg Buscopan)
- contraceptives
- decongestant (eg Pseudoephedrine)
- DEET-based insect repellent
- anti-diarrhoeal treatments – consider an oral-rehydration solution (eg Gastrolyte), diarrhoea 'stopper' (eg Loperamide) and anti-nausea medication (eg Prochlorperazine)
- first-aid items such as scissors, elastoplasts, bandages, gauze, thermometer (but not mercury), sterile needles and syringes, safety pins and tweezers
- anti-inflammatory (eg Ibuprofen)
- indigestion tablets (eg Quick Eze or Mylanta)
- iodine tablets (unless you are pregnant or have a thyroid problem) to purify water
- Laxative (eg Coloxyl)
- migraine medicine – sufferers should take their personal medicine
- paracetamol
- Permethrin for clothing and mosquito nets
- steroid cream for allergic/itchy rashes (eg 1% to 2% hydrocortisone)
- sunscreen and hat
- throat lozenges
- thrush (vaginal yeast infection) treatment (eg Clotrimazole pessaries or Diflucan tablet)
- Ural or equivalent if you're prone to urine infections

HEALTH

IN TRANSIT

DEEP VEIN THROMBOSIS (DVT)

Deep vein thrombosis occurs when blood clots form in the legs during plane flights, chiefly because of prolonged immobility. The longer the flight, the greater the risk. Though most blood clots are reabsorbed uneventfully, some may break off and travel through the blood vessels to the lungs, where they may cause life-threatening complications.

The chief symptom of DVT is swelling or pain of the foot, ankle, or calf, usually but not always on just one side. When a blood clot travels to the lungs, it may cause chest pain and difficulty in breathing. Travellers who find that they have any of these symptoms should immediately seek medical attention.

To prevent the development of DVT on long flights, you should walk about the cabin, perform isometric compressions of the leg muscles (ie contract the leg muscles while sitting), drink plenty of fluids, and avoid alcohol and tobacco.

JET LAG & MOTION SICKNESS

Jet lag is common when crossing more than five time zones; it results in insomnia, fatigue, malaise or nausea. To avoid jet lag, try drinking plenty of fluids (nonalcoholic) and eating light meals. Upon arrival, seek exposure to natural sunlight and readjust your schedule (for meals, sleep etc) as soon as possible.

Antihistamines such as dimenhydrinate (Dramamine), prochlorperazine (Phenergan) and meclizine (Antivert, Bonine) are generally the first choice for the treatment of motion sickness. Their major side effect is drowsiness. A herbal alternative is ginger, which works like a charm for some people.

IN KOREA

AVAILABILITY & COST OF HEALTH CARE

South Korea is a well-developed country, and the quality of medical care reflects this. Standards of medical care are higher in Seoul and other cities than in rural areas, although making yourself understood can be a problem anywhere.

North Korea is poverty-stricken and medical care is completely inadequate throughout the country including Pyongyang. Shortages of routine medications and supplies are a common problem.

A recommended hospital in Seoul is the government-run **Samsung Medical Center & International Health Service** (Map pp84-5; ☎ 02-3410 0200; 50 Ilwon-Dong, Gangnam-gu).

INFECTIOUS DISEASES

Filariasis

A mosquito-borne disease that is very rare in travellers; mosquito-avoidance measures are the best way to prevent this disease. It's widespread in rice-growing areas in southwest Korea.

Hepatitis A

A problem throughout the country, this food- and water-borne virus infects the liver, causing jaundice (yellow skin and eyes), nausea and lethargy. There is no specific treatment for hepatitis A; you just need to allow time for the liver to heal. All travellers to Korea should be vaccinated against hepatitis A.

Hepatitis B

The only sexually transmitted disease that can be prevented by vaccination, hepatitis B is spread by body fluids, including sexual contact. Up to 10% of the population are carriers of hepatitis B, and usually are unaware of this. The long-term consequences can include liver cancer and cirrhosis.

HIV

HIV is also spread by body fluids. Avoid unsafe sex, sharing needles, invasive cosmetic procedures such as tattooing, and needles that have not been sterilised in a medical setting.

Influenza

Influenza (flu) symptoms include high fever, muscle aches, runny nose, cough and sore throat. It can be very severe in people over the age of 65 or in those with underlying medical conditions such as heart disease or diabetes – vaccination is recommended for these individuals. There is no specific treatment, just rest and paracetamol.

Japanese B Encephalitis

This viral disease is transmitted by mosquitoes, but is very rare in travellers. Most cases occur in rural areas, and vaccination is recommended for travellers spending more than one month outside cities. There is no treatment, and a third of infected people will die, while another third will suffer permanent brain damage. The highest risk is in the southwest rice-growing areas.

Leptospirosis

Leptospirosis is contracted after exposure to contaminated fresh water (eg rivers). Early symptoms are very similar to the 'flu' and include headache and fever. It can vary from a very mild to a fatal disease. Diagnosis is through blood tests, and it is easily treated with Doxycycline.

Lyme Disease

This tick-borne disease occurs in the summer months. Symptoms include an early rash and general viral symptoms, followed weeks to months later by joint, heart or neurological problems. Prevention is by using general insect-avoidance measures and checking yourself for ticks after walking in forest areas. Treatment is with Doxycycline.

Rabies

This sometimes fatal disease is spread by the bite or lick of an infected animal – most commonly a dog. You should seek medical advice immediately after any animal bite and commence post-exposure treatment. If an animal bites you, gently wash the wound with soap and water, and apply iodine-based antiseptic. If you are not pre-vaccinated, you will need to receive rabies immunoglobulin as soon as possible.

STDs

Sexually transmitted diseases are common throughout the world and the most common include herpes, warts, syphilis, gonorrhoea and chlamydia. People carrying these diseases often have no signs of infection. Condoms will prevent gonorrhoea and chlamydia but not warts or herpes. If after a sexual encounter you develop any rash, lumps, discharge or pain when passing urine, seek immediate medical attention. If you have been sexually active during your travels, have an STD check on your return home.

Tuberculosis

Only North Korea has significant risk. While tuberculosis is rare, travellers, medical and aid workers, and long-term travellers who have significant contact with the local population,

should take precautions. Vaccination is usually only given to children under the age of five, but adults at risk are recommended to undertake pre- and post-travel TB testing. The main symptoms are fever, cough, weight loss, night sweats and tiredness.

Typhoid

This serious bacterial infection is spread via food and water. It gives a high and slowly worsening fever and headache, and may be accompanied by a dry cough and stomach pain. It is diagnosed by blood tests and treated with antibiotics. Vaccination is recommended for all travellers spending more than a week in Korea and travelling outside Seoul. Be aware that vaccination is not 100% effective, so you must still be careful with what you eat and drink.

Typhus

Scrub typhus is present in the scrub areas of Korea. This is spread by a mite and is very rare in travellers. Symptoms include fever, muscle pains and a rash. Following general insect-avoidance measures when walking in the scrub will help you avoid this disease. Doxycycline works as a prevention and treatment for typhus.

TRAVELLERS' DIARRHOEA

Travellers' diarrhoea is the most common problem which affects travellers – between 10% and 20% of people visiting South Korea will suffer from it. The risk in North Korea is more like 40% to 60%. In the majority of cases, travellers' diarrhoea is triggered by a bacteria (there are numerous potential culprits), and therefore responds promptly to treatment with antibiotics, which will depend on your circumstances: how sick you are, how quickly you need to get better, where you are etc.

Travellers' diarrhoea is defined as the passage of more than three watery bowel actions within 24 hours, plus at least one other symptom such as fever, cramps, nausea, vomiting or feeling generally unwell. Treatment consists of staying well hydrated; rehydration solutions like Gastrolyte are the best for this. Antibiotics such as Norfloxacin, Ciprofloxacin or Azithromycin will kill the bacteria quickly.

Loperamide is just a 'stopper' and doesn't get to the cause of the problem. It can be helpful, for example, if you have to go on a long bus ride. Don't take Loperamide if you have

---

DRINKING WATER

- never drink tap water

- bottled water is generally safe – check the seal is intact at purchase

- check ice has not been made with tap water

- boiling water is the most efficient method of purifying it

- the best chemical purifier is iodine, but it should not be used by pregnant women or those with thyroid problems

- water filters should also filter out viruses; ensure your filter has a chemical barrier such as iodine and a small pore size (eg less than four microns)

---

a fever, or blood in your stools. Seek medical attention quickly if you do not respond to an appropriate antibiotic.

Giardiasis

Giardia is a parasite that is relatively common in travellers. Symptoms include nausea, bloating, excess gas, fatigue and intermittent diarrhoea. 'Eggy' burps are often attributed solely to Giardia, but work in Nepal has shown that they are not specific to Giardia. The parasite will eventually go away if left untreated but this can take months. The treatment of choice is Tinidazole, with Metronidazole being a second-line option. Giardia is not common in South Korea.

ENVIRONMENTAL HAZARDS
Air Pollution

Air pollution, particularly from vehicles, is an increasing problem in Seoul. If you have severe respiratory problems, speak with your doctor before travelling to any heavily polluted urban centres. This pollution also causes minor respiratory problems such as sinusitis, dry throat and irritated eyes. If troubled by the pollution, leave the city for a few days and get some fresh air.

Food

Eating in restaurants is the biggest risk factor for contracting travellers' diarrhoea. Ways to avoid it include eating only freshly cooked food and avoiding shellfish and food that has been sitting around in buffets. Peel all fruit

and cook vegetables. Eat in busy restaurants with a high turnover of customers.

Insect Bites & Stings

Insects are not a major issue in Korea; however, there are some insect-borne diseases present.

Ticks are contracted after walking in rural areas. Ticks are commonly found behind the ears, on the belly and in armpits. If you have had a tick bite and experience symptoms such as a rash at the site of the bite or elsewhere, fever or muscle aches, you should see a doctor. Doxycycline prevents and treats tick-borne diseases.

Bee and wasp stings mainly cause problems for people who are allergic to them. Anyone with a serious bee or wasp allergy should carry an injection of adrenaline (eg an Epipen) for emergency treatment. For others pain is the main problem – apply ice to the sting and take painkillers.

Parasites

The most common parasite in Korea is Clonorchis. Infection occurs after eating infected fresh-water fish – these may be raw, pickled, smoked or dried. Light infections usually cause no symptoms; however, heavy infections can cause liver problems. In some areas up to 20% of the local population are infected.

WOMEN'S HEALTH

In most well-developed areas of Korea, supplies of sanitary products are readily available. Birth-control options may be limited, so bring adequate supplies of your own form of contraception. Heat, humidity and antibiotics can all contribute to thrush. Treatment is with antifungal creams and pessaries such as Clotrimazole. A practical alternative is a single tablet of Fluconazole (Diflucan). Urinary tract infections can be precipitated by dehydration or long bus journeys without toilet stops; bring suitable antibiotics.

Pregnant women should receive specialised advice before travelling. The ideal time to travel is in the second trimester (between 16 and 28 weeks), when the risk of pregnancy-related problems are at their lowest and pregnant women generally feel at their best. During the first trimester there is a risk of miscarriage and in the third trimester complications such as premature labour and high blood pressure are possible. It's wise to travel with a companion. Always carry a list of quality medical facilities available at your destination and ensure you continue your standard antenatal care at these facilities. Avoid rural travel in areas with poor transportation and medical facilities. Most of all, ensure travel insurance covers all pregnancy-related possibilities, including premature labour.

Travellers' diarrhoea can quickly lead to dehydration and result in inadequate blood flow to the placenta. Many of the drugs used to treat various diarrhoea bugs are not recommended in pregnancy. Azithromycin is considered safe.

TRADITIONAL & FOLK MEDICINE

Traditional medicine in Korea is known as Oriental medicine and is based on traditional Chinese medicine (TCM). Although Korean traditional medicine is heavily influenced by TCM, it has developed its own unique methods of diagnosis and treatment. Acupuncture techniques and herbal medicines are widely used.

Unique to Korean traditional medicine is Sasang Constitutional Medicine, which classifies people into four types (Taeyangin, Taeumin, Soyangin and Soeumin) based on their body type, and treats each differently according to their constitution. In Korea 'fusion medicine', which combines both traditional and Western medical systems, is increasingly popular. The World Health Organization has more than one research facility looking into traditional medicine in Seoul.

Be aware that 'natural' doesn't always mean 'safe', and there can be drug interactions between herbal medicines and Western medicines. If you are utilising both systems, ensure you inform both practitioners what the other has prescribed.

HEALTH

Language

Korean is a knotty problem for linguists. Various theories have been proposed to explain its origins, but the most widely accepted is that it is a member of the Ural-Altaic family of languages. Other members of the same linguistic branch are Turkish and Mongolian. In reality Korean grammar shares much more with Japanese than it does with either Turkish or Mongolian. Furthermore, the Koreans have borrowed nearly 70% of their vocabulary from neighbouring China, and now many English words have penetrated their language.

Chinese characters (hanja) are usually restricted to use in maps, government documents, the written names of businesses and in newspapers. For the most part Korean is written in Han·geul, the alphabet developed under King Sejong's reign in the 15th century. Many linguists argue that the Korean script is one of the most intelligently designed and phonetically consistent alphabets used today.

Han·geul consists of only 24 characters and isn't that difficult to learn. However, the formation of words using Han·geul is very different from the way that Western alphabets are used to form words. The emphasis is on the formation of a syllable, and

the end result bears some resemblance to a Chinese character. For example, the first syllable of the word Han·geul (한) is formed by an 'h' (ㅎ) in the top left corner, an 'a' (ㅏ) in the top right corner and an 'n' (ㄴ) at the bottom, the whole syllabic grouping forming a syllabic 'box'. These syllabic 'boxes' are strung together to form words.

ROMANISATION

In July 2000, the Korean government adopted a new method of Romanising the Korean language. Most of the old Romanisation system was retained, but a few changes were introduced to ensure a more consistent spelling throughout Korea and overseas. The new system has been energetically pushed throughout the government and tourist bureaus, but some corporations, individuals, academics and news outlets are reluctant to adopt it.

We use the new Romanisation style throughout this book, but you'll come across many spelling variations. To avoid confusion it's always best to go back to the original Korean script. In fact, it's well worth the few hours required to learn the Korean alphabet, even though we've provided Korean script throughout this book for map references and points of interest.

PRONUNCIATION

In the words and phrases in this chapter, the use of the variants **ga/i, reul/eul** and **ro/euro** depends on whether the preceding letter is a vowel or a consonant respectively.

Vowels & Vowel Combinations

ㅏ	a	as in 'are'
ㅑ	ya	as in 'yard'
ㅓ	eo	as the 'o' in 'of'
ㅕ	yeo	as the 'you' in 'young'
ㅗ	o	as in 'go'
ㅛ	yo	as in 'yoke'
ㅜ	u	as in 'flute'
ㅠ	yu	as the word 'you'
ㅡ	eu	as the 'oo' in 'look'
ㅣ	i	as the 'ee' in 'beet'
ㅐ	ae	as the 'a' in 'hat'
ㅒ	yae	as the 'ya' in 'yam'
ㅔ	e	as in 'ten'

ㅖ	**ye**	as in 'yes'
ㅘ	**wa**	as in 'waffle'
ㅙ	**wae**	as the 'wa' in 'wax'
ㅚ	**oe**	as the 'wa' in 'way'
ㅝ	**wo**	as in 'won'
ㅞ	**we**	as in 'wet'
ㅟ	**wi**	as the word 'we'
ㅢ	**ui**	as 'u' plus 'i'

Consonants

Unaspirated consonants are generally difficult for English speakers to render. To those unfamiliar with Korean, an unaspirated **k** will sound like 'g', an unaspirated **t** like 'd', and an unaspirated **p** like 'b'.

Whether consonants in Korean are voiced or unvoiced depends on where they fall within a word. The rules governing this are too complex to cover here – the following tables show the various alternative pronunciations you may hear.

Single Consonants

The letter ㅅ is pronounced 'sh' if followed by the vowel ㅣ, even though it is transliterated as **si**.

In the middle of a word, ㄹ is pronounced 'n' if it follows ㅁ (**m**) or ㅇ (**ng**), but when it follows ㄴ (**n**) it becomes a double 'l' sound (**ll**); when a single ㄹ is followed by a vowel it is transliterated as **r**.

ㄱ	g/k
ㄴ	n
ㄷ	d/t
ㄹ	r/l/n
ㅁ	m
ㅂ	b/p
ㅅ	s/t
ㅇ	–/ng
ㅈ	j/t
ㅊ	ch/t
ㅋ	k
ㅌ	t
ㅍ	p
ㅎ	h/ng

Double Consonants

Double consonants are pronounced with more stress than their single consonants counterparts.

ㄲ	kk
ㄸ	tt
ㅃ	pp

ㅆ	ss/t
ㅉ	jj

Complex Consonants

These occur only in the middle or at the end of a word.

ㄱㅅ	–/ksk/–
ㄴㅈ	–/nj/n
ㄴㅎ	–/nh/n
ㄹㄱ	–/lg/k
ㄹㅁ	–/lm/m
ㄹㅂ	–/lb/p
ㄹㅅ	–/ls/l
ㄹㅌ	–/lt/l
ㄹㅍ	–/lp/p
ㄹㅎ	–/lh/l
ㅂㅅ	–/ps/p

POLITE KOREAN

Korea's pervasive social hierarchy means that varying degrees of politeness are codified into the grammar. Young Koreans tend to use the very polite forms a lot less than the older generation, but it's always best to use the polite form if you're unsure. The sentences in this section use polite forms.

ACCOMMODATION

I'm looking for a ...
... reul/eul chatgo isseoyo   ...를/을 찾고 있어요
   guesthouse
   yeogwan/minbak jip   여관/민박집
   hotel
   hotel   호텔
   youth hostel
   yuseu hoseutel   유스호스텔

Where is a cheap hotel?
ssan hoteri eodi isseoyo?
싼 호텔이 어디 있어요?
What is the address?
jusoga eotteoke dwaeyo?
주소가 어떻게 돼요?
Could you write the address, please?
juso jom jeogeo juseyo?
주소 좀 적어 주세요?
Do you have any rooms available?
bang isseoyo?
방 있어요?

I'd like (a) ...
... ro/euro juseyo   ...로/으로 주세요
   bed
   chimdae   침대

single bed
singgeul chimdae 싱글 침대
double bed
deobeul chimdae 더블 침대
twin beds
chimdae dugae 침대 두개
room with a bathroom
yoksil inneun bang juseyo 욕실있는 방 주세요
to share a room
gachi sseuneun bang 같이 쓰는 방
Western-style room
chimdae bang juseyo 침대 방 주세요
a room with sleeping mats
ondol bang juseyo 온돌 방 주세요

How much is it ...?
e ... eolma eyo? 에...얼마에요?
per night
harutbam 하룻밤
per person
han saram 한사람

May I see it?
bang jom bolsu 방 좀 볼수
isseoyo? 있어요?
Where is the bathroom?
yoksiri eodi-e 욕실이 어디에
isseoyo? 있어요?
I'm/We're leaving now.
jigeum tteonayo 지금 떠나요

Making a reservation
(for written or phone requests)

To/From ... e-ge/buteo ... 에게/부터...
Date naljja 날짜

I'd like to book ...
(see the list on this page for bed and room options)
... yeyak haryeogo haneundeyo ...
예약 하려고 하는데요...
in the name of ...
ireum euro ... 이름으로...
for the night/s of ...
naljjalro ... 날짜로...
credit card ...
sinyong kadeu ... 신용 카드...
number
beonho 번호
expiry date
manryo il 만료일

Please confirm availability and price.
sayonghal su inneunji wa gagyeok hwaginhae juseyo
사용할 수 있는지 와 가격 확인해
주세요

CONVERSATION & ESSENTIALS
Hello. (polite)
annyeong hasimnikka
안녕 하십니까
Hello. (informal)
annyeong haseyo
안녕 하세요
Goodbye. (to person leaving)
annyeong-hi gaseyo
안녕히 가세요
Goodbye. (to person staying)
annyeong-hi gyeseyo
안녕히 계세요
Yes.
ye/ne 예/네
No.
aniyo 아니요
Please.
juseyo 주세요
Thank you.
gamsa hamnida 감사 합니다
That's fine/You're welcome.
gwaenchan seumnida 괜찮습니다
Excuse me.
sillye hamnida 실례 합니다
Sorry (forgive me).
mian hamnida 미안 합니다
See you soon.
tto mannayo/najung-e 또 만나요/나중에
buteobwayo 봐요
How are you?
annyeong haseyo? 안녕 하세요?
I'm fine, thanks.
ne, jo-ayo 네 좋아요
May I ask your name?
ireumeul yeojjwobwado 이름을 여쭤봐도
doelkkayo 될까요?
My name is ...
je ireumeun ... imnida 제 이름은...입니다
Where are you from?
eodiseo oseosseoyo? 어디서 오셨어요?
I'm from ...
jeoneun ... e-seo 저는...에서
wasseumnida 왔습니다
I (don't) like ...
jeoneun ... jo-a hey/ 저는...좋아해요/
... jo-a haji anhayo ...좋아하지 않아요
Just a minute.
jamkkan manyo 잠깐만요

DIRECTIONS
Where is ...?
... i/ga eodi isseoyo? ...이/가 어디 있어요?

SIGNS

입구 **Entrance**
ipgu

출구 **Exit**
chulgu

안내 **Information**
annae

영업중 **Open**
yeong eop jung

휴업중 **Closed**
hyu eop jung

금지 **Prohibited**
gumji

방있음 **Rooms Available**
bang isseum

방없음 **Full/No Vacancies**
bang eopseum

경찰서 **Police Station**
gyeongchalseo

화장실 **Toilets**
hwajangsil

신사용 **Men**
sinsayong

숙녀용 **Women**
sungnyeoyong

Go straight ahead.
ttokbaro gaseyo 똑바로 가세요

Turn left.
oenjjogeuro gaseyo 왼쪽으로 가세요

Turn right.
oreunjjogeuro gaseyo 오른쪽으로 가세요

at the next corner
da eum motungi e-seo 다음 모퉁이에서

at the traffic lights
sinhodeung e-seo 신호등에서

behind ...	*... dwi-e*	...뒤에
in front of ...	*... ap-e*	...앞에
far	*meolli*	멀리
near	*gakka-i*	가까이
opposite	*bandae pyeon-e*	반대편에
beach	*haesu yokjang*	해수욕장
	haebyeon	해변
bridge	*dari*	다리
castle	*seong*	성
cathedral	*seongdang*	성당
island	*do*	도

(when used in place names)
seom 섬
(when used as a generic noun)

EMERGENCIES

Help!
saram sallyeo! 사람살려!

There's been an accident.
sago nasseoyo 사고 났어요

I'm lost.
gireul ireosseoyo 길을 잃었어요

Go away!
jeori ga! 저리가!

Call ...!
... bulleo juseyo!
...불러 주세요!

a doctor	*ui-sareul*	의사를
the police	*gyeongchareul*	경찰을
an ambulance	*gugeupcha jom*	구급차좀

market	*sijang*	시장
palace	*gung*	궁
ruins	*yetteo*	옛터
sea	*bada*	바다
tower	*ta-wo/tap*	타워/탑

HEALTH

I'm ill.
jeon apayo 저 아파요

It hurts here.
yeogiga apayo 여기가 아파요

I'm ...	*... isseoyo*	...있어요
asthmatic	*cheonsik*	천식
diabetic	*dangnyo byeong-i*	당뇨병이
epileptic	*ganjil byeong-i*	간질병이

I'm allergic to ...
... allereugiga isseoyo
...알레르기가있어요

antibiotics	*hangsaengje*	항생제
aspirin	*aseupirin*	아스피린
penicillin	*penisillin*	페니실린
bees	*beol*	벌
nuts	*ttang kkong*	땅꽁

antiseptic	*sodong yak*	소독약
condoms	*kondom*	콘돔
contraceptive	*pi imyak*	피임약
diarrhoea	*seolsa*	설사
hospital	*byeongwon*	병원
medicine	*yak*	약
sunblock cream	*seon keurim*	선크림
tampons	*tampon*	탐폰

LANGUAGE

LANGUAGE DIFFICULTIES

Do you speak English?
  yeong-eo haseyo?
  영어 하세요?

Does anyone here speak English?
  yeong-eo hasineunbun gyeseyo?
  영어 하시는 분계세요?

How do you say ... in Korean?
  ... eul/reul hangug-euro eotteoke malhaeyo?
  …을 한국어로 어떻게 말해요?

What does ... mean?
  ... ga/i museun
  …가/이무슨
  tteusieyo?
  뜻 이에요?

I understand.
  algeseoyo
  알겠어요

I don't understand.
  jalmoreugenneun deyo
  잘 모르겠는데요

Please write it down.
  jeogeo jusillaeyo
  적어 주실래요

Can you show me (on the map)?
  boyeo jusillaeyo
  보여 주실래요?

NUMBERS

Korean has two counting systems. One is of Chinese origin, with Korean pronunciation, and the other is a native Korean system – the latter only goes up to 99 and is used for counting objects, expressing your age and for the hours when telling the time. They're always written in *Han·geul* or digits, but never in Chinese characters. Sino-Korean numbers are used to express minutes when telling the time, as well as dates, months, kilometres, money, floors of buildings; numbers above 99 and can also be written in Chinese characters. Either Chinese or Korean numbers can be used to count days.

	Sino-Korean		Korean	
1	*il*	일	*hana*	하나
2	*i*	이	*dul*	둘
3	*sam*	삼	*set*	셋
4	*sa*	사	*net*	넷
5	*o*	오	*daseot*	다섯
6	*yuk*	육	*yeoseot*	여섯
7	*chil*	칠	*ilgop*	일곱
8	*pal*	팔	*yeodeol*	여덟
9	*gu*	구	*ahop*	아홉
10	*sip*	십	*yeol*	열

Combination

11	*sibil*	십일
12	*sibi*	십이
13	*sipsam*	십삼
14	*sipsa*	십사
15	*sibo*	십오
16	*simnyuk*	십육
17	*sipchil*	십칠
18	*sippal*	십팔
19	*sipgu*	십구
20	*isip*	이십
21	*isibil*	이십일
22	*isibi*	이십이
30	*samsip*	삼십
40	*sasip*	사십
50	*osip*	오십
60	*yuksip*	육십
70	*chilsip*	칠십
80	*palsip*	팔십
90	*gusip*	구십
100	*baek*	백
1000	*cheon*	천

PAPERWORK

name	*ireum/*	이름/
	seongmyeong	성명
nationality	*guk jeok*	국적
date of birth	*saengnyeon woril/*	생년월일/
	saeng-il	생일
place of birth	*chulsaengji*	출생지
sex (gender)	*seongbyeol*	성별
passport	*yeogwon*	여권
visa	*bija*	비자

QUESTION WORDS

Who? (as subject)	*nugu*	누구
What? (as subject)	*mu-eot*	무엇
When?	*eonje*	언제
Where?	*eodi*	어디
How?	*eotteoke*	어떻게

SHOPPING & SERVICES

I'd like to buy ...
  ... reul/eul sago sipeoyo
  …를/을 사고 싶어요

How much is it?
  eolma yeyo?
  얼마예요?

I don't like it.
  byeollo mam-e
  별로 맘에
  andeuneyo
  안드네요

May I look at it?
  boyeo jusillaeyo?
  보여 주실래요?

I'm just looking.
  geunyang gugyeong
  그냥 구경
  haneungeo-eyo
  하는 거에요

It's cheap.
  ssa-neyo
  싸네요

It's too expensive.
  neomu bissayo
  너무 비싸요

I'll take it.
igeoro haraeyo 이걸로 할래요

Do you accept ...?
... jibul haedo dwaeyo? ...지불해도 돼요?
 credit cards
 keurediteu kadeu-ro 크레디트 카드로
 travellers cheques
 yeohaengja supyo 여행자 수표

more deo 더
less deol 덜
smaller deo jageun 더작은
bigger deo keun 더큰

I'm looking for ...
... reul/eul chatgo isseoyo ...를/을 찾고 있어요
 a bank
 eunhaeng 은행
 a church
 gyohoe 교회
 the city centre
 sinae jung simga 시내 중심가
 the ... embassy
 dae sigwan 대사관
 the market
 sijang 시장
 the museum
 bangmulgwan 박물관
 the post office
 uche-guk 우체국
 a public toilet
 hwajangsil 화장실
 the telephone centre
 jeonhwa guk 전화국
 the tourist office
 gwan gwang annaeso 관광 안내소

I want to change ...
... reul/eul bakku ryeogo haneun deyo
...를/을 바꾸려고 하는데요
 money
 don 돈
 travellers cheques
 yeohaengja supyo 여행자 수표

TIME & DATES
What time is it?
 jigeum myeot si-eyo? 지금 몇시 에요?
It's (10 o'clock).
 (yeol) siyo (열)시요

in the morning achim-e 아침에
in the afteroon ohu-e 오후에

in the evening jeonyeok-e 저녁에
When? eonje 언제
today o-neul 오늘
tomorrow nae-il 내일
yesterday eo-je 어제

Monday woryoil 월요일
Tuesday hwayoil 화요일
Wednesday suyoil 수요일
Thursday mogyoil 목요일
Friday geumyoil 금요일
Saturday toyoil 토요일
Sunday iryoil 일요일

January irwol 일월
February iwol 이월
March samwol 삼월
April sawol 사월
May owol 오월
June yu-gwol 육월
July chirwol 칠월
August parwol 팔월
September guwol 구월
October siwol 시월
November sibirwol 십일월
December sibiwol 십이월

TRANSPORT
Public Transport
What time does the ... leave/arrive?
 ... i/ga (eonje tteonayo/eonje dochak-haeyo)?
 ...이/가 언제 떠나요/언제 도착해요?
airport bus gonghang beoseu 공항버스
boat (ferry) yeogaekseon 여객선
bus beoseu 버스
city bus sinae beoseu 시내버스
intercity bus si-oe beoseu 시외버스
plane bihaeng-gi 비행기
train gicha 기차

Two other types of intercity bus are:

gosok beoseu 고속 버스
(high frequency express bus)
u-deung beoseu 우등 버스
(less frequent, more comfortable and a little more expensive)

I'd like a ... ticket.
 ... hanjang juseyo ...한장 주세요
one-way pyeondo pyo 편도표
return wangbok pyo 왕복표
1st class il-deung seok 일등석
2nd class i-deung seok 이등석

LANGUAGE

I want to go to ...
... e gago sipseumnida
...에 가고 싶습니다
The train has been (delayed).
gichaga (yeonchak) doe-eosseumnida
기차가(연착) 되었습니다.
The train has been (cancelled).
gichaga (chwiso) doe-eosseumnida
기차가 (취소) 되었습니다

the first
cheot 첫
the last
maji mak 마지막
bus station
beoseu jeongnyu jang 버스정류장
platform number
peuraetpom beonho 플랫폼번호
subway station
jihacheol yeok 지하철역
ticket office
pyo paneun got 표 파는곳
ticket vending machine
pyo japangi 표 자판기
timetable
sigan pyo 시간표
train station
gicha yeok 기차역

Private Transport
I'd like to hire a/an ...
... reul/eul billi-go sipeoyo
...를/을 빌리고 싶어요
car
jadongcha 자동차
(or simply cha, 차)
4WD
jipeu cha 지프차
motorbike
otoba-i/moteo sai-keul 오토바이/모터사이클
bicycle
jajeongeo 자전거

Is this the road to ...?
i-gil daragamyeon ... e galsu isseoyo?
이길 따라가면...에갈수 있어요?
Where's a service station?
annae soga eodi isseoyo?
안내소가 어디있어요?
Please fill it up.
gadeuk chaewo juseyo
가득 채워 주세요
I'd like (30) litres.
(samsip) liteo neo-eo juseyo
(삼십)리터 넣어 주세요

ROAD SIGNS

우회로	Detour
uhwoe-ro	
길없음	No Entry
gil-eupseum	
추월금지	No Overtaking
chuwol geumji	
주차금지	No Parking
jucha geumji	
입구	Entrance
ipgu	
접근금지	Keep Clear
jeopgeun geumji	
통행료	Toll
tonghaeng-ryo	
톨게이트	Toll Gate
tol geiteu	
위험	Danger
wi heom	
서행	Slow Down
seo haeng	
일방통행	One Way
il-bang tonghaeng	
나가는길	Freeway Exit
naganeun gil	

diesel dijel 디젤
petrol/gas hwi baryu 휘발유

(How long) Can I park here?
(eolmana) jucha halsu isseoyo?
(얼마나) 주차 할수 있어요?
Where do I pay?
eodiseo jibul hamnikka?
어디서 지불합니까?
I need a mechanic.
jeongbi gong-i biryo haeyo
정비공이 필요해요
The car/motorbike has broken down at ...
... eseo chaga/otoba-i ga gojang nasseoyo
...에서차가/오토바이가 고장 났어요
The car/motorbike won't start.
chaga/otoba-i ga sidong-i geolli-ji annayo
차가/오토바이가 시동이 걸리지
않아요
I have a flat tyre.
taieo-e peongkeu nasseoyo
타이어에펑크났어요
I've run out of petrol.
gireumi tteoreo jeosseoyo
기름이 떨어졌어요
I've had an accident.
sago nasseoyo
사고 났어요

TRAVEL WITH CHILDREN

Is there (a/an) ...
... isseoyo? ...있어요?
I need (a/an) ...
piryo haeyo ...필요해요
baby change room
gijeogwi galgosi 기저귀 갈 곳이
baby car seat
yu-a jadongcha 유아자동차안전의자
anjeon uija
child-minding service
agi bwajuneun seobiseu 아기봐주는 서비스
children's menu
eorini menyu 어린이 메뉴
(disposable) nappies/diapers
ilhoeyong gijeogwi 일회용 기저귀

infant milk formula
bunyu 분유
(English-speaking) babysitter
agi bwajuneun saram 아기 봐주는 사람
highchair
agi uija 아기의자
potty
agi byeon-gi 아기변기
stroller/pusher
yu-mocha 유모차

Do you mind if I breastfeed here?
yeogi-seo agi jeotmeok yeodo doenayo?
여기서 아기 젖먹여도 되나요?
Are children allowed?
eorinido doennikka?
어린이도됩니까?

Glossary

For more food and drink terms, see the Menu Decoder (p69); for general terms see the Language chapter (p410).

ajumma – a married or older woman
~am – hermitage
anju – snacks eaten when drinking alcohol

bang – room
bawi – large rock
~bong – peak
buk~ – north
buncheong – Joseon-era pottery with simple folk designs

celadon – green-tinged pottery from the early-12th century
cha – tea
~cheon – small stream
Chuseok – Thanksgiving Day

dae~ – great, large
dancheong – ornate, multicoloured eaves that adorn Buddhist temples and other buildings
Dan-gun – mythical founder of Korea
DMZ – the Demilitarized Zone that runs along the 38th parallel of the Korean peninsula, separating North and South
-do – province
~do – island
-dong – neighbourhood or village
dong~ – east
donggul – cave
DPRK – Democratic People's Republic of Korea (North Korea)
DVD bang – room for watching DVDs

-eup – town

-ga – section of a long street
~gang – river
geobukseon – 'turtle ships'; iron-clad warships of the late 16th century
gil – small street
-gu – urban district
gugak – traditional Korean music
~gul – cave
-gun – county
~gung – palace
gwageo – Joseon government service exam

hae – sea
haenyeo – traditional female divers of Jejudo
hagwon – private language school where students study after school or work
hallyu –(Korean Wave) increasing interest in Korean pop culture from other parts of Asia
hanbok – traditional Korean clothing
hang – harbour
Han-geul – Korean phonetic alphabet
hanja – Chinese characters
hanji – traditional Korean handmade paper
hanok – traditional Korean one-storey wooden house with a tiled roof
harubang – lava-rock statues found only on Jejudo
~ho – lake
hof – local pub

insam – ginseng

jaebeol – huge family-run corporate conglomerate
~jeon – hall of a temple
~jeong – pavilion
jjimjilbang – upmarket spa and sauna
Juche – North Korean ideology of economic self-reliance

KTO – Korea Tourism Organisation
KTX – Korea Train Express; fast 300km/h train service

minbak – private homes with rooms for rent
mudang – female shaman
Mugunghwa – semi-express train
~mun – gate
-myeon – township
~myo – shrine

nam~ – south
~neung – tomb
~no – street
noraebang – karaoke room
~nyeong – mountain pass

oncheon – hot-spring bath
ondol – underfloor heating system

pansori – traditional Korean solo opera
PC bang – internet café
pension – upmarket accommodation in the countryside or near beaches
pocketball – pool
pokpo – waterfall

pyeong – a unit of real estate measurement equal to 3.3 sq metres

~reung – tomb
-ri – village
~ro – street
ROK – Republic of Korea (South Korea)
~ryeong – mountain pass

~sa – temple
Saemaul – luxury express train
samul·nori – drum-and-gong dance
~san – mountain
sanjang – mountain hut
sanseong – mountain fortress
seo~ – west
Seon – Korean version of Zen Buddhism
~seong – fortress
seowon – Confucian academy

shamanism – set of traditional beliefs; communication with spirits is done through a mudang
~si – city
sijang – market
sijo – short poems about nature and life; popular in the Joseon period
soju – the local firewater; often likened to vodka
ssireum – Korean-style wrestling

taekwondo – Korean martial art
tap – pagoda
tonggeun – commuter-class train

yangban – aristocrat
yeogwan – motel with small en suite
yeoinsuk – small, family-run budget accommodation with shared bathroom
yo – padded quilt that serves as a mattress or futon for sleeping on the floor

Behind the Scenes

THIS BOOK

Lonely Planet's first Korea guide was published in 1988. The 5th edition was written by Robert Storey and Eunkyong Park. The last edition was updated by Martin Robinson, Andrew Bender and Rob Whyte. For this 7th edition, Martin and Rob were joined by Ray Bartlett. The History chapter was written by Dr Bruce Cumings.

This guidebook was commissioned in Lonely Planet's Melbourne office, and produced by the following:

Commissioning Editors Jane Thompson; Rebecca Chau; Jay Cooke
Coordinating Editor Dianne Schallmeiner
Coordinating Cartographer Corey Hutchison
Coordinating Layout Designer Steven Cann
Managing Editor Suzannah Shwer
Managing Cartographer Julie Sheridan; Corie Waddell
Assisting Editors Jackey Coyle; Simon Williamson
Proofreader Simon Sellars
Assisting Cartographer Helen Rowley
Cover Designer Jane Hart
Project Manager Chris Love
Language Content Coordinator Quentin Frayne

Thanks to Jessa Boanas-Dewes; Helen Christinis; Sally Darmody; Jennifer Garrett; JD Hilts; Korea Tourism Organisation; Averil Robertson; Celia Wood

THANKS
MARTIN ROBINSON

Thanks to KTO, particularly Kang Soon-deog and Moon Young-nam; all the helpful TIC staff; the ever-generous English teachers at Sinheung middle school in Jeonju; kind and helpful Mr Kim at Gimnyeong Maze; the merry pensioners on the Lake Chungju ferry; and the young cop on Sapsido. Thanks also to Rolfe in Yeosu, Ralf in Seogwipo, the driver who rescued me outside Suanbo Hot Springs, the ute driver who gave me a lift at Sangumburi Crater, the two bus drivers who went out of their way, BJ Song, Youngbok Jang, and my dad, Evelyn and Paul for accommodation. Above all thanks to my wife and constant companion Marie.

RAY BARTLETT

Humble thanks to so many great people, all of whom helped me along the way: Jane, Martin, Rebecca and all the other Lonely Planet folks behind the scenes – your professionalism, dedication and help are what make this a dream job. Thanks to new friends: my 'Amazon Baby' and your kind family, Micky, Joy, EP, Heonsu, Anyeong and the FullHouse goshiwon girls. Thanks to old friends: Kiyeon, for forcing a cellphone upon me, among other things; JaeYoung, for proofing, questions, and beers (mmmm, beeeeeers!); Kyoung-ee (Where can I start…in Tulum, I guess?) for putting me up, stopping trains, braving torrential rains, midnight laundry runs, and more. And to sweet 'Sugar Magnolia' for such cheerful, patient enduring of just about everything: cold rain, sweltering heat, seasickness, matching outfits, those crazy bus rides – I cannot thank you enough. Korea wouldn't have been the same.

As always, a huge thank you to my folks behind the scenes as well: friends and family who remain

---

THE LONELY PLANET STORY

The story begins with a classic travel adventure: Tony and Maureen Wheeler's 1972 journey across Europe and Asia to Australia. There was no useful information about the overland trail then, so Tony and Maureen published the first Lonely Planet guidebook to meet a growing need.

From a kitchen table, Lonely Planet has grown to become the largest independent travel publisher in the world, with offices in Melbourne (Australia), Oakland (USA) and London (UK). Today Lonely Planet guidebooks cover the globe. There is an ever-growing list of books and information in a variety of media. Some things haven't changed. The main aim is still to make it possible for adventurous travellers to get out there – to explore and better understand the world.

At Lonely Planet we believe travellers can make a positive contribution to the countries they visit – if they respect their host communities and spend their money wisely. Every year 5% of company profit is donated to charities around the world.

supportive despite my frequent lengthy disappearances. To the proud citizens of Korea – thank you for sharing your beautiful country with me; may you treat each reader of this guide as kindly and generously as you've treated me.

ROB WHYTE

First, thanks to my wife and daughter for their patience, support and occasional nagging to finish this project. To my colleagues Jason Russell, Trey Coffie, Pablo Zatylus and Eric Bravo for their unique insights into some of Busan's lesser known corners. Thanks to the KIT administration for granting me a flexible schedule to work on this book and Kim Ah-young for her invaluable research assistance. On the road there was Pastor Lee, Captain Nam, Mr Cho for his brilliant historical insights and Monsieurs Lee, Park and Ha at the Namhae County office who showed me that the Korean spirit of generosity is alive and well in the countryside.

OUR READERS

Many thanks to the travellers who used the last edition and wrote to us with helpful hints, useful advice and interesting anecdotes:

A Sung-Eun Ahn, Raymond Ang, Rj Arndt, **B** Chris Baik, Orlando Barone, Nathalie Beauval, Joachim Bergmann, Rosswyn Blair, Gabriele Bolognini, B Bolton, Nathan Braun, Kathy Brenner, Brenda Bryan, Peter Button, Ji Young Byun, **C** Matthew Campbell, Larry Castle, Jim Cathcart, Bethany Cerella, Inju Cho, Wonchung Chung, Alex Cole, James Colyn, David Combs, Michael Cop, Tamzin Costello, Anna Crosland, Philip Cutuli, Joanie Dawson, Willem J De Wit, **D** Katleen Dobek, Andrew Dopheide, **E** Helen Eames, **F** Scott Fallis, Ian Fleming, James Fox, **G** Jame Gallagher, Eric Gankerseer, Michael Gershowitz, Bernhard Goebel, Jack Goldstein, Alison Greene, **H** Marcus Hand, Eleanor Handreck, Matthew Haswell, Andrea Helbig, Jacqueline Hewitt, Andreas Hippin, Susan Holland, Minsuk Hong, Genevieve Howard, Gina Hwang, **I** Ingrid Ifversen, **J** Larry Jackson, Jang, Ben Jordan, **K** Ronen Kalish, Ute Keck, Eugene Kim, Ho Kim, Hun Kim, Vinnie Kim, Yumi Kim, George Kitching, **L** Joann Landingham, Elizabeth Lipes, Eve Marie Little, Lisa Lloyd, Hector Lopez, Bill Lovegrove, **M** Diana Maestre, Yamada Manabu, Carla Martin, David Mccann, Berthold Melcher, Josh Mink, Carolyn Mitchell, Craig Mitchell, Mola Mola, Marie-Loe Molenaar, Dávid Molnár, **O** Michal Obrebski, Dax Oliver, **P** Deborah P, Jade Pak, Robert Papelier, Ramon Pacheco Pardo, Jens Paulsen, Cory Pettit, Laura Phipps, Harnpon Phungrassami, Donata Piccolo, Daniela Praborini, Gregor Prahl, **R** Rebecca Redwood, Lance Reegan-Deihl, Beth Rice, Sarah Riches, Lars Ritterhoff, Soo Hyun Roh, Marc Rumminger, **S** Jared Sandler, Colin Schrader, Jana Seaman, Rama Sellappan, Emanuel Serra, Sanne Severinsen, Christopher Shanley, Peter & Florence Shaw, Francis Shillitoe, Michael Siegler, Lim Wei Siong, Richard Smith, Sang-Hyun Son, Elizabeth Standal, Joann Stock, **T** Nicole Thinnes, Marc Tillotson, Ima Traveler, Ian Turner, **V** K V, Omni Vagus, Erwin van Engelen, Jef Van Hout, **W** Becky Wadey, Suzanne Walker, Seth Wallace, Moshe Wallach, Dryden Watner, Charles Wei Siong Lim, Pei Ching Wen, A West, Nancy Wichers, James Wickens, Darryn Wilson, Julie Wilson, Gordon Wisotzki, Curt Wold, Matt Wood, **Y** Carl Yamada, Kim Yangjung, Jee Young Yu.

SEND US YOUR FEEDBACK

We love to hear from travellers – your comments keep us on our toes and help make our books better. Our well-travelled team reads every word on what you loved or loathed about this book. Although we cannot reply individually to postal submissions, we always guarantee that your feedback goes straight to the appropriate authors, in time for the next edition. Each person who sends us information is thanked in the next edition – and the most useful submissions are rewarded with a free book.

To send us your updates – and find out about Lonely Planet events, newsletters and travel news – visit our award-winning website: **www.lonelyplanet.com/contact**.

Note: we may edit, reproduce and incorporate your comments in Lonely Planet products such as guidebooks, websites and digital products, so let us know if you don't want your comments reproduced or your name acknowledged. For a copy of our privacy policy visit www.lonelyplanet.com/privacy.

ACKNOWLEDGMENTS

Many thanks to the following for the use of their content:

Seoul Subway transport map (c) 2006 Seoul Metropolitan Rapid Transport Corporation

Index

000 Map pages
000 Photograph pages